'CANNON PLAYED FROM THE GREAT FORT'

Sieges in the Severn Valley During the English Civil War 1642–1646

Richard Israel

'This is the Century of the Soldier', Fulvio Testi, Poet, 1641

Helion & Company

Helion & Company Limited
Unit 8 Amherst Business Centre
Budbrooke Road
Warwick
CV34 5WE
England
Tel. 01926 499 619
Email: info@helion.co.uk
Website: www.helion.co.uk
Twitter: @helionbooks
blog.helion.co.uk/

Published by Helion & Company 2021
Designed and typeset by Mach 3 Solutions Ltd (www.mach3solutions.co.uk)
Cover designed by Paul Hewitt, Battlefield Design (www.battlefield-design.co.uk)

ISBN 978-1-913336-50-9

British Library Cataloguing-in-Publication Data.
A catalogue record for this book is available from the British Library.

Contents

List of Plates

List of Figures

List of Maps

List of Tables

List of Abbreviations

AD	Anno Domini
aOD	Above Ordnance Datum (height above sea level)
BC	Before Christ
c.	circa
cm	centimetre
d	pence
ft	foot/feet
g	gram
in	inch
kg	kilogram
km	kilometre
lb	pound
m	metre
oz	ounce

Acknowledgments

I would first like to thank my editor, Charles Singleton, as without his support this book would not exist. Thank you to Helion & Company Ltd. It has been an incredible opportunity and privilege to write this book.

I am indebted to my friend, Dr Philip R. Rowe, with whom I have discussed all aspects of archaeology since meeting him in 2003.

Thanks must also go to the Historic Environment Records (HERs), namely Peter Insole of Bristol City Council, Andrew Armstrong of Gloucester City Council, Sheena Payne-Lunn of Worcester City Council and Giles Carey of Shropshire Council. The HERs are wonderful resources, and I would encourage people to visit and use these assets as they contain a wealth of information.

In addition, I would like to thank the staff of all of the Record Offices I have visited throughout the years, namely Bristol Archives, Gloucestershire Archives, the Archive and Archaeology Service at The Hive in Worcester, and Shropshire Archives.

Thank you to Ellie Ramsey of the Council for British Archaeology (West Midlands branch), for providing me with a copy of Annette Roe's article on Bridgnorth (Panpudding Hill) from the *West Midlands Archaeology* journal.

Thanks must go to the following for giving me permission to use the following images:

ProQuest® as part of Early English Books Online www.proquest.com, with the assistance of Corye L. Bradbury, for giving permission to reproduce the illustrations from the works of Henry Hexham, Nicholas Stone and Robert Ward in Figures 1–11 and 13.

The British Library, with the assistance of Sandra Powlette, for permission to reproduce the illustrations in Figures 1 and 4.

The University of Illinois (Urbana-Champaign Campus) Library, with the assistance of Sara R. Benson, for permission to reproduce illustrations in Figures 3 and 8–11.

The Beinecke Rare Book and Manuscript Library, Yale University, with the assistance of Rebecca Aldi and Natalia Sciarini, for permission to reproduce the illustrations in Figures 5–7 and 13.

Antonia Parker Jones, heir of Patrick McGrath, for permission to use 'The Royalist attack on Bristol 1643', pp. 26–27, and 'The Attack by the

Parliamentary forces 1645', p. 39, from his pamphlet *Bristol and Civil War*, along with the assistance of Mary Feerick of the Bristol Historical Association.

Jon Day, with the assistance of Isabelle FitzGerald, for his permission to use Map 2, from *Gloucester & Newbury 1643: The Turning Point of the Civil War*.

Gloucestershire Archives for permission to use plan D 12862 of Gloucester city's defences.

Shropshire Archives and the Museum Curator for permission to use *Prospect Town of Shrewsbury Great Frost 1739* (PH.5.13.5.22.219) and Shropshire Archives for permission to use Bridgnorth *c.* 1660 map (SRO P40.V.2.5).

Dr Jonathan Worton and Rosemary Thornes of the Shropshire Archaeological and Historical Society for the plan of Civil War defences of Shrewsbury contained within the Society's *Transactions* at p.103.

Taylor & Francis Ltd (http://www.tandfonline.com) on behalf of the Society for Landscape Studies for permission to use Figure 2 at p. 53 titled 'Bridgnorth, to the west of the River Severn (north to top)' in article by Jeremy Haslam titled 'The articulation of burgages and streets in early medieval towns, part 1: the case of Bridgnorth, Shropshire', *Landscape History*, Vol. 37 (1) (2016), pp. 51–68, as a base map for Map 8.

The Archive Enquiry Team, Worcestershire Archive and Archaeology Service of Worcestershire County Council, for permission to use *An Exact Ground Plot of the City of Worcester, As It Stood Fortified 3. Sep: 1651* (899:41 BA510).

Malcolm Atkin and Worcestershire Archive and Archaeology Service for permission to use the reconstruction of the defences as a result of the archaeological excavations at King's School on Severn Street from p. 61 of *The Civil War in Worcestershire*; and the plan of defences of Worcester during the 1646 siege at p. 124 of *Worcestershire Under Arms: an English County During the Civil Wars* as a base map for Map 10.

Finally, I would like to thank my family, in particular my mum, Vanessa, for all of her support throughout my research.

I dedicate this book to my beautiful twin sister, Rebecca Israel (14 February to 15 February 1985).

Chronology

Brief summary of the main events of the English Civil War (1642–51) relating to the Severn Valley region

1642

Charles I raises the standard on 22 August 1642 at Nottingham to declare Civil War.

1643

Siege of Worcester, 29 May–31 May 1643. Unsuccessful Parliamentarian siege.

Siege of Bristol, 26 July 1643. Successful Royalist siege.

Siege of Gloucester, 10 August–5 September 1643. Unsuccessful Royalist siege.

1645

Siege of Shrewsbury, 9 February 1645. Successful Parliamentarian siege.

Siege of Bristol, 21 August–11 September 1645. Successful Parliamentarian siege.

1646

Siege of Bridgnorth, 31 March–26 April 1646. Successful Parliamentarian siege.

Siege of Worcester, 20 May–23 July 1646. Successful Parliamentarian siege.

Charles I surrenders.

1648

Second Civil War, after which Charles I is arrested and put on trial; he is found guilty and executed on 30 January 1649.

1651

The monarchy is abolished in England and Ireland, but not Scotland, where Charles I's son is crowned Charles II, King of Great Britain. The final battle of the war is fought at Worcester on 3 September 1651. The Commonwealth under Lord Protector Oliver Cromwell continues until 1658. The monarchy is restored in 1660.

Introduction

Siege warfare is often the forgotten aspect of the English Civil War. When most people think of the conflict, they immediately think of the battlefields of Edgehill, Newbury and Marston Moor. Whilst these battles are significant, the resources, men and equipment to stage them came from the towns and cities throughout the land.

This book will focus on five towns of the Severn Valley region – Bristol, Gloucester, Worcester, Bridgnorth and Shrewsbury – that were under siege during the First Civil War (1642–46). This area has been chosen because the region, including Bristol, was critical to success for both the Royalists and Parliamentarians. The Upper Severn was an important centre for coal and iron, amongst other products, which was carried along the River Severn – navigable from Shrewsbury, and the second busiest river in Europe, after the Maas – to the ports of Gloucester and Bristol. In return, imports were disembarked at towns along the river. The region also had key road networks to the rest of England, including London, as well as to Wales.[1]

To analyse the strategy, tactics, and offensive and defensive fortifications during this period, the techniques of landscape archaeology will be employed. This means that, wherever available, sieges will be looked at based on the available information and an understanding of the geology, topography and cartographic and historical data, along with the archaeological record of the five towns and their surrounding landscapes.

The sieges will be examined in chronological order. Chapter 1 analyses the sieges of 1643, looking at the events of Worcester, Bristol and Gloucester. The second chapter examines the sieges of Shrewsbury and Bristol in 1645, then Chapter 3 looks at the two sieges of 1646, Bridgnorth and Worcester. The fourth chapter compares and contrasts the outcomes, strategy and tactics for all the sieges, seeing what changes occurred, if any, as a result of the conflicts.

To understand siege warfare of the mid-17th century, it is necessary to briefly look at the development of warfare to that point in history, followed by a focus on the impact of the Thirty Years' War (1618–48), the military manuals available at the time, and the development of artillery.

---

1 Ian Roy, 'England Turned Germany? The Aftermath of the Civil War in Its European Context', *Transactions of the Royal Historical Society*, Vol. 28 (1978), pp. 133–34.

Pre-Historic and Ancient Warfare

Warfare is first depicted in cave paintings at Morella La Vella in Spain dating from the Mesolithic (middle stone age) era *c.* 20,000 BC, which illustrates men using bows.[2] The first evidence from history of siege engines comes in the form of a relief illustrating a wheeled siege tower from the tomb of the general Intef in Egyptian Thebes from the late 11th Dynasty.[3] There are references to sieges in the Bible. One such example is the siege of Jericho, although there is very little evidence archaeologically dating to the 13th century BC. Siege warfare continued to develop in Mesopotamia, with the first documentary evidence of embankments, siege towers, battering rams and sapping dating from the reign of Ishme-Dagan I (1797–1757 BC). The Persians specialised in embankments, undermining and the creation of large-scale earthworks. Archaeological excavations of the town of Paphos in Cyprus showed an extensive embankment built by the Persians around 497 BC.[4]

The Classical World

The city states of the area now referred to as Ancient Greece had a profound impact on siege warfare. One of the key periods was the Peloponnesian War (431–404 BC). There is evidence of battering rams being used at Plataea in 427 BC, along with an increase in the use of fire, with a flamethrower being used at Delium by the Boeotians in 423 BC. By 398 BC, Dionysius of Syracuse used towers, rams and arrow-firing catapults against the city of Motya.[5]

Thucydides described key elements of the Spartan siege of Plataea in 429 BC. After failing to take the city by assault using siege engines, the Peloponnesians began construction of a line of circumvallation. To protect their siegeworks, they were also required to construct a line of contravallation.[6] A line of circumvallation is a series of siegeworks facing the town or city being besieged, theoretically designed to enclose the besieged and cut them off from the outside world. A line of contravallation is constructed around the line of circumvallation to protect it from an approaching relief army, meaning that the besiegers can continue the assault.

The Romans under the command of Julius Caesar conducted one of the great sieges of the ancient world in 52 BC against the Gauls and their leader, Vercingetorix, at the town of Alesia. Caesar's own account of the siegeworks begins with the construction of siegeworks that were 10 miles (16.1km) in length, with 23 forts along their course. After a cavalry battle,

2 Robert L. O'Connell, *Of Arms and Men: A History of War, Weapons, and Aggression* (Oxford: Oxford University Press, 1989), pp. 26–27.

3 Barry J. Kemp, *Ancient Egypt: Anatomy of a Civilization* (Abington: Routledge, 2006), p. 235.

4 Konstantin Nossov, *Ancient and Medieval Siege Weapons* (Guilford: First Lyons Press, 2012), pp. 10, 13, 26.

5 O'Connell, *Of Arms and Men*, p. 59.

6 Thucydides, *History of the Peloponnesian War*, trans. Rex Warner (London: Penguin Group, 1954), Book Two 71, 75, 76, 77, 78, pp. 168, 170–73, Book Three, 21, p. 204.

which resulted in Vercingetorix sending his mounted forces away to find men to join in the war effort, Caesar began construction of a ditch that was 20ft (6.09m) wide, with vertical sides. Then, 400 paces behind the ditch, he built further fortifications. At a further distance he constructed two more ditches 15ft (4.57m) in width, and filled the inner ditch with water. Behind this was an earthwork that was 12ft (3.65m) high, containing a rampart, parapet and battlements, with stakes projecting where the earthwork met the parapet. Finally, towers were placed at 80ft (24.38m) intervals around the siegeworks. Additional defences were constructed to hinder sorties by the Gauls. Thick branches and tree trunks were cut, stripped of bark and sharpened at one end. Small ditches, 5ft (1.52m) in depth, were also dug, with five interlocking stakes placed in each ditch. These were referred to as 'gravestones'. In front of these, in diagonal rows in a quincunx pattern, were pits 3ft (0.91m) in depth. Smooth, thick stakes were sunk into the pits, with only a maximum of 3in (7.6cm) exposed, and the pits were camouflaged with brushwood and twigs. At 3ft (0.91m) intervals, eight rows of the pits were dug. As they resembled a flower, they were referred to as 'lilies'. In front of the lilies were logs 1ft (30cm) in length, with iron hooks, which were referred to as 'spurs'. A further 14-mile (22.53km) circuit of defences was then commenced to protect the besieging forces.[7]

Between 66 and 73 AD, the emperor Vespasian and his son Titus conducted several well-known sieges in the Jewish Wars, including at Jotapata, Jerusalem, Machaerus and Masada. At each siege they built a circumvallation, camps and a large mound to get over the walls they were attacking. To protect battering rams, the Roman armies constructed towers and sheds. Catapults fired iron or stone blots. They also used the ballista to fire a large single stone, which required eight men to operate it. The Romans were successful in these sieges due to their overwhelming numbers and their ability to conduct attritional warfare.[8]

Medieval Warfare

Siege towers, also known as belfries, were essential elements in medieval warfare, having previously been used by the Romans. The towers were normally made of wood, ran on wheels and had an outer cover of ox hides to protect against weapons and fire. Whilst Richard the Lionheart was said to have dined in a siege tower at Messina in Sicily in 1190, the tower's main functions were to provide cover for those attacking the lower sections of the enemy wall, and as a bridge to reach the top of the wall. Weapons used from the towers included spears, crossbows and bows; however, the tower also acted as cover for a battering ram, in addition to mining operations. In medieval siege warfare, it is difficult to determine what is classified as an 'engine' or a 'machine', as the documentary evidence intersperses the

7 Julius Caesar, *The Gallic War*, edited and trans. Carolyn Hammond (Oxford: Oxford University Press, 2008), The Seventh Book: 52 BC, 7.68–7.74, pp. 181–85.

8 David John Breeze, *The Roman Army* (London: Bloomsbury, 2016), pp. 70–72.

different words. However, the positioning of siege engines was essential. For the besiegers, an assessment had to be made of the main targets; for example, whether to focus on a particular section of wall. The projectiles used during medieval sieges included metal, inflammable objects and even human heads, corpses and other dead animals; however, stone was the most common.[9]

Documentary evidence records the continued use of the ballista and catapult during this period, along with the introduction of the trebuchet. An important example of siege warfare occurred at Acre between 1189 and 1191, pitting Richard the Lionheart against Saladin during the Third Crusade to the Holy Land. The siege lasted for approximately two years and has been described by historian John D. Hosler as an ideal example of 12th century warfare. The most up-to-date military technology of the time was available, including trebuchets, siege towers, battering rams, the construction of ramparts and sapping, and even biological and chemical warfare with the polluting of the water supply by using corpses.[10]

The medieval era also ushered in two key developments – the castle and the cannon. Castles developed in Europe, following the collapse of the Holy Roman Empire of Charlemagne in the late 9th and early 10th centuries. It was the Normans who brought *castella* to England, and by 1086 at least 50 castles had been built around the country to secure their hold on the kingdom.[11]

Castles developed from a motte construction on a natural or artificial mound with a timber palisade and ditch. The feature then developed, using timber before stone as the key building material. A basic design could follow the tower of Houdan in northern France. From inside a square and its diagonals, a circle is drawn, with the side of the square acting as its diameter. Where the diagonals of the square and the circumference meet at the intersection, four circles can be drawn to represent the turrets. The interior walls are represented by a smaller square drawn inside the first.[12]

With the introduction of gunpowder from the late 13th century, it began to have an impact on siege warfare. The development of artillery slowly changed warfare. Whilst the French made significant developments in field artillery, it was the Italians who rose to prominence in siege weaponry, with their first recorded use in the 13th century. For the English, the first prominent use of artillery was at Harfleur in 1415.[13] Muskets were also introduced during the Middle Ages, with matchlocks appearing in Europe from the 15th century.[14]

---

9 Jim Bradbury, *The Medieval Siege* (Woodbridge: The Boydell Press, 1992), pp. 241–42, 251.

10 John D. Hosler, *The Siege of Acre 1189–1191: Saladin, Richard the Lionheart and the Battle that Decided the Third Crusade* (London: Yale University Press, 2018), pp. 162–63, 172.

11 Stuart Prior, *A Few Well-positioned Castles: The Norman Art of War* (Stroud: Tempus Publishing Ltd, 2006), p. 36.

12 Malcolm Hislop, *Castle Builders: Approaches to Castle Design and Construction in the Middle Ages* (Barnsley: Pen & Sword Books Ltd, 2016), pp. 9–10, 29, 54.

13 John Rigby Hale, 'The early development of the bastion: an Italian Chronology *c.* 1450–*c.* 1534', in John Rigby Hale, John Roger Loxdale Highfield and Beryl Smalley (eds) *Europe in the late Middle Ages* (London: Faber and Faber, 1965), p. 471; Peter Hoskins, *Siege Warfare During the Hundred Years War 'Once More unto the Breach...'* (Barnsley: Pen & Sword Books Ltd, 2018), p. 31.

14 Michael Spencer, *Early Firearms 1300–1800* (Oxford: Shire Publications Ltd, 2008), p. 6.

The response to this new technology was two-fold – either the thickness of the walls could be increased or the walls could be scarped. Scarping the wall was as an attempt to limit the impact of cannonballs. Scarping was preferred, as it weakened the effect of siege ladders designed to scale the defences by increasing the angle required to set them up against the wall. Taller towers were interposed along the length of walls so that if a wall was being scaled by an advancing enemy, they could be shot at from the flanks. The use of medieval siege engines did have an impact on the ability to break through walls; however, these weapons were unwieldly and largely inaccurate, so much so that they were unable to specifically attack one focal point regularly. The role of siege engines was eventually overtaken by the use of the mortar.[15]

There was also the critical introduction of the angled bastion, a move away from the rounded bastion. The round bastion meant that there was 'dead ground' immediately in front of the feature, which attackers could exploit. Indeed, the series of coastal 'device' castles constructed under the orders of Henry VIII (reigned 1509–47) were obsolete at the time of construction. Developed around 1500 in Italy, the angled bastion meant that there was no such 'dead ground' and reduced the number of artillery pieces required.[16] The angled bastion marked the introduction of the *Trace Italienne* style of fortification, with fortifications made in stone and masonry as well as earth.[17] The late introduction of *Trace Italienne* fortification in England was because the country had been largely peaceful since the Wars of the Roses (1455–85).

The key siege techniques during this period included blockade and bombardment by mechanical machines, including the ballista and trebuchets. In addition, there was bombardment with artillery, although this focused more on individuals rather than targeting the fortifications. Then there was the assault. Wherever possible, assault was preferred if a gap in the fortification could first be made by either mining or bombardment; battering rams and the use of fire, including burning arrows, were also key components.[18]

The Thirty Years' War (1618–48)

The 17th century was a violent period in history, as for only three of its years was there peace in Europe. Indeed, conflict had plagued Europe since the end of the 15th century: the Italian wars between 1494 and 1559; the French religious wars of 1562–98 and 1621–29; the wars in the Netherlands of 1572–1607 and 1621–47; and war in Hungary between 1593 and 1606. The most relevant prolonged conflict to this study was the Thirty Years' War.[19]

15 Hale, 'The early development of the bastion', p. 474.

16 Bernard Lowry, *Discovering Fortifications from the Tudors to the Cold War* (Princes Risborough: Shire Publications Ltd, 2006), p. 13.

17 Quentin Hughes, *Military Architecture* (London: Hugh Evelyn Ltd, 1974), pp. 77, 105.

18 Hoskins, *Siege Warfare During the Hundred Years War 'Once More unto the Breach…'*, pp. 29–34.

19 Charles Carlton, *Going to the Wars: The Experience of the British Civil Wars 1638–1651* (London: Routledge, 1992), p. 8; Geoffrey Parker, *The Military Revolution: military innovation and the rise of the West 1500–1800* (Cambridge: Cambridge University Press, 1996), p. 43.

Essentially, there were two different techniques of siege warfare at the time of the Thirty Years' War. The first was utilised by Prince Maurice of Nassau, who controlled territory with a series of fortified towns and cities, which made pitched battles largely irrelevant because the focus was on the fortifications having to be besieged. This meant that armies were relatively small – a maximum of 10,000 men. The Dutch laid siege to the fortress of Maastricht in 1632 by controlling all communication between Brussels and Westphalia. The Dutch influence over English siege techniques was observed by Prince Maurice, along with the future Parliamentarian commanders Thomas Fairfax and George Goring, who served under Frederick Henry of Nassau at the siege of Breda in 1637. Their techniques for siege warfare included a mixture of blockade, mining and bombardment which could take days, weeks or even years.[20]

The leading Royalist, Prince Rupert, favoured the approach of Gustavus Adolphus, the Swedish king who operated a different method to the Dutch. His approach required control of large areas of territory and being successful in battle, while his siege techniques included early assault, heavy bombardment and intimidation.[21]

Military Manuals

Two of the most important military manuals that influenced 17th century warfare came from the classical world. The first was *De Re Militari* by Flavius Vegetius Renatus, written in the late 5th century, which explores such themes as the use of missiles, bows, camps, organisation, officers, cavalry, drills and battle formations.[22]

The second book was written in the mid-second century by Aelian, who drew on Hellenistic works and the tactics of Alexander the Great. Indeed, the musket and pike armies of the Civil War period were heavily influenced by the approaches taken by the Macedonian phalanx some 2,000 years before. Aelian's work covers tactics, files, formations and cavalry, amongst other aspects of warfare.[23]

There were almost 100 military manuals produced in Britain between 1600 and 1642.[24] One such example was Henry Hexham, who in 1637 wrote *The Principles of the Art Militarie*, based on the wars of the United Netherlands in mainland Europe. Hexham, who had a 42-year career in

20 Christopher Duffy, *Siege Warfare: The Fortress in the Early Modern World 1494–1600* (London: Routledge & Kegan Paul Ltd, 1979), p. 145; Geoffrey Parker (ed.), *The Thirty Years' War* (London: Routledge, 1997), pp. 116, 185; Jon Day, *Gloucester & Newbury 1643: The Turning Point of the Civil War* (Barnsley: Pen & Sword Books Ltd, 2007), p. 65.

21 Parker, *The Thirty Years' War*, pp. 62, 185; Day, *Gloucester & Newbury 1643: The Turning Point of the Civil War*, p. 65.

22 Flavius Vegetius Renatus, *De Re Militari (Concerning military affairs): the classic treatise on warfare at the pinnacle of the Roman Empire's power* (Leonaur, 2012), pp. 23, 29, 41, 43, 50, 60, 94.

23 Christopher Matthew, *The Tactics of Aelian or On the Military Arrangements of the Greeks* (Barnsley: Pen & Sword Books Ltd, 2012), pp. xiii, xv, 5.

24 John Barratt, *Sieges of the English Civil War* (Barnsley: Pen & Sword Books Ltd, 2009), p. 3.

the Dutch army and was a quartermaster to Colonel Goring, was based at Portsmouth when he wrote his second volume – *The Second Part of The Principles of the Art Militarie, Practised In the Warres of the United Provinces: Consisting of the severall formes of battell, represented by the illustrious Maurice Prince of Orange, of famous memorie, and his highnesse Frederick Henrie Prince of Orange that now is, Lord Generall of the Armie of the high & mightie lords the States Generall, of the United Netherlands, &c. Together with the order, and forme of quartering, encamping, and approching in a warre offensive, and defensive* – which was published in London in 1639.[25]

Key segments of Hexham's work focus on approaches towards capturing a town or fortification. This includes an understanding of soil, topography and use of parapets, along with faggots (bundles of wood) and gabions, which were baskets filled with soil and designed to protect artillery positions. There is also a discussion on redoubts, demi-bastions and full bastions.[26]

When approaching a town or fortification, Hexham stated that the focus should be to attack the curtain wall *or* the bastion. Approaching a single bastion was more efficient because the bastion itself was positioned before the curtain wall and had support from a single defensive position – from the opposite bastion – rather than a series of bastions when approaching a curtain wall. Before approaching the main bastion (or curtain wall), he said the besiegers should move against the fortifications constructed in front of those defences, including hornworks, half-moons and ravelins.[27]

When approaching with trenches as seen in Figure 1, the besiegers were under continual fire from the enemy, which Hexham said meant that another style of trench known as a 'sapp' (sap) was necessary. From this trench, a kneeling man excavated the ground using a short spade to a depth of 3ft (0.91m), and dispersed the earth either side of him. The sapper moved forward, whilst a second digger expanded the trench to 6ft (1.82m). This continued until a third man completed the sap. The saps had to be kept dry and not excavated to such depths as to allow water to settle in them. It is important to note that Hexham suggests that there must be either 200, 300, 400 or even 500 soldiers designated to work beside the artillery.[28]

Further literature includes Robert Ward's 1639 work *Animadversions of Warre; or, A militarie magazine of the truest rules, and ablest instructions,*

25 Laurence Spring, *The First British Army 1624–1628: The Army of the Duke of Buckingham* (Solihull: Helion & Company Limited, 2016), p. 20; Henry Hexham, *The Principles of the Art Militarie; practised in the warres of the Vnited Netherlands* (London: M.P. for Matthew Symmons, 1637); Henry Hexham, 'The Second Part of The Principles of the Art Militarie, Practised In the Warres of the United Provinces : Consisting of the severall formes of battell, represented by the illustrious Maurice Prince of Orange, of famous memorie, and his highnesse Frederick Henrie Prince of Orange that now is, Lord Generall of the Armie of the high & mightie lords the States Generall, of the United Netherlands, &c. Together with the order, and forme of quartering, encamping, and approching in a warre offensive, and defensive', in *The Principles of the Art Militarie; practised in the warres of the Vnited Netherlands* (London: Printed by Robert Young, at the signe of the Starre upon Bread-street-hill, 1639), pp. 1–40.

26 Hexham, 'The Second Part of The Principles of the Art Militarie', pp. 13–16.

27 Hexham, 'The Second Part of The Principles of the Art Militarie', pp. 15–16.

28 Hexham, 'The Second Part of The Principles of the Art Militarie', pp. 15–17.

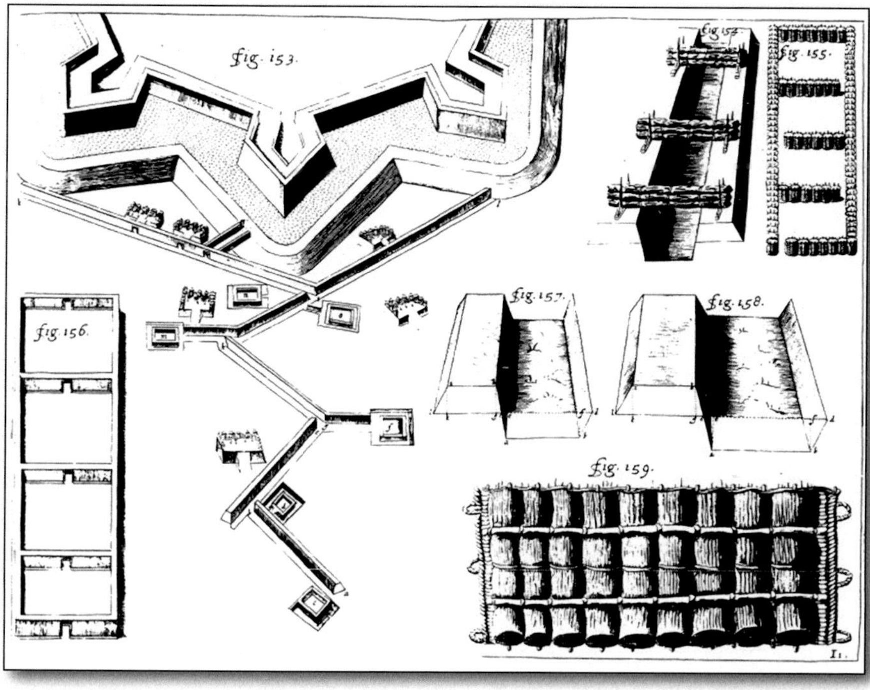

Figure 1 Illustration from Henry Hexham's *The Second Part of The Principles of the Art Militarie* (1639, pp. 18–19), showing how to approach a fortification. (Reproduced by permission of the British Library – Shelfmark: General Reference Collection C.122.i.4.(3.). Image published with permission of ProQuest®. Further reproduction is prohibited without permission. Image produced by ProQuest® as part of Early English Books Online. www.proquest.com)

for the managing of warre. A particularly important section is his analysis of the siege of Breda (1624–25). Chapters 41 and 42 examine the redoubts, fortifications and batteries used by the Spanish general Spinola in his successful campaign to besiege the town.[29]

Ward described three batteries in detail, noting that each side of those which faced the town were made cannon-proof, that is to say that the curtain walls/bastions were 25ft (7.62m) thick (Figure 2). Looking at the first battery, it was described as 160ft (48.76m) long and 125 ft (38.1m) wide, with the rear and flank wall 15ft (4.57m) thick; one wall was thicker as it contained a parapet on the inside. The front of the fortification contained two exterior angles with nine windows; each window was 2½ft (0.76m) wide to allow for the positioning of cannon. A raised area inside the fortification was approximately 8ft (2.43m) in height and 35ft (10.66m) broad, covered with planks designed for the recoil and repositioning of the artillery pieces. The outer wall and underneath the cannon windows were palisaded with sharp long stakes. Around the battery was a ditch which was 7ft (2.13m) deep and 48ft (14.63m) in width. The ditch was cut so that it sloped from top to bottom. The bottom of the ditch was 38ft (11.58m) in width. The outer section of the ditch contained a palisade and was designed to block assaults. Before gaining access to the battery, a half-moon, which contained a guard of musketeers, was constructed outside of the fortification; it was contained within a counterscarp and palisade.[30]

29 Robert Ward, *Animadversions of Warre; or, A militarie magazine of the truest rules, and ablest instructions, for the managing of warre* (London: John Dawson, 1639), pp. 94–105.

30 Ward, *Animadversions of Warre*, p. 95.

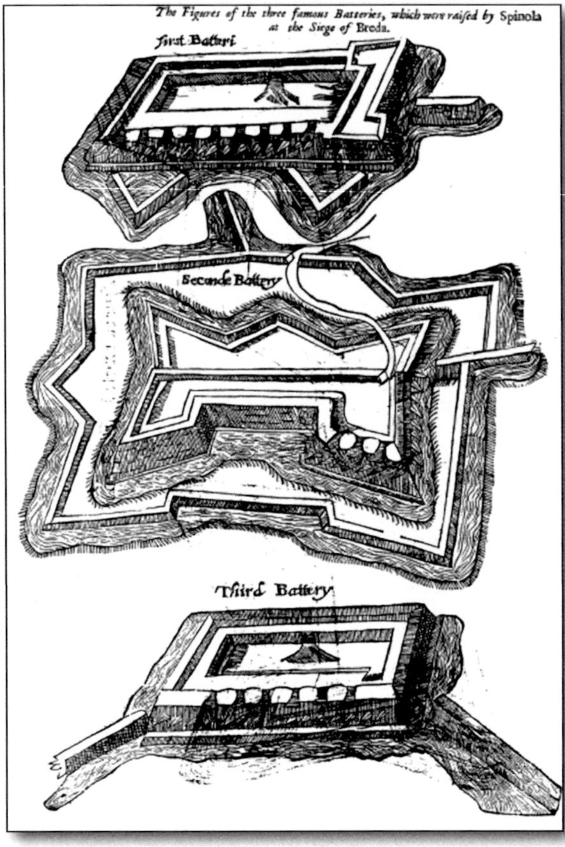

Figure 2 Illustration from Robert Ward's *Animadversions of Warre* (1639, p. 94) showing a series of batteries constructed for the siege of Breda (1624–25). (Reproduced by permission of Beinecke Rare Book and Manuscript Library, Yale University. Image published with permission of ProQuest®. Further reproduction is prohibited without permission. Image produced by ProQuest® as part of Early English Books Online. www.proquest.com)

Ward added that the other forts were covered with green turf. The bastions were 35ft (10.66m) thick and 13ft (3.96m) high. The curtain walls were 100ft (30.48m) long and were supported by a ditch that was 12ft (3.65m) in width and 8ft (2.43m) deep. It was these fortifications that would endure the battering of the cannon from the besieged town.[31]

What can be seen from these last two accounts is the amount of detail, precision, effort, men and resources required to construct approaches, batteries and fortifications to the 17th century military manual standard. This includes Hexham's suggestion of having between 200 and 500 soldiers near the artillery, and the imposing dimensions of the first battery given by Ward – 160ft (48.76m) long and 125ft (38.1m) wide. These represent the 'perfect', the idealised versions of what to construct – not the reality of warfare. Interestingly, both Ward and Hexham – along with other writers – were influenced by Diego Ufano's *Tratado de Artilleria* published in 1613, demonstrating the continued Continental impact on fortification design.[32]

The Artillery of the Age

Since the Elizabethan period, writers such as William Bourne – who in 1587 wrote *The Arte of Shooting in Great Ordnaunce* – and Thomas Smith – who produced *The Art of Gunnery* in 1600 – had written books, in English, on how to effectively position and utilise the artillery of the age. By the start of the Civil War, Robert Norton had also published *The Gunner* in 1628, and in addition to this, William Eldred had written *The Gunners Glasse* in 1646. Another important work is Nathaniel Nye's 1647 *The Art of Gunnery*, which was the subject of a later edition published in 1670.[33] Figure 3 illustrates some of the available types of cannon in the Civil War period.

31 Ward, *Animadversions of Warre*, p. 99.

32 Christopher Duffy, *Siege Warfare: The Fortress in the Early Modern World 1494–1600* (London: Routledge & Kegan Paul Ltd, 1979), p. 146; David Flintham, 'They have sent to Holland for Engineers', in Serena Jones (ed.), *'Britain Turned Germany': The Thirty Years' War and its impact on the British Isles, 1638–1660*, Proceedings of the Helion and Company 'Century of the Soldier' Conference (Warwick: Helion & Company Ltd, 2019), p. 90.

33 William Bourne, *The Arte of Shooting in Great Ordnaunce* (London: Thomas Woodcocke, 1587); Thomas Smith, *The Art of Gunnery* (London: William Ponsonby, 1600); William Eldred, *The Gunners Glasse* (London: Robert Boydel, 1646); Nathaniel Nye, *The Art of Gunnery* (London: William Leak, 1647); Nathaniel Nye, *The Art of Gunnery* (London: William Leak, 1670).

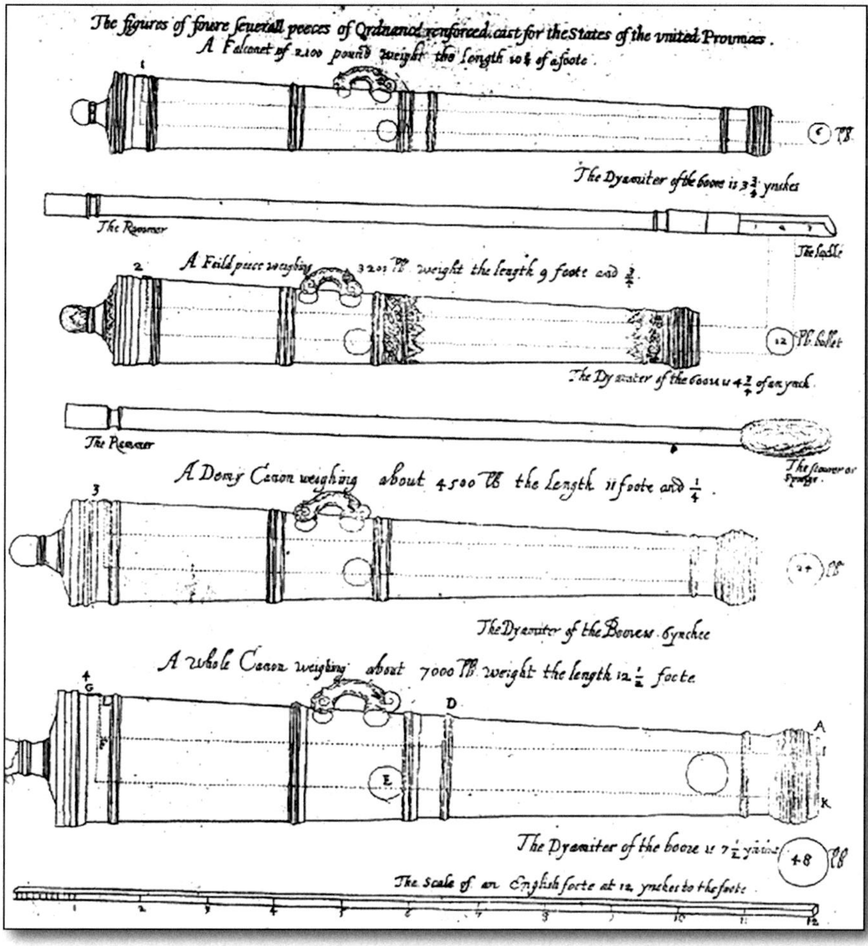

Figure 3 Illustration from Henry Hexham's *The Third Part of the Principles of the Art Military* (1643, between pp. 4–5) showing some of the available types of cannon. (Reproduced by permission of the University of Illinois (Urbana-Champaign Campus) Library. Image published with permission of ProQuest®. Further reproduction is prohibited without permission. Image produced by ProQuest® as part of Early English Books Online. www.proquest.com)

Thomas Smith published *The Art of Gunnery* in 1600. Table 1 illustrates three key artillery pieces – the minion, saker and demi-culverin. One of the most important aspects for this study is the range of the weapons. The data reveals that the optimum (point-blank) range for all of the cannon would have been between 213.36m and 289.56m, with the maximum ranges between 1,066.8m and 1,371.6m.

Table 1: Artillery data from Thomas Smith's *The Art of Gunnery* (1600), pp. 87–88

Artillery	Weight of cannon	Weight of shot	Length of cannon	Point-blank range	Maximum range
Demi-culverin	3,000lb 1,360.77kg	11¾lb 5.32kg	11ft 3.35m	380 paces 289.56m	1,800 paces 1,371.6m
Saker (ordinary)	1,900lb 861.82kg	6lb 2.72kg	9½ft 2.89m	300 paces 228.6m	1,500 paces 1,143m
Minion	1,100lb 498.95kg	4¾lb 2.15kg	8ft 2.43m	280 paces 213.36m	1,400 paces 1,066.8m

We now move onto an examination of Robert Norton's work, *The Gunner*. By examining Table 2, the essential figure of point-blank range reveals that in order to be fully effective, the artillery had to be positioned within *c*. 265m for a demi-culverin, and as close as *c*. 137m for a falconet piece. This information illustrates how, theoretically, warfare was enacted in such close quarters during the 17th century.

Table 2: Artillery data from Robert Norton's *The Gunner* (1628), pp. 52–53

Artillery	Weight of cannon	Weight of shot	Length of cannon	Point-blank range (paces)	Point-blank range (metres)
Demi-culverin	2,200–2,500lb	9–12½lb	11ft	348	265.17
	997.90–1,133.98kg	4.08–5.66kg	3.352m		
Saker	1,400–1,600lb	5–5½lb	9ft	300	228.6
	635.02–725.74kg	2.26–2.49kg	2.74m		
Minion	1,200lb	3¾(?)lb	7½(?)feet	240	182.88
	544.31kg	1.70kg	2.28m		
Falcon	700lb	2⅖(?)lb	7ft	260	198.12
	317.51kg	1.08kg	2.13m		
Falconet	500lb	1⅔(?)lb	6ft	180	137.16
	226.79kg	0.75kg	1.82m		
Rabinet (Robinet)	300lb	¼lb	4ft	–	–
	136.07kg	0.11kg	1.21m		

Examining William Eldred's 1646 work *The Gunners Glasse* (Table 3), there is the now familiar theme linking the weight and length of the weapons; while the shot weight appears to be standardised, albeit, for example, with Norton giving the weight of shot for a demi-culverin as between 4.08kg and 5.66kg, in comparison to Eldred specifying 4.08kg.

Eldred states that the most important pieces for a field army are the demi-cannon, whole culverins, demi-culverins and sakers. For a siege, he notes that for the assault of every individual fortification, there should be nine cannons, eight demi-cannons, six quarter-cannons and seven pieces of field artillery.[34]

He notes that for each 15 days of a siege, cannons should fire eight shots per day, the demi-cannons 10 shots and the culverins 12 shots, with the demi-culverins and sakers firing 14 shots each day. The artillery train should carry a significant supply of munitions, including 5,000 shots for cannons, 12,000 for demi-cannons, 14,000 for culverins and 16,000 for demi-culverins.[35]

34 Eldred, *The Gunners Glasse*, p. 114.
35 Eldred, *The Gunners Glasse*, pp. 116, 118.

Table 3: Artillery data from William Eldred's *The Gunners Glasse* (1646), p. 15

Artillery	Weight of cannon	Weight of shot	Length of cannon
Demi-culverin	3,600lb	9lb	10ft
	1,632.93kg	4.082kg	3.04m
Saker	2,500lb	5lb	9½ft
	1,133.98kg	2.26kg	2.89m
Minion	1,500lb	4lb	8ft
	680.38kg	1.81kg	2.43m
Falcon	700lb	2.25lb	6ft
	317.51kg	1.02kg	1.82m
Falconet	210lb	1.25lb (?)	4ft
	95.25kg	0.56kg	1.21m
Rabinet (Robinet)	120lb	¾lb	3ft
	54.43kg	0.34kg	0.91m

Table 4 analyses the first 1647 version of Nye's *The Art of Gunnery*, published one year after his direct involvement in the Siege of Worcester. The data illustrates important information regarding the weight of cannon, weight of shot and the length of the pieces, but does not detail any ranges of the weapons. The weight of the shot is described in intricate detail, for example describing the shot used for the robinet as being 8oz (0.22kg) of iron and 10oz (0.28kg) of lead.

Comparing Nye's data with that of Eldred's, published one year earlier, similar weights are discussed. This is evident when comparing the weight of the shot for the minion piece, with Nye stating it weighs 3¾lb (1.70kg), but Eldred producing a figure of 4lb (1.81kg). These minor differences continue to illustrate a degree of standardisation in the size and weight of the shot and, thereby, the weight and length of the cannon being produced in the foundries throughout the land. Nye himself is an interesting character; as Cliff Mitchell notes, he was willing to criticise rival publications, such as William Bourne's work.[36]

Moving to the final artillery table (Table 5), Nye's updated 1670 version of *The Art of Gunnery*, a plethora of artillery is listed, with no less than 18 different pieces named. This includes three different types of demi-cannon, three variations of the culverin, three types of demi-culverin and three different sakers, including a Tudor-era artillery piece, which has a larger weight of shot, weighing in at 7lb 5oz (3.31kg), compared to the (ordinary) saker, which has a shot of 6lb (2.72kg).

Of particular note is the data demonstrating that the culverin (ordinary whole) artillery piece had a point-blank range of 400 yards (365.7m) and a maximum range of 800 yards (731.5m). The weight of the shot fired by this culverin is listed as 17lb 5oz (7.85kg). Each piece firing 12 rounds per day, as previously noted by Eldred, may have caused some damage to the enemy's position, if correctly targeted.

36 Nathanael Nye, *The Art of Gunnery (1647) together with A Treatise of Artificial Fire-Works*, introduction and transcription by Cliff Mitchell (Farnham: The Pike and Shot Society, 2004), p. ii.

Table 4: Artillery data from Nathaniel Nye's *The Art of Gunnery* (1647), pp. 74–79

Artillery	Weight of cannon	Weight of shot	Length of cannon	Point-blank range	Maximum range
Demi-culverin (ordinary)	2,700lb	10lb 10½oz	10ft	–	–
	1,224.69kg	4.833kg	3.04m		
Saker (ordinary)	1,500 lb	6lb	9ft	–	–
	680.38kg	2.72kg	2.74m		
Minion	1,000lb	3¾lb	8ft	–	–
	453.59kg	1.70kg	2.43m		
Falcon	750lb	2½lb	7ft	–	–
	340.19kg	1.13kg	2.13m		
Falconet	400lb	1lb 5oz	6ft	–	–
	181.43kg	595.33g	1.82m		
Robinet	300lb	8oz iron and 10oz lead	5½ft	–	–
	136.07kg	510.29g	1.67m		

Table 5: Artillery data from Nathaniel Nye's *The Art of Gunnery* (1670), pp. 71–79

Artillery	Weight of cannon	Weight of shot	Length of cannon	Point-blank range	Maximum range
Cannon	8,000lb	58lb	12ft	–	–
	3,628.73kg	26.30kg	3.65m		
Demi-cannon	6,000lb	36lb	12ft	–	–
	2,721.55kg	16.32kg	3.65m		
Demi-cannon (ordinary)	5,600lb	36lb	10–11ft	–	–
	2,540.11kg	16.32kg	3.04–3.35m		
Demi-cannon (another)	5,400lb	30lb	10 or 12ft	–	–
	2,449.39kg	13.60kg	3.04 or 3.65m		
Culverin	4,800lb	20lb	10, 12 or 13ft	–	–
	2,177.24kg	9.07kg	3.04, 3.65 or 3.96m		
Culverin (ordinary whole)	4,500lb	17lb 5oz	12ft	400 yards	800 yards (by the metal)
	2,041.16kg	7.85kg	3.65m	365.7m	731.5m
Culverin (least size)	4,000lb	Almost 15lb	12ft	–	–
	1,814.36kg	Almost 6.80kg	3.65m		
Demi-culverin	3,000lb	12lb 11oz	10, 12 or 13ft	–	–
	1360.77kg	5.75kg	3.04, 3.65 or 3.96m		
Demi-culverin (ordinary)	2,700lb	10lb 10.5oz	10ft	–	–
	1,224.69kg	4.83kg	3.04m		
Demi-culverin (lower)	2,000lb	9lb	9 or 10ft	–	–
	907.18kg	4.08kg	2.74 or 3.04m		

Artillery	Weight of cannon	Weight of shot	Length of cannon	Point-blank range	Maximum range
Sakers (Tudor era)	1,800lb	7lb 5oz	9 or 10ft	–	–
	816.46kg	3.31kg	2.74 or 3.04m		
Sakers (ordinary)	1,500lb	6lb	9ft	–	–
	680.38kg	2.72kg	2.74m		
Sakers (lower)	1, 400lb	4.75lb	8ft	–	–
	635.02kg	2.15kg	2.43m		
Minion	1,000lb	3.75lb	8ft	–	–
	453.59kg	1.70kg	2.43m		
Minion (ordinary)	750lb	3.75lb	7ft	–	–
	340.19kg	1.70kg	2.13m		
Faucons (Falcon)	750lb	2.5lb	7ft	–	–
	340.19kg	1.13kg	2.13m		
Fauconets (Falconets)	400lb	1lb 5oz	6ft	–	–
	181.43kg	0.59kg	1.82m		
Rabanet (Robinet)	300lb	8oz of iron, 12oz of lead	5.5feet	–	–
	136.07kg	0.22kg of iron, 0.34kg of lead	1.67m		

Figure 4 Illustration from Henry Hexham's *The Third Part of The Principles of the Art Militarie…* (1640, between pp. 24–25) showing how to attack a curtain wall (top) and how to assault a bastion (bottom). (Reproduced by permission of the British Library – Shelfmark: General Reference Collection C.122.i.4.(4.). Image published with permission of ProQuest®. Further reproduction is prohibited without permission. Image produced by ProQuest® as part of Early English Books Online. www.proquest.com)

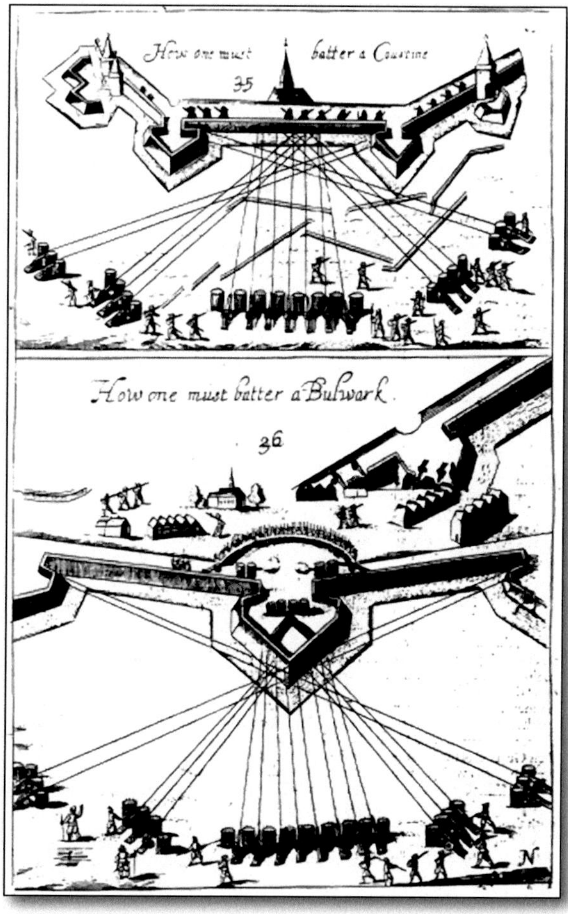

An understanding and appreciation of the evidence found in the literature of the period is critical to comprehending how artillery impacted on the development of defences and the besiegers' use of this weapon. For example, Smith notes that from the end of the Elizabethan period, the range of the demi-culverin was between *c.* 1,370m and a point-blank range of *c.* 289m, whilst Norton in 1628 revises the point-blank range down to *c.* 265m. The effectiveness, or at least the function of the artillery of the age in assaulting the ramparts and bastions discussed, is perhaps most clearly expressed in the literature of the period by Henry Hexham's work (Figure 4).

The historian Chris Henry categorises cannons into two main types, the battering and the culverin. The battering or siege artillery consisted of the cannon, the perrier and the demi-cannon. The culverin type usually had a lighter shot and theoretically a longer range. It important to note that the term culverin refers not only to a particular gun, but also to a group of guns. Guns in this class include the saker and the falcon. The categorisation is further complicated with the introduction of the drake and the bastard. Drake refers to a shorter and lighter version of the weapon; for example, a drake culverin is a smaller version of the culverin. The term 'bastard' refers to a gun that has a specific calibre and weight but does not have a specific length. The most common shot of the period consisted of cast iron; however, lead and stone were also used, if necessary.[37]

However, according to the historian David Blackmore, sieges generally involved very specific artillery, such as culverins, cannons and demi-cannons, whilst demi-culverins and smaller weapons were used in the field,[38] though the historian John Barratt notes that the demi-culverin was frequently utilised against fortifications.[39] The reality of war probably meant that regardless of what type of artillery piece was available, even if it was not specifically designed for siege warfare, it would have been used in any event. Chris Henry further complicates the matter by including the perrier in the category of siege guns. The complexity of the issue is perhaps best summed up by Henry himself, who summarised that there was a "bewildering variety of ordnance in use and that the technical authors of the day only agreed in part of lengths and sizes".[40]

Summary

On the eve of the Civil War, it can be seen that some of the techniques of warfare were thousands of years old – including mining, sapping, scaling ladders, use of missiles and large-scale earthworks. The introduction of gunpowder to Europe in the 13th century, and the subsequent development of the *Trace Italienne* style of fortification, had seen a move away from the stone-built castles of the medieval era.

Whilst the relative peace and prosperity on the British Isles saw the expansion of towns and cities over their medieval walls and ditches, the experiences on the Continent in the Thirty Years' War brought advances in fortification design and artillery. The landscape of the Severn Valley – with its important rivers and road networks to Wales, Oxford and London – was not ready for the construction of weapons and fortifications as seen in the military manuals of Henry Hexham and Robert Ward. However, war was approaching, and control of these towns and ports was vital to the success of both the King and Parliament.

37 Chris Henry, *English Civil War Artillery 1642–51* (Oxford: Osprey Publishing Ltd, 2005), pp. 9–10, 18.

38 David J. Blackmore, *Arms and Armour of the English Civil Wars* (London: The Trustees of the Royal Armouries, 1990), p. 83.

39 Barratt, *Sieges of the English Civil War*, p. 4.

40 Henry, *English Civil War Artillery 1642–51*, p. 9.

Chapter 1

The Sieges of 1643

On 22 August 1642, in a theatrical medieval theme, King Charles I raised the standard at Nottingham; the Civil War was underway. Neither side was victorious at the first major engagement of the war at Edgehill on 23 October that year. Moving into 1643, both sides controlled equal amounts of territory, although Parliament held London and Hull, which contained large arsenals of weapons, in addition to several key ports.[1] On the offensive, it was Parliament that undertook the first siege in the area focused on by this study.

The Parliamentarian Siege of Worcester, 29–31 May 1643

The city of Worcester lies on the east bank of the River Severn on a gravel terrace overlaying Keuper Marl geology. At this point the river moves through a 500m floodplain cutting into the terrace, which means that the banks of the river are well drained. The south-facing promontory demarcated by the River Severn in the west and the Frog Brook in the east provides two naturally defensive positions. The city sits between 23.8m and 25.9m aOD (above Ordnance Datum, a term used by archaeologists for the height above sea level) at its northern circuit whilst falling southwards towards the cathedral, before a distinct drop to Frog Brook and the alluvium at Diglis. Worcester holds an important position on the Severn, with Gloucester 25 miles (40.23km) to the south and Bridgnorth 25 miles (40.23km) away heading north.[2]

Writing from Worcester on 30 September 1642, the Parliamentarian Nehemiah Wharton[3] pronounced that the county of Worcestershire was

---

1 Peter Gaunt, *The English Civil Wars 1642–51* (Oxford: Osprey Publishing Ltd, 2003), pp. 34–35, 37; Peter Gaunt, *The English Civil War: A Military History* (London: I.B. Tauris & Co Ltd, 2014), p. 46.

2 Nigel Baker and Richard Holt, *Urban Growth and the Medieval Church: Gloucester and Worcester* (Aldershot: Ashgate Publishing Ltd, 2004), pp. 139, 142.

3 Henry Ellis, 'Letters from a subaltern officer of the Earl of Essex's army, written in the summer and autumn of 1642; detailing the early movements of that portion of the Parliament forces

"pleasaunt, fruitfull, and rich country, abounding in corne, woods, pastures, hills and valleys".[4] He described the city of Worcester as follows:

> "[It is] on the east bank of that famous river Severne. The wall in the forme of a triangle, the gates seaven, the bulwarkes five, but much decayed: no castle, only a mount of earth ... This citty hath also a stronge stone bridge over Severne, consistinge of sixe arches, with a gate in the middle of the bridge, as stronge as that on London Bridge, with a percullis."[5]

What this account demonstrates is that the medieval wall, despite some decay, is still intact. The description refers to seven gates entering the city, with reference to five bulwarks – the surviving medieval towers. It appears that the castle had been robbed of any stone, and no longer existed, with only a mound of earth (perhaps a reference to the original motte and bailey structure) at the site. The importance of the stone bridge over the River Severn is signified by an interesting description of six arches, while there is also a portcullis to monitor entry to the town from the west.

Wharton remained in Worcester, and on 7 October 1642[6] wrote that he observed on the Monday that soldiers were being paid 12d every day to construct fortifications around the town. On Wednesday he went to observe their progress, and noted that "scaunces, half moones, redouts"[7] were being constructed on "on one side of the city, and goe round the city unto Seuerne againe. It will be finished with all convenient speede."[8] This is the first known account of any fortifications being constructed at Worcester. Of particular importance is the reference to a sconce, half-moon and redoubt. If Wharton's words are interpreted correctly, it appears that the new fortifications would stop at the River Severn, being a natural barrier; John Speed's 1610 plan of the city show a medieval wall enclosing the majority of the western section of the town on the bank of the Severn.

So what exactly was a sconce, half-moon and redoubt? Robert Ward, in his 1639 work *Animadversions of Warre; or, A militarie magazine of the truest rules, and ablest instructions, for the managing of warre*, illustrates that the most common sconce is a square feature, with four 'bulworkes' (bastions) at each corner, as illustrated in Figure 5. Ward says this type of sconce should be positioned on rocky high ground or near a river, with thick cannon-proof ramparts and bastions, and the ability to withstand the enemy's artillery.[9]

Reference is also made to a triangular sconce, with three bastions at each corner. Ward notes that this sconce should be constructed at a position that is naturally defensive, partly because it is a small feature, not much better than a redoubt. The advantage of this type of sconce is that it is quick to

which was formed by the volunteers of the metropolis; and their further movements when amalgamated with the rest of the Earl of Essex's troops', *Archaeologia*, Vol. 35 (1853), p. 330.

4 Ellis, 'Letters from a subaltern officer of the Earl of Essex's army...', p. 328.

5 *Ibid.*

6 *Ibid.*, p. 334.

7 *Ibid.*, p. 333.

8 *Ibid.*, p. 333.

9 Ward, *Animadversions of Warre*, pp. 38, 88.

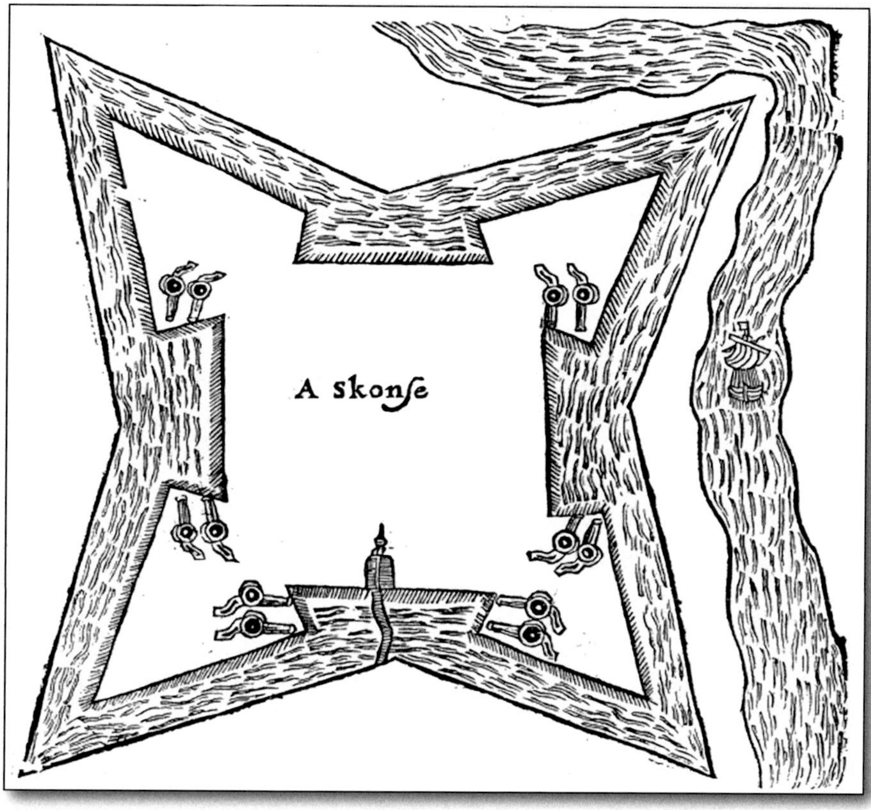

Figure 5 Illustration from Robert Ward's *Animadversions of Warre* (1639, p. 88) showing a four-sided sconce fortification. (Reproduced by permission of Beinecke Rare Book and Manuscript Library, Yale University. Image published with permission of ProQuest®. Further reproduction is prohibited without permission. Image produced by ProQuest® as part of Early English Books Online. www.proquest.com)

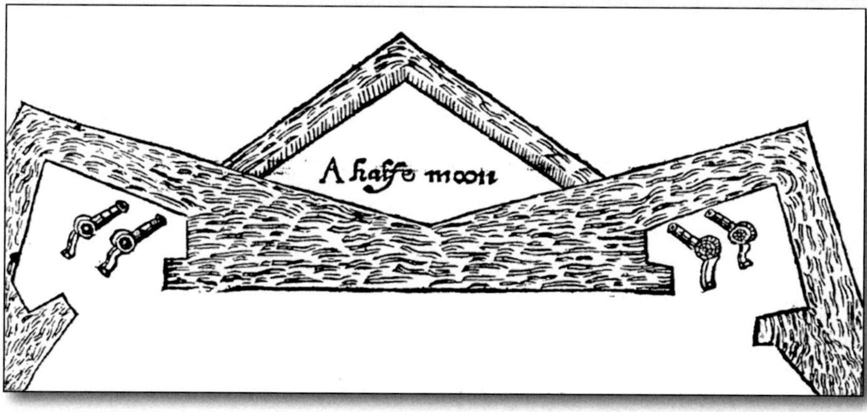

Figure 6 Illustration from Robert Ward's *Animadversions of Warre* (1639, p. 89) showing a half-moon fortification. (Reproduced by permission of Beinecke Rare Book and Manuscript Library, Yale University. Image published with permission of ProQuest®. Further reproduction is prohibited without permission. Image produced by ProQuest® as part of Early English Books Online. www.proquest.com)

construct, made of earth, and that it should only be constructed to the height of the artillery pieces. In addition, Ward illustrates a sconce design of six bastions that has the ability to hold up to 200 soldiers.[10] Ward depicts the half-moon feature (illustrated in Figure 6) stylistically as an almost semi-circular/arrow point construction, consisting of two bastions' faces joined to two flanks, located in front of the main ditch and between the main bastions. He states that they are suitable features from which to hinder any approach from a besieging army that attempts to use mines, and refers to the experience

10 Ward, *Animadversions of Warre*, pp. 84, 89.

of Dutch engineers regarding this.[11] The final feature, the redoubt, comes in a variety of forms, including triangular and square. What form is constructed depends on the number of men a commander had available to man it. The main purposes of the redoubt was to stop the enemy from making any surprise attacks, prevent a cavalry approach or hinder the enemy's approach over a water ford, with two redoubts working in tandem on occasion. Ward said the breastwork should be between 4ft (1.21m) and 5ft (1.52m) thick, and 8ft (2.43m) in height, with a palisade and a ditch 6ft (1.82m) to 8ft (2.43m) wide. Entrance to the fortification should be via a drawbridge. The square redoubt should hold 150 soldiers, be palisaded and placed between two fortifications, either by itself or with another redoubt.[12]

Based on Ward's descriptions of the various fortifications, it would seem that the sconce or half-moon features would be the most suitable to be constructed to defend Worcester, particularly as the four-sided sconce and the triangular redoubt were designed to be positioned by rivers. The pluralisation of the language used by Wharton suggests that more than one of the features were being constructed. Given the time and resources at the beginning of the conflict, it would appear that the most likely feature to be constructed at that time would be the triangular redoubt.

A Parliamentarian intelligence report dated 9 October 1642 recorded: "We have made some small works upon the hill neere Worcester ... neere Severn."[13] This source describes further works being undertaken at Worcester, this time on a hill near the town. Given the language, it appears that a series of works may refer to a number of redoubts, and that the engineers in charge of construction had recognised the obvious advantages of high ground. As the nearest high ground, now aptly named Fort Royal Hill, is detached and away from the main medieval town, it can be inferred that the features were connected to the town via a series of banks (ramparts) and ditches.

Following the Battle of Edgehill on 23 October 1642, and the Parliamentarian Colonel Essex's withdrawal from Worcester to Gloucester, the Royalists took control of the city. It is fortunate that the *Chamber Order Book of Worcester* survives and has some important information regarding the construction of the fortifications throughout the town. For example, on 2 March 1642/3,[14] it records that Sir William Russell, the governor, was considering raising charges "upon the cittizens concerning the raysing of money for the souldiers and fortiff[ic]acions of the citty".[15]

A few weeks later, on 11 March 1642/3, the *Chamber Order Book* records further attempts to prepare the town for conflict, noting that:

11 *Ibid.*, pp. 47–48.

12 *Ibid.*, pp. 85–87.

13 R. Howes, *Weekly Intelligence from Severall parts of this Kingdome, and other places, from the 10 of Octob. to the 18.* (London: 1642), p. 13.

14 Shelagh Bond (ed.), *The Chamber Order Book of Worcester 1602–1650* (Leeds: The Worcestershire Historical Society, 1974), p. 361.

15 Bond, *The Chamber Order Book of Worcester 1602–1650*, p. 362.

> "£180 the moneth upon this cittie for the payment of souldiers and for fortificacion of this cittie, and that it is here affirmed that the souldiers doe not expect any paie and that they are willing to prepare and raise threescore men every day to worke for the fortification of this cittie."[16]

Another example notes that:

> "It is ordered that there shall be raised fowertie shillings every day in the weeke (except Sundaie) for the payment of 60 men dayly that shall worke in the fortification of this cittie soe long as the worke shall continue."[17]

What these records note is the increased reliance, and expenditure, being put upon the citizens of Worcester for the construction of the fortifications. According to Richard Norwood, one man could excavate 500 cubic feet (14.1 cubic metres) every day.[18] This means that for six days worked, one man could move 3,000 cubic feet (84.95 cubic metres) of earth. Multiplying this by 60 (the number of men mentioned in the *Chamber Order Book*) means that the men working on the fortifications of Worcester should have been able to excavate 180,000 cubic feet (5,097.03 cubic metres) of earth. This is a significant amount of earth moved for the creation of ditches and ramparts for the defence of the town.

An important defensive feature was the city ditch. The ditch had been scoured in 1638; however, it appears to have fallen into disrepair, as in 1643, Richard Wylde complained of a smell coming from it.[19] This suggests that unmaintained, the ditch was used as a rubbish tip and was probably prone to flooding. However, as the archaeologist and historian Malcolm Atkin states, because there is no evidence that the ditch – flat-bottomed and 10–16m in width to the east of the city (modern-day City Walls Road) – was cleaned in this period, the boggy nature of the fill would have actually provided the besieged with a tactical advantage if the city was stormed.[20]

The historian John Barratt describes the fortifications of Worcester at the time of the 1643 siege as consisting of the medieval walls lined with banks of earth between 6ft (1.82m) and 9ft (2.74m) thick, with the ditches in front of them a maximum of 36ft (10.97m) in width and 10ft (3.04m) deep.[21] According to Malcolm Atkin, the extent of the defences ran from the old bridge (between Newport Street and Tyebridge Street to the west) along the bank of the river, with the church of St Clement's inside the wall. The line turned east towards The Butts and Sansome Street, which was interposed by

---

16 Bond, *The Chamber Order Book of Worcester 1602–1650*, p. 363.

17 *Ibid.*, p. 364.

18 Richard Norwood, *Fortification or Military Architecture* (London: Andrew Crooke, 1639), p. 123.

19 Clive Beardsmore, 'Documentary Evidence for the History of Worcester City Defences', in M.O.H. Carver (ed.), 'Medieval Worcester: an archaeological framework: reports, surveys texts and essays', *Transactions of the Worcestershire Archaeological Society* (3rd Series) Vol. 7 (1980), p. 63.

20 Malcolm Atkin, *Worcester 1651* (Barnsley: Pen and Sword Books Ltd, 2008), p. 33.

21 John Barratt, *Sieges of the English Civil War*, p. 98.

Plate: 1 St Martin's Tower, City Walls Road, Worcester (facing north-north-west). (Author's photo)

Foregate Street and the gate here. The wall, and accompanying ditch, then followed what is now City Walls Road to St Martin's Gate on the southern side of Cornmarket. Moving off City Walls Road, the wall continued to Sidbury Gate. Turning west, the wall enclosed the site of St Peter's Church and continued along King Street towards the mound where the medieval castle once sat. Keeping along the quayside, the wall ran north along the bank of the River Severn to Bridge Gate. The medieval wall is described as being 1.8m (6ft) thick and having banks of earth along the wall at least 2m (6½ft) thick.[22] Some of the medieval city wall has survived to the present day, including St Martin's Tower on City Walls Road, which can be seen in Plate 1.

Both Atkin and Barratt reference the use of earth again the medieval walls, which was intended to lessen the impact of cannon shot. Given that the construction of fortifications of this time consisted of earthen banks and ditches, it appears logical to put earth against old medieval walls to strengthen them. However, the engineer David Papillon, writing in 1645, stated that "If the towne hath walls … it is not the lining of these walls … that will secure the same."[23] In addition to this, Robert Ward mentions

22 Atkin, *Worcester 1651*, pp. 29–30.

23 David Papillon, *A practicall abstract of the arts of fortification and assailing containing foure different methods of fortifications with approved rules, to be set out in the feild all manner of*

regarding medieval walls, "the imperfections of our walled Townes here in England, that we may not bee deceived in putting our confidence in the strength of them".[24]

Consequently, on the eve of the first siege of Worcester, the city had a series of sconces, half-moons and redoubts of unknown size, shape and quality, albeit with some works on a nearby hill, a medieval wall lined with earth – that two period authors said would be insufficient to keep out an attacking force – and a boggy ditch.

On the morning of 29 May 1643, Sir William Waller and his Parliamentarian army of 3,000 men, with eight cannon, approached the city. Governor Sir William Russell was in Oxford, so the city was under the control of Colonel William Sandys. As the Royalists did not surrender, the Parliamentarians attacked, with their focus on the south and east sections of the city. The right flank moved towards St Martin's Gate, while the centre targeted Green Hill. Accompanied by an artillery barrage, there followed assaults on Diglis and Friar's Gate, both of which failed. The cannon fire, however, destroyed the cathedral organist's house. The Royalists returned fire with 200 shots, having used 11 barrels of gunpowder. Waller's men had made it as far as medieval wall below Castle Hill, to the blockhouse of William Berkeley. The Royalists then conducted a cavalry sally from St Martin's Gate, and were able to successfully clear the east section of the city. Casualties were high after two days of fighting. With Prince Maurice and his Royalist relief army approaching the city, Waller retreated, having lost around 160 men.[25]

If it is assumed that some of the eight artillery pieces Waller brought with him were demi-culverins, sakers and minions, in order for the cannon to be effective, by utilising data from Smith's *The Art of Gunnery* (Table 1) (p. xxi) and Norton's *The Gunner* (Table 2) (p. xxii), the demi-culverin would have to be sited either 290m (Smith) or 265m (Norton) from the city walls, with the saker being 228m and the minion artillery piece between 213m (Smith) and 183m (Norton). Consequently, any engagement would have been at extremely close quarters, notwithstanding the charge of cavalry from St Martin's Gate by the Royalists.

The historical record notes that the Royalists fired 200 shots over two days. If it is assumed that 100 shots were fired per day, based on William Eldred's analysis of the number of rounds fired per day (p. xxii), this could have equated to them having two demi-cannon, two culverins, two demi-culverins and two sakers; then the Royalists would have had around eight cannons positioned along the east and south sections of the city. If the Royalists only had eight sakers, they could have theoretically fired 112 shots per day. If again referring to Eldred (p. xxii), it can be noted that the number of artillery pieces brought by Waller fell well short of the recommended 30

superficies, intrenchments, and approaches by the demy circle, or with lines and stakes (London: R. Austin, 1645), pp. 11–12.

24 Ward, *Animadversions of Warre*, p. 55.

25 Malcolm Atkin, *The Civil War in Worcestershire* (Stroud: Alan Sutton Publishing Ltd, 1995), pp. 50–51; Malcolm Atkin, *Worcestershire under Arms: an English County During the Civil Wars* (Barnsley: Pen & Sword Ltd, 2004), p. 65.

by bringing just eight. Based on the arithmetical calculation of the Royalist cannons, it can be found that both sides were similarly matched in terms of firepower.

It is not clear whether or not the fortifications on what was later named Fort Royal Hill had functioning artillery pieces that were fired. However, it can be said that, despite Papillon's warning against lining the medieval walls and gates with earth p. 32), and Ward's lack of faith in the medieval walls (p. 33) as suitable defensive features, the evidence appears to demonstrate that in conjunction with the artillery pieces – and a cavalry charge – they were effective: the Royalists were able to hold their positions, forcing the Parliamentarians to retreat.

Events at Worcester showed that, the Royalists understood the need to control the high ground by constructing fortifications on Fort Royal Hill, some 38m above sea level,[26] and that the nature of the geology (Keuper Marl) did not affect the construction of new defences. There is an unfortunate lack of archaeological evidence for this siege. However, considering that the events took place over just two days, it would be unlikely to feature in the archaeological record, in part due to the ephemeral nature of English Civil War archaeology. Nevertheless, as shall be seen with the siege at Gloucester, it is possible to date archaeological evidence to precise time frames.

Following on from the brief siege, Henry Townshend, a magistrate from Worcestershire, recorded that the preparation of the town's defences was stepped up, including the removal of the following:

> "... trees, hedges, mounds and fences which might any manner prejudice the City and help and succour the Assailants or enemies and likewise all Houses or buildings be immediately plucked down and levelled ... the ordinary sort of women out of every ward within the City joined in companies and with colours and drums, striking up with spades, shovels and mattocks did begin to work upon Tuesday last being the 30th day of June who were to the number of 400 on a day going in a warlike manner like Soldiers, and did so behave themselves therein in slighting all such fortifications as were left by the Earl of Essex at his being here, and throwing down of ditches that by their own Industry and free service (in imitation of the She Citizens of London) as they within one week will perfect the levelling of the same ... by reason some of them were killed in the siege (though casually) and also to ease the soldiers, who being weary of the late hot service desiring some rest, and to prevent Sir W. Waller's approach near, if he should return suddenly against them."[27]

Analysing this extract, an increase in the number of people working on the defences is evident, including women, along with the destruction of large areas to prepare a better field of fire. This destruction can be clearly seen with the clearance of the suburbs outside of the medieval town walls, including

26 Memory Map Inc. © Crown Copyright Ordnance Survey 2008 Licence No: PU100034184 (Central England).

27 John William Willis Bund (ed.), *Diary of Henry Townshend of Elmley Lovett 1640–1663*, Vol. 2 (London: The Worcestershire Historical Society, 1916), pp. 123–24.

about 600m outside Fore Gate.[28] This, combined with the removal of any mounds of earth, trees, hedges and fences, illustrates how much more work was necessary to prepare the defences of Worcester to a suitable standard. For some of the Parliamentarians, the irony must not have been lost that they were later attacking the very same fortifications they had been constructing only weeks earlier.

Worcester continued to prepare itself for another siege, which would eventually come in three years' time. However, the story now moves on to Bristol and the Royalists' attempt to take the city from Parliament.

The Royalist Siege of Bristol, 26 July 1643

In the summer of 1642, the Royalist council of the city of Bristol ordered guns to be positioned on the medieval walls and the gates to be repaired. Following the arrival of Colonel Thomas Essex in November, Parliament took control of the city. By February 1643, Colonel Nathaniel Fiennes was installed as governor, and an earthwork was constructed on Brandon Hill.[29]

This was important, as the core of the city of Bristol is situated between the Rivers Avon and Frome on a low sandstone ridge. It was necessary to secure the high ground surrounding Bristol to the north. As shall be seen, geology affected the nature and type of fortifications that were constructed. The fortifications of Water Fort, Brandon Hill and Windmill Hill Fort were constructed on Quartzitic Sandstone. The sites of Essex Fort, Colston's Fort and Prior's Hill Fort were all built on Mercia Mudstone, previously known as 'Keuper Marl'; Bristol Castle, the earliest parts of which dated back to the 11th century, was constructed on a promontory of Redcliffe Sandstone, which can be 40m in thickness. Topographically, sites such as Brandon Hill and Windmill Hill Fort sat at 79m and 76m above sea level respectively.[30]

Unfortunately, there are no surviving contemporary maps of Civil War-era Bristol. However, an examination of John Speed's 1610 plan of the city does illustrate the importance of the Rivers Avon and Frome, in addition to Bristol Castle – shown as an impressive fortification, along with the medieval Portwall to the south of the city. Whilst James Jacobus Millerd's 1673 *An*

28 Atkin, *The Civil War in Worcestershire*, p. 51; Atkin, *Worcester 1651*, p. 31.

29 Barratt, *Sieges of the English Civil War*, p. 27.

30 James Russell, *The Civil War Defences of Bristol: Their Archaeology & Topography* (Bristol: Author, 2003), pp. 6–7; Cai Mason, *Water Fort, Brandon Hill, Bristol: Historic Environment Desk-Based Assessment and Topographical Survey* (Unpublished Report Ref: 109410.01: Wessex Archaeology, 2015), p. 1; Andy King, *Archaeological Excavation at the site of the Royal Fort, St Michael's Hill for University of Bristol* (Unpublished Report No. 2142/2012: Bristol and Region Archaeological Services, 2012), p. 6; Allan N. Insoll, with additions by Robert Jones, 'Chapter 2: The setting of Bristol: its geology and topography; deposit model', in Nigel Baker, Jonathan Brett and Robert Jones (eds), *Bristol: A Worshipful Town and Famous City: An Archaeological Assessment* (Oxford: Oxbow Books, 2018), p. 26; Andy King, *Archaeological Evaluation at Brandon Hill, Bristol for Bristol City Council* (Unpublished Report No. 2515/2011: Bristol and Region Archaeological Services, 2011), p. 2.

exact delineation of the famous citty of Bristoll... is important, it does not present any information regarding the topography of the landscape.[31]

It is fortunate that there is an account of the defences and fortifications that the Parliamentarians had constructed in 1643, by the Royalist engineer Bernard de Gomme. It reads as follows:

> "The Cittye of Bristoll stands in a hole: & upon the Northside towards Durdham downe, be 3 eminenter knolls or rockye hills, now crowned with so many forts. Next the river on the Southern skirt of Brandon hill is the Water fort, & on the knapp of the hill more Northward, is Brandon fort it selfe, some 18 foote square, & as many high; its Graff or mote but shallow & narrow, by reason of the rockynesse of the grownd. This is the highest of the fort hills. From whence the Line or Curtayne runnes Eastward, down the hill at the bottom of which stands the Barne & Spurre, where wee first entred which is since calld Washingtons Breache. Thence trends the Line still eastward, up St. Michael's hill on ye knoll of which stands the Windmill fort (though not fullye so Loftye as Brandon hill), yet with 420 passes by a Line of it. At the bottome of this, & upon the Highwayes side, stands Alderman Jones howse, with a Batterye crosse the way, which the Line crookes a Little northward to fetch in. Up the hill, againe, more Easterlye, & within muskett shott, there is another Redoubt some 18 foote square, against wch Col. Bellasses Batterye played. Within Lesse then Muskett shott of this, is Priorshill fort: fower square, ech side 24 of my passes. And hence trends the Line Southerlye, towards the Town where in the bottome of the hill in the medow calld Stokes Croft, upon Gloucester highway, & within Little more than half musket shot of Priors fort, there is a great Spurreworck in the Line, & a strong high Traverse, or Fore worck, watching & shutting up the highway, with a strong port of timber barres on the East side of it. And these be the mayn worcks wee had to attack on our side: having in all 5 Cavalliers or Batteryes: in the middle of everye twoe of which, be allso Little Ravelins or Tenailles, thrusting out sharp angles, to flancker & skowre along the Curtaine. I measured no further, because wee had to deale no further. These forts be all pallisadoed, but have no Fauxbrayes or fore-defences: nor on some sides, not so much as a Barm, Corridore, or footebank. Theyr drye rockye Graffs, be allso narrowe & shallowe. These forts command all the valley towarde Durdham downe, Northwards: & back againe over the whole Cittye, Southwards. Thorow all these forts from river to river, runnes a continued Line or Curtaine of meane strength & not comparable to those at Oxford. Its height, commonlye, about a yeard & halfe: or 6 foote where highest. The thicknesse on the top, above a yard, usuallye. The Graff or Ditche, commonly, 2 yards broade, but somewhere a foote or twoe, more. The depth scarce considerable; as being hardlye 5 foote, usuallye; & in many rockye places not so deepe. The ditches about the Redoubts, ordinarilye, about 8 or 9 foote deepe, & and so much over.
>
> "And thus was the Cittye fortified on our Northside, but the Southside where Prince Maurice fell on, though it hath not such forts, yet is the Line there something stronger; besides that it is fenced with the River. The whole Circumvallation, is full 5 miles. The grownd in most parts is rockye, that it being at a Councell of warre debated, whither to fall on by Approaches, or by Storme: the former waye (though

31 Jeff Bishop, *Bristol through Maps: Ways of Seeing a City* (Bristol: Redcliffe Press Ltd, 2016), pp. 35–36.

> safer) was rejected, for that the Stonynesse admitts nor mines nor sapping. Within the Cittye, is a large old Castle: but weake, still: notwithstanding the Enemyes had something repayrd & fortified it. A Mote was begun; & some howses pulled down for it. Tis wett, but in some places: nor hath it Fauxbrayes on all sides: & towards the South next the River, a Redoubt."[32]

Scrutinising this historical source, it can be seen that de Gomme understood the importance of observation and analysis. Being able to undertake such an examination of the defences, particularly on the northern side, identifying where the fortifications were sited, and the strengths and weaknesses of the line, is – as the Duke of Wellington's maxim states – time well spent,[33] especially as de Gomme was responsible for refortifying the city.

It is unclear which "3 eminenter knolls or rockye hills" de Gomme is referring to in his account. They could have been Brandon Hill, Windmill Hill, Colston's Fort and/or Prior's Hill. As Colston's Fort was sometimes referred to as a redoubt, due to the interchangeable use of language used to describe fortifications as 'redoubts', 'forts' and/or 'citadels', the three hills would have probably been Brandon, Windmill and Prior's. The location of the Water Fort shows that it was constructed to monitor any potential activity on the River Avon, illustrating the importance of rivers to the minds of 17th century military theorists, and thus highlighting another reason why Bristol was a key target for both the Royalists and Parliamentarians.

De Gomme highlights the importance of understanding the local terrain and topography by noting that the fortification at Brandon Hill was constructed on the highest point in the landscape. The 1643 fortification is described as 18ft (5.48m) square and 18ft (5.48m) in height; it is a small fort, and appears to be of similar form to a Second World War pillbox. The height of the wall is curious, because it does not appear to represent what can be found in the literature of the period when compared to Richard Norwood's *Fortification or Military Architecture*, for example.[34] The height of the wall and small size of the fort can be explained by the difficulty in constructing a fortification in this landscape. The key problem is the geology, in this case Quartzitic Sandstone. De Gomme himself records that "drye rockye Graffs [ditches], be allso narrowe & shallowe", illustrating that the construction of any fortification on this geology would have problems. The shallow and narrow nature of the ditches would have caused strategic and tactical problems for either side: strategic because of the importance of Bristol as as port and manunfacturing centre, and tactical because of the question of how to hold a large defensive line when facing a siege.

De Gomme also describes Colston's Fort (or Redoubt) as being "18 foote square". This is an indication that the Parliamentarians constructed key

---

32 Bernard de Gomme (Charles Firth and J.H. Leslie, eds), 'The Siege and Capture of Bristol by the Royalist Forces in 1643', *Journal of Army Historical Research*, Vol. 4 (1925), pp. 184–85.

33 Jim Storr, *King Arthur's Wars: The Anglo-Saxon Conquest of England* (Warwick: Helion & Company Ltd, 2018), p. 34.

34 Norwood, *Fortification or Military Architecture*, p. 112; John Lynch, *Bristol and the Civil War: For King and Parliament* (Stroud: The History Press, 2009), p. 37.

fortifications of the same size. Furthermore, it suggests that they constructed what they could, given the time, resources and manpower available, and is another reason why the ditches are narrow and shallow. This is perhaps best highlighted by the construction of "Little Ravelins or Tenailles", as it has been seen that Henry Hexham (p. xviii) stated that these types of features should be *in addition* to main fortifications such as bastions and curtain walls, rather than the main defences themselves.

Interestingly, all of the forts were described as having been palisaded, suggesting an understanding of contemporary 17th century military thinking, as palisades were placed on and around batteries at the siege of Breda (1624–25), as described by Robert Ward p. xix). Critically, the five main fortifications were constructed on high ground, on what are, in effect, slopes. Standing on these slopes, the one in front is called the forward slope, while that behind is the reverse slope. Depending on the status of a siege or battle, and the weapons available, it may have been necessary to defend the reserve slope rather than the forward one.[35] Therefore, this presented a tactical difficulty, and the construction of a series of fortifications on the north side of Bristol was carried out in necessary haste.[36]

De Gomme pronounces Bristol Castle to be "weake", despite some attempts at repairs. The castle had been in decline for many years; William Worcestre noted on 12 September 1480 that it was "broken down and in an extremely bad state of repair".[37]

De Gomme also describes the circuit of the defences as being 5 miles (8.04km) in length. This figure is exaggerated, as the historian James Russell notes that it was actually just over 3 miles (4.82km) around.[38] This fact is an important reminder not to take historical sources at face value, and to question why they were written and for whom.

An important and unrivalled source is Samuel Fawcett's list of the artillery pieces recorded after the Royalists' capture of Bristol, made on 28 July 1643. It states that the city had the following artillery, and notably records the positions they occupied:

> "At Gibb tayler in the marsh – 3 Minions, 1 Rabonett
> In the marsh next the key – 1 Minion
> At the Topp of the key – 1 Minion
> Within ffroome Gate – 2 Sakers
> Vpon the Redoubt by the Limekill neare Clifton – 2 Minions
> Vpon Brandon Hill Redoubt – 3 Minions, 1 Rabonett
> Vpon Windmill Hill Redoubt – 2 Sakers, 1 Minion
> Vpon the platform by Mile Hill gate – 1 Minion, 1 falcon
> In the Redoubt between Mr. Jones house & prior hill – 1 Minion, 1 falcon

---

35 Storr, *King Arthur's Wars: The Anglo-Saxon Conquest of England*, p. 54.

36 Nigel Baker, Jonathan Brett and Robert Jones (eds), *Bristol: A Worshipful Town and Famous City: An Archaeological Assessment* (Oxford: Oxbow Books, 2018), p. 255.

37 Frances Neale, *William Worcestre: The Topography of Medieval Bristol* (Bristol: Bristol Record Society, 2000), p. 253.

38 Russell, *The Civil War Defences of Bristol: Their Archaeology & Topography*, p. 10.

Vpon the Redoubt one prior Hill – 3 Sakers, 1 Murderers
Vpon the platform in the Norneworke at Harrillgate – 1 Minion
On the Spurr by Newfoundland House – 1 Saker
Vpon the platform at Stapleton way – 1 falcon
Vpon the platform at Lappers gate – 1 Minion
At newgate over the gate – 1 falcon
Within Newgate – 1 demi Cullv, 2 falconets, 4 Rabonetts
In broad mead – 1 Minion, 1 falcon
Before Prince Ruperts Lodgin – 1 Rabonett, 1 falcon
Over the Bridge
At Tower Harris over the bridge – 1 Saker, 2 Minions
In the Square Tower next to tower Harris – 2 falconets
In the Round Tower next Temple gate – 1 Minion
Vpon Temple gate – 1 Saker
Platform without Temple gate – 1 Saker, 1 Minion, 1 falcon
In the Spurr next the Gate – 1 Rabonett
In the next Angle – 1 falconet
Vpon the platform behind Ratcliff Church – 1 Saker
In the next Angle to bedmester Gate – 1 falconet
In the Hornworke at Bedmester gate – 1 Saker, 1 Minion, 1 Rabonett
In the demibastion by Trayne mills – 1 Minion, 3 Rabonetts
Vpon Ratcliff Church – 1 Saker, 2 Minions
Within Ratcliff gate – 1 demi Cullv
In the Castle
In the Castle walls by the drabridge neare ye gate – 3 Murderers
At the Angle vpon the Right hand on the wall – 1 Minion
In the Halfe moone below the Castle – 2 Minions
Vpon the platform in the Angle of the wall – 1 Minion
Vpon the wall behind the Armorey – 2 Minions, 1 Rabonett
Vpon the wall in the Courtayne – 1 Minion
Vpon the wall ouer the Coffer – 1 Minion
In the yard two falconets of Brasse mounted and three Iron vnmounted and one new minion of Brasse vnmounted together wth. fouer Rabonetts mounted & two vnmounted – 1 minion, 5 falconets and 6 rabonetts
Within the Castle gate one six pound of brasse – 1 Saker
Vpon the Castle Tower – 2 demi Cullv, 4 Sakers
Vpon the greene one whole Cannon morter-peece brasse – 1 Morter peece."[39]

What this source uniquely demonstrates are the positions of artillery, their size and the numbers and locations of fortifications throughout Bristol at the 1643 siege. In total, it indicates the city had 98 artillery pieces, of which there were 11 falconets, seven falcons, 19 robinets, four murderers, 19 sakers, 33 minions, four demi-culverins and one mortar. In all, 42 separate positions are listed, of which 11 focused on the castle. The castle itself had 32 artillery pieces. This fact illustrates that the "broken down" and "weake"

39 Ian Roy (ed.), *The Royalist Ordnance Papers 1642–1646 Part 2* (Oxfordshire Record Society, Vol. 49, 1975), pp. 261–63.

castle described by William Worcestre and de Gomme respectively had close to one-third of the city's artillery defending it. Using William Eldred's discussion (p. xxii) on how many shots a piece could fire within one day, Bristol's four demi-culverins could fire 56 shots per day, with the 19 sakers firing 266 rounds. This means that for just these 23 pieces, they could theoretically fire 322 shots per day if manned efficiently. Including the other 75 pieces of artillery mentioned, this would have been a lot of firepower at the disposal of the Parliamentarians. Eldred states that three people were required to fire an artillery piece,[40] so to effectively man the 98 artillery pieces would have required 294 men.

Interestingly, this list of artillery includes a series of fortifications that are only found in this historical source – namely the defences "Over the Bridge", including defences at St Mary Redcliffe Church (as seen in Plate 2), a hornwork at Bedminster Gate and a demi-bastion at Trin Mills. The construction of a hornwork (as illustrated in Figure 7) appears to be similar in use to that of a ravelin described earlier by de Gomme, but it should have been, according to the military manuals, an addition to rather than the main section of defences. This evidence continues to add weight to the theory that the fortifications around Bristol were hurriedly constructed by the Parliamentarians.

Figure 7 Illustration from Robert Ward's Anima'dversions of Warre (1639, p. 90) showing a hornwork fortification. (Reproduced by permission of Beinecke Rare Book and Manuscript Library, Yale University. Image published with permission of ProQuest®. Further reproduction is prohibited without permission. Image produced by ProQuest® as part of Early English Books Online. www.proquest.com)

Turning to the siege itself, as has been stated, de Gomme notes that the decision was taken to storm the city rather than approach it using saps and mining. This is partly because of the geology of the landscape of Bristol.

Approaching from Oxford under the command of Prince Rupert, the Royalists had a small artillery train. It contained several heavy siege artillery pieces – two demi-cannons (27-pdr; 12.24kg), along with two culverins (15-pdr; 6.80kg), which appear to correspond with the figures given in Table 5 (pp. xxiv–xxv). In addition, there were two demi-culverins and two 6-pdrs (2.72kg). The two 6-pdr pieces appear to have been (ordinary) sakers when compared to Table 5 containing data from Nye's 1670 version of *The Art of Gunnery*.[41] Based on Eldred's calculation of the number of shots fired per

40 Chris Henry, *English Civil War Artillery 1642–51* (Oxford: Osprey Publishing Ltd, 2005), p.34.

41 Barratt, *Sieges of the English Civil War*, pp. 28–29; Lynch, *Bristol and the Civil War: For King and Parliament*, p. 71.

Plate 2 St Mary Redcliffe Church, Bristol (facing east). (Author's photo)

day, and if the artillery was operating at full capacity, the two demi-cannons should have been able to fire 20 shots per day, and the two culverins another 24 shots. With the two demi-culverins and the two sakers each able to fire 28 rounds daily, the total shots fired per day by the Royalist besiegers should have been 100.

In addition to the Royalist artillery being accompanied by de Gomme and Fawcett, there was also a French explosives expert named de la Roche. The Oxford Army contained 4,500 foot soldiers and 6,000 horsemen.[42] The newly formed Royalist Western Army, meanwhile, under the command of Prince Maurice, consisted of Cornish troops and had some 3,000 infantry and between 1,500 and 1,600 cavalry. This gave the besieging Royalist forces around 7,500 foot and 7,500 horse.[43] Despite the lack of ammunition for the artillery, this was a considerable force, against which Colonel Fiennes, the Parliamentarian commander, had only around 2,000 infantry and possibly 2,500 men in total.[44]

The Royalists closed in on Bristol on 23 July, with Prince Rupert establishing his headquarters at Westbury, whilst Colonel Washington occupied Clifton Church near the fortification at Brandon Hill with his force of dragoons. On Monday, 24 July, ships in Kingswood were taken over by Royalist sympathisers, thereby cutting off Parliamentarian contact by sea, whilst Prince Maurice and his troops settled around the village of Bedminster and positioned artillery on a small hill facing Temple Gate.[45]

The siege began in earnest on 25 July. The general positions of attack can be seen in Map 1, illustrating that the bulk of the Royalist forces focused their assault on the northern section of the city's defences.

The attack was due to commence at dawn on Wednesday, 26 July. However, synchronisation of the attack was proving difficult, and the Western Army attacked at 3:00 a.m. As the uniforms of the opposing sides were similar, the password 'Oxford' was given so that the Royalist troops could identify their compatriots. Upon hearing the launch of the assault, Prince Rupert ordered Lord Grandison to attack the works at Stokes Croft and Prior's Hill Fort. Despite Grandison's men launching grenades and a petard (as illustrated in Figure 8), after 30 minutes of inconclusive fighting, the attack moved fully to Prior's Hill Fort, but the Royalists were unable to scale the walls despite making it to the ditch, as their ladders had not arrived. After finding a ladder, Colonel Lunsford managed to scale the fortification, but he could not make it over the palisade.[46]

Colonel Bellasis's men attacked either side of Windmill Hill Fort, but despite using firepikes (literally flaming pikes), they were unable to scale

---

42 Barratt, *Sieges of the English Civil War*, p. 28.

43 *Ibid.*, p. 29; Lynch, *Bristol and the Civil War: For King and Parliament*, p. 73.

44 Lynch, *Bristol and the Civil War: For King and Parliament*, p. 41.

45 Barratt, *Sieges of the English Civil War*, p. 29; Lynch, *Bristol and the Civil War: For King and Parliament*, pp. 74–75.

46 Patrick McGrath, *Bristol and the Civil War* (Bristol: Bristol Branch of the Historical Association, 1981), pp. 23–24; Barratt, *Sieges of the English Civil War*, p. 30; Lynch, *Bristol and the Civil War: For King and Parliament*, p. 77.

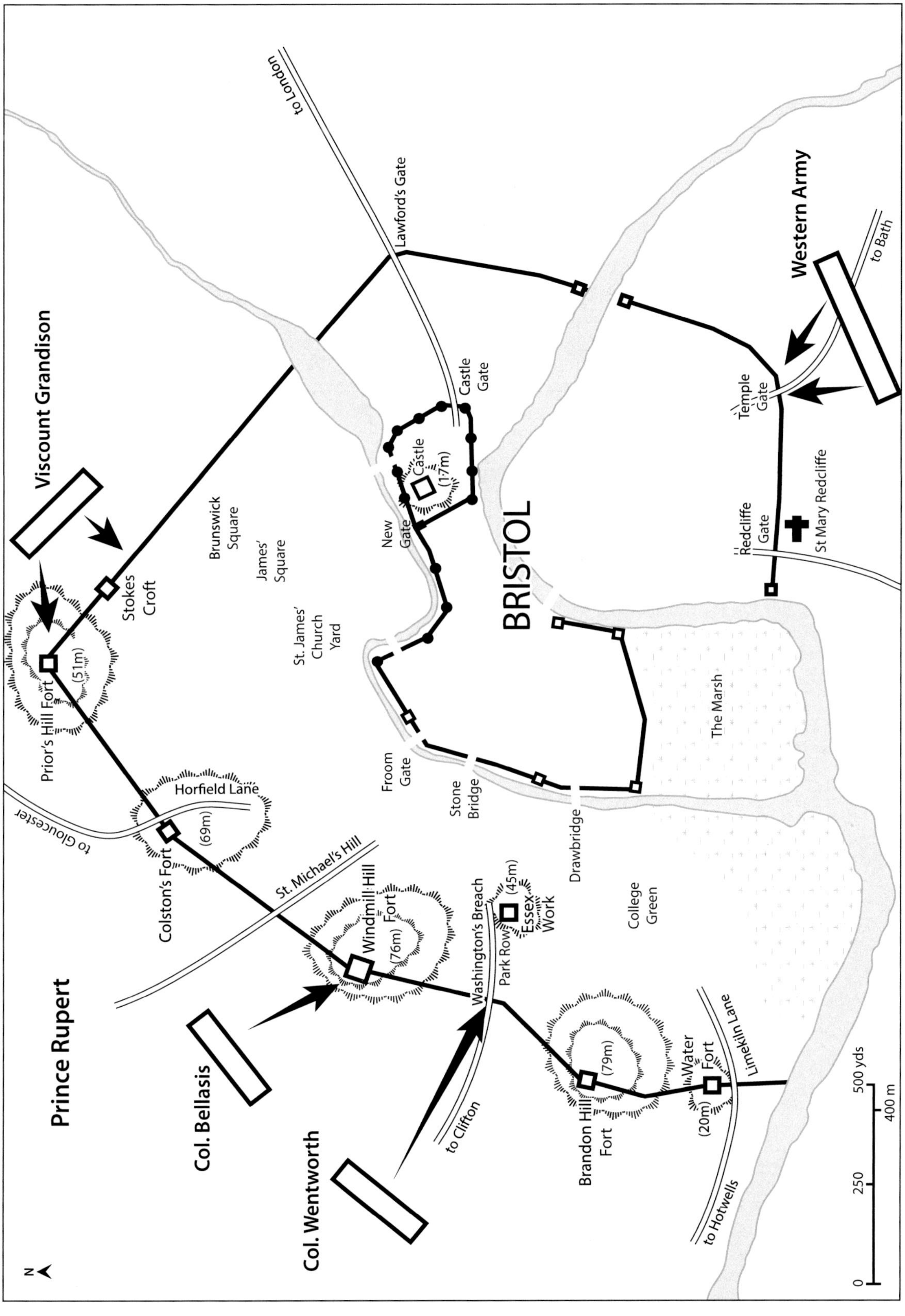

Map 1 The Royalist assault on Bristol on 25 July 1643 (Redrawn from Patrick McGrath's *Bristol and the Civil War* (1981), pp. 26–27.)

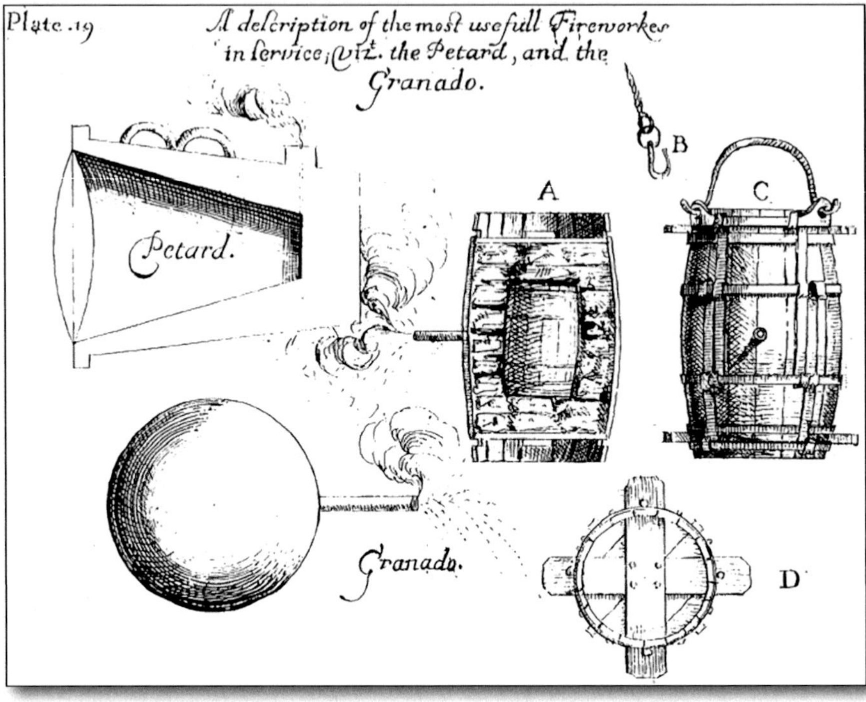

Figure 8 Illustration from Nicholas Stone's Enchiridion of Fortification (1645, p. 67, Plate 19) showing a petard and grenade. (Reproduced by permission of the University of Illinois (Urbana-Champaign Campus) Library. Image published with permission of ProQuest®. Further reproduction is prohibited without permission. Image produced by ProQuest® as part of Early English Books Online. www.proquest.com)

the feature without ladders and lacked any faggots to fill the ditches.[47] The Western Army, meanwhile, was also unsuccessful in its assault to the south. Finding the ditch too deep, and losing two regimental commanders – along with the commanders of the three assault columns – the Cornishmen withdrew. However, Prince Maurice managed to keep the southern defenders occupied until the breakthrough was made in the northern section.[48]

The troops of Colonel Wentworth, assaulting between Brandon Hill Fort and Windmill Hill Fort, along with dragoons under the command of Colonel Washington, made a successful breach in the defences with the aid of firepikes. This section was outside of the range of the defenders' artillery and represented a blind spot. The Parliamentarians, understanding this, had cover in form of a body of cavalry under the command of a Sergeant Langrish.[49]

After breaking through, the Royalists encountered the Essex Work or Essex Fort, which was positioned at the top of what is now Park Street. Wentworth's men, supported by a force of horsemen, successfully captured the position, with witnesses reporting defenders running out of the fort.[50] Minus the addition of pikemen, the fighting here was a variation of the basic

47 McGrath, *Bristol and the Civil War*, p. 24. Barratt, *Sieges of the English Civil War*, p. 32.

48 Lynch, *Bristol and the Civil War: For King and Parliament*, pp. 78–80.

49 McGrath, *Bristol and the Civil War*, pp. 24, 28; Lynch, *Bristol and the Civil War: For King and Parliament*, p. 80.

50 McGrath, *Bristol and the Civil War*, p. 28; Lynch, *Bristol and the Civil War: For King and Parliament*, p. 81; Barratt, *Sieges of the English Civil War*, p. 34.

deployment of units as they would be in the field, as developed by Maurice of Nassau in 1593, with the Dutch technique of musketeers flanked by cavalry.[51]

Interestingly, in 1994, at the junction of Woodland Road and Park Row, archaeological excavations revealed evidence of a significant ditch. A trench (known as 'Trench Two') was dug by machine to a depth of 2.2m, and then continued by hand. The northern section discovered a ditch which had a steep angle of 40–60 degrees. At a minimum, the ditch was 50m in length and 7.5–9m wide. The angle of the outer face rarely went below 40 degrees, possibly indicating a counterscarp. In front of the ditch were deposits of clean sandy clay, with evidence of tip lines above these, with a small depression. It is possible that the northern section of the ditch was observed in what was termed 'Trench Four'. The western section of the ditch became narrower and shallower as it made a sharp turn to the south, possibly indicating a bastion corner. Despite no dating evidence being recovered, because of the significant size of the ditch it was inferred that it was part of the Essex Work.[52]

Artillery at Brandon Hill Fort and Water Fort was turned by its Parliamentarian handlers and began to fire into the city, targeting Wentworth as he and his troops tried to secure College Green. Despite being under attack from surrounding houses, including light artillery and infantry, the street fighting continued.[53] The historian John Lynch suggests that light artillery produced under the orders of Sir Edward Hungerford were akin to modern heavy machine guns or mortars.[54]

Despite house-to-house fighting, Bellasis's infantry and Aston's cavalry managed to work their way to the Frome Gate. According to legend, Mrs Dorothy Hazzard and around 200 women and girls attempted to block up the gate with woolsacks of earth, creating a barrier some 16ft (4.87m) thick, whilst ordering the defending men to stand firm.[55]

After six hours of fighting, by around 9:00 a.m., the Royalists had not made any significant breakthroughs. They had only made one successful breach in the northern section, and had been repulsed in the south (despite attempts here to fill the ditch with carts and faggots), whilst other troops were being held in street fighting and around the Frome Gate.[56] Between 100 and 300 of the Cornish troops had been killed or injured, while reports of casualties for the Oxford Army varied from 1,000–1,400, a loss of between 23 and 31 percent. The Parliamentarians, meanwhile, still held fortifications on the high ground. Prince Rupert, realising the importance of these fortifications, ordered the arriving Western Army to attack those positions,

---

51 Warwick Louth, 'Organised Chaos: Applying seventeenth-century military manuals to conflict archaeology', in Ismini Pells (ed.), *New approaches to the military history of the English Civil War* (Solihull: Helion & Company Ltd, 2016), p. 132.

52 John Bryant, 'Archaeological Evaluation of Park Row and Woodland Road, Clifton, Bristol' (Unpublished Report: Bristol and Region Archaeological Services, 1994), pp. 7, 8, 11.

53 Lynch, *Bristol and the Civil War: For King and Parliament*, p. 81; Barratt, *Sieges of the English Civil War*, pp. 34–35.

54 Lynch, *Bristol and the Civil War: For King and Parliament*, p. 82.

55 McGrath, *Bristol and the Civil War*, p. 30; Lynch, *Bristol and the Civil War: For King and Parliament*, p. 83; Barratt, *Sieges of the English Civil War*, p. 35.

56 Lynch, *Bristol and the Civil War: For King and Parliament*, p. 83; McGrath, *Bristol and the Civil War*, p. 29.

rather than support the Royalist troops already in the city. The inner section of the defences on the River Frome was also still in the hands of Parliament; some accounts suggest that the defenders here had lost less than 10 men.[57]

Nevertheless, despite their apparent tactical advantage, morale amongst the Parliamentarians was deteriorating fast. Fiennes issued a rallying call, but only 200 men of the 1,000–1,200 he expected to attend arrived. Seeing the small number, Fiennes panicked and offered to surrender. The Royalists, however, rejected the proposal, fearing trickery. At around 11:00 a.m., the Parliamentarians launched a final sally. This lasted about 30 minutes, and when they returned, Fiennes again asked for negotiations. This time the Royalists accepted.[58]

Later that day, Fiennes agreed to 10 articles of surrender. The terms were a strategic disaster for the Parliamentary cause, as they had to "leave behind them all Cannon and Ammunition".[59] Whilst the Royalists had gained the city, it had come at a heavy price: only around 1,400 men of the Oxford Army could be found afterwards. It was because of the cost of the storming of Bristol that a different approach was taken at Gloucester the following month.[60]

Despite having a numerical advantage in infantry and cavalry, in addition to using firepikes and a petard, after six hours of fighting the Royalists had struggled to make any real gains in the city, apart from the section between Brandon Hill Fort and Windmill Hill Fort, now known as Washington's Breach. This can partly be blamed on 'eagerness' or lack of discipline/communication in the Western Army. For example, if they had not launched their attack early, then the Royalists would have been in a much better position to approach the northern fortifications with the necessary scaling ladders.

Around 2,000 men had held out against a numerically superior force for several hours, holding the high ground and the fortifications, despite fierce fighting in and around the streets of Bristol. The use of firepikes and turning light artillery into the equivalent of modern machine guns had added a frightening element to siege warfare, whilst also illustrating the ingenuity of the combatants.

Neither the lack of contemporary 'state of the art' fortifications, the using of hornworks and ravelins as complete fortifications in their own right, rather than as part of a more complex picture, nor the impact of the local geology on the forts that were constructed appear to have limited the ability of the Parliamentarians to hold large sections of Bristol, despite the chaotic and disorganised approaches of both sides. The archaeological record near the Essex Work has shown how much effort was put into preparing the city for conflict. A critical factor for the Parliamentarians appears to have

57 Lynch, *Bristol and the Civil War: For King and Parliament*, p. 84; Barratt, *Sieges of the English Civil War*, p. 35.

58 Lynch, *Bristol and the Civil War: For King and Parliament*, pp. 85–86; Barratt, *Sieges of the English Civil War*, p. 36.

59 Anonymous, *A copie of the articles agreed upon at the surrender of the city of Bristol* (London: 1643), p. 6.

60 Barratt, *Sieges of the English Civil War*, p. 37.

been their ineffective use of or ability to man their artillery pieces. It is also surprising, given that theoretically the Royalists could have fired 100 shots per day, that they did not commence the siege with a few days of artillery bombardment, if not to make a great impact on the fortifications, then to give the Parliamentarian soldiers something additional to think about whilst performing their daily tasks.

What this storm approach to siege warfare demonstrated was that, despite problems, the Royalists actually captured Bristol because of the defenders' fall in morale and, in part, the fear of those (excluding Mrs Dorothy Hazzard and the women near Frome Gate) engaged in holding the city. What is often forgotten is the terror in soldiers' eyes, the sounds of artillery and musket fire, the smells and smoke of gunpowder from those weapons and the general confusion that comes from being in battle. Perhaps the siege is best summarised by someone who served in it:

> "That day I came over the Rhiver and view'd that side where I found very many of our Men slaine especially in those places where my Lord Grandyson, and my Lord Henry Bellasis fell on; they were commaunded to assault Brandon, and Prior hill ffortts, which is not to bee taken by a storme; they were both wounded, and left the grafts full of dead bodys.
>
> "This is all I can remember of the Siege of Bristoll; but thus muche I can say is perfectly true."[61]

Nevertheless, with the Royalists in the ascendency in the region, they now moved on in an attempt to take the nearby city of Gloucester.

The Royalist Siege of Gloucester, 10 August–5 September 1643

Until recently, the city of Gloucester marked the lowest bridgeable point over the River Severn, hence why the Romans constructed Glevum there. Topographically, Gloucester is relatively flat, with the majority of fortifications having been constructed on land that is at most 15m above sea level. The initial fortress constructed there was approximately 250m from the riverbank on the eastern edge of a floodplain; at the south it was positioned on a gravel terrace and a small knoll lying west–east, with stream beds running north–south. The course of the River Severn has been altered throughout late pre-history to the modern era as a result of both natural and human processes. The Roman road network meant that by the medieval period, five main roads marked entrances and exits of the town, in addition to the River Severn.[62]

61 de Gomme (Charles Firth and J.H. Leslie (eds)), 'The Siege and Capture of Bristol by the Royalist Forces in 1643', p. 201; Lynch, *Bristol and the Civil War: For King and Parliament*, p. 87.

62 Baker and Holt, *Urban Growth and the Medieval Church: Gloucester and Worcester*, pp. 27–29; Mark Brett, *Gloscat Gloucester Archaeological Evaluation* (Unpublished Report No. 06022: Cotswold Archaeology, 2006), p. 5.

The modern historian is fortunate to have two primary sources concerning the siege of Gloucester in 1643. However, it is crucial to remember that these testimonies are, as Atkin and Howes quite rightly state, "partisan accounts written from the viewpoint of the successful defenders".[63] Published two years after the siege, in 1645, John Corbet described the defences of Gloucester on 10 August 1643, at the start of the siege, as:

> "The works of a large compasse, not halfe perfect; from the south-gate eastward almost to the north port, the city was defended with an ancient wall lined with earth to a reasonable height; thence to the north-gate, with a slender work upon a low ground, having the advantage of a stone barn that commanded severall wayes: upon the lower part of the city, from the north to the west-gate, (being a large tract of ground) there was no ancient defence, but a small work newly raysed, with the advantage of marish grounds without, and a line drawn from the inner north-gate under the colledge wall to the priory of St. Oswald's.
>
> From the west towards the south-gate along the river side, no more defence than the river itselfe, and the meadows beyond levell with the town: from the castle to the south-port, a firme and lofty work to command the high ground in the suburbs. The ditches narrow, but watered round. In this posture did the city stand when the king's forces hovoured over the hills, and now and then skirted upon the town, before a close siege was laid: upon the tenth of August."[64]

What this evidence suggests is that the fortifications facing the Royalists at the beginning of the siege were not of a sufficient standard, if compared to the military manuals of the time. Such were its inefficiencies that the ancient wall would have dated from the Roman period, and 17th century theorists and writers would have criticised lining the wall with earth. One such was engineer David Papillon, who in 1645 wrote that lining town walls would not secure them against cannon fire.[65] Papillon would have no doubt been critical of the fortifications at the time of the siege, and stated that they were decayed when he presented a plan for new defences in 1646.[66]

The historian John Rhodes has noted that Corbet's "south-gate eastward almost to the north port" is the city's South Gate, the stone wall (of Roman origin), the scons (bastion) at Rignell Stile, East Gate and The Sallie Gate, moving towards the North Gate. Similarly, the "stone barn" is Friars' Barne, the "inner north-gate" is Northgate Prison, and the "north to the west-gate" section includes the Outer North Gate, Captain Singleton's bastion, Alvin Gate and Chapple House. The "west towards the south-gate along the river

63 Malcolm Atkin and Russell Howes, 'The use of archaeology and documentary sources in identifying the Civil War defences of Gloucester', *Post-Medieval Archaeology*, Vol. 27 (1993), p. 17.

64 John Corbet, 'An Historicall relation of the military government of Gloucester: from the beginning of the Civill Warre betweene King and Parliament to the removal of Colonell Massie from that Government to the command of the Westerne Forces' (1645), in J. Washborn (ed.), *Bibliotheca Gloucestrensis* (Gloucester: J. Washborn, 1825), pp. 42–43.

65 Papillon, *A practicall abstract of the arts of fortification*, pp. 11–12.

66 Malcolm Atkin, 'David Papillon and the Civil War Defences of Gloucester', *Transactions of the Bristol and Gloucestershire Archaeological Society*, Vol. 111 (1993), p. 149.

side", Rhodes says, is West Gate and The Key towards the bastion under the Castle, with the final section "from the castle to the south-port" being Barbycon (Barbican) Hill, with two dams finishing at the aforementioned South Gate.[67] Corbet's description notes the utilisation of the marshy 'marish' ground, and that a large section of the defences consisted of the River Severn, illustrating that, where possible, the Parliamentarian troops under the command of Colonel Massey understood the importance of using the topography and the landscape to their advantage.

Along with Corbet's description, it is known that the population of Gloucester was around 5,000, the walls between the South Gate and East Gate were around 6ft (1.82m) thick and two storeys high, and a second line of defence was provided by a bank and ditch system which ran from the Inner North Gate, underneath the cathedral walls, to St Oswald's Priory.[68] A ditch existed measuring between 13ft and 16½ft (4–5m) in width from the South Gate to Almesham Postern.[69] Archaeological research at 31 Parliament Street has revealed evidence of the backfill of this ditch to a depth of almost 11ft (3.3m).[70] Detached from the main circuit of fortifications was a sconce at the Vineyard, by the River Severn at old Bishop's palace, and defences on Alney Island.[71]

One of the most critical events in the preparation of the defences was the clearance of suburbs, which resulted in destroying 241 homes – about one-third of the city.[72] Evidence for this destruction can be seen in the archaeological record. Excavations in 1988 on the Bank of England site on Southgate Street discovered evidence of a thin layer of burning and collapsed masonry. Clay pipes recovered there dated the activity to between 1640 and 1660. Malcolm Atkin dates this to 10 August 1643, when the citizens burnt the suburbs to stop the Royalists from using the buildings as cover on their approach.[73] The creation of a defensive ditch, approximately 10m in width and 4m in depth, required the destruction of Green Dragon Lane.[74] No doubt the clearance of the suburbs was to create an effective field of fire; however, this was incomplete, as Corbet notes the Royalists' "entrenchments on the south and east parts, the night before in the shadow and shelter of the houses which the flame had not catched, within musket-shot of the walls".[75] The distance for musketry shot would have been between 45.72m and 91.44m,[76]

67 John Rhodes, 'The Civil War Defences of Gloucester', *Transactions of the Bristol and Gloucestershire Archaeological Society*, Vol. 132 (2014), pp. 163–64, 170–85.

68 Jon Day, *Gloucester & Newbury 1643: The Turning Point of the Civil War* (Barnsley: Pen & Sword Books Ltd, 2007), pp. 33, 38.

69 Malcolm Atkin and Wayne Laughlin, *Gloucester and the Civil War: a city under siege* (Stroud: Alan Sutton Publishing Ltd, 1992), p. 50.

70 Anthony P. Garrod, '31 Parliament Street, Gloucester', *Glevensis*, Vol. 19 (1985), p. 47.

71 Day, *Gloucester & Newbury 1643: The Turning Point of the Civil War*, p. 38.

72 Atkin and Laughlin, *Gloucester and the Civil War: a city under siege*, p. 66.

73 Malcolm Atkin, 'Excavations in Gloucester, 1988', *Glevensis*, Vol. 23 (1988), pp. 5, 9.

74 Malcolm Atkin, 'Excavations in Gloucester 1989 – An Interim Report', *Glevensis*, Vol. 24 (1990), p. 3.

75 Corbet, 'An Historicall relation of the military government of Gloucester', p. 45.

76 Malcolm Wanklyn and Frank Jones, *A military history of the English Civil War 1642–1646: Strategy and Tactics* (Harlow: Pearson Education Limited, 2005), p. 28.

clearly demonstrating the short distance between the besiegers and the besieged. Indeed, such short distances equates this area to the landscape of 'no man's land' during the First World War, and was clearly in range of the artillery of the age (see Tables 1 and 2).

At the start of the siege, the Royalists held a strong numerical advantage, with 6,000 infantry and cavalry facing 1,500 Parliamentarian defenders.[77]

Turning in more detail to the Royalists siegeworks, Corbet notes the following:

> "The enemy was indefatigable and swift in the entrenchments. The workes from the south and east gates, hasted to meete each other; their preparations seemed more tedious, yet effectuall and certain and tended withal to save the lives of their men. Wherefore they chused not a sudden storme on lower and weaker parts of the city, but rather to prepare the assault on the strongest side, yet most easy to their intention. For there only could they rayse the workes without the annoyance of the water-springs, that issued in the lower grounds ; there only could they make battery within pistoll shot of the walls, that wanted flankers; and when they had once entred a breach there, they were instantly possest of the highest part of the of the town."[78]

What is clear from this evidence is the impact the geology (Blue Lias and Charmouth Mudstone) had on the construction of both defensive and offensive fortifications. The high water-table, meanwhile, affected what siegeworks could be constructed in the immediate vicinity of the South Gate and East Gate. This is an important example illustrating that any tactician/commander should know, to the best of their ability, the geology and terrain that is to be the arena of conflict.

Continuing with the examination of the Royalists' movements, John Dorney, the Town Clerk, noted that on Friday, 11 August:

> "[W]e discovered that the enemy had the night before began their entrenchments in Gawdy-Greene, on the south part of the city, and about Issold's house on the east part ... likewise cut the pipes that conveied our water from Robinhood's-hill to our conduits, and diverted the course of the water that drove our corne-mills."[79]

The account clearly reveals the initial positions of the Royalists in relation to the defences of Gloucester, namely on Gawdy Green (now Brunswick Square) to the south and near Issold's House to the east. Another important tactic is revealed, namely the cutting of the water supply from Robinhood's Hill. This would have caused hardship to the 1,500 soldiers and the population of the town. The cutting of the water supply was employing similar tactics to those that occurred at the siege of Breda in 1624, when the besiegers "blockt

77 Day, *Gloucester & Newbury 1643: The Turning Point of the Civil War*, pp. 37, 58.

78 Corbet, 'An Historicall relation of the military government of Gloucester', pp. 46–47.

79 John Dorney, 'A briefe and exact relation of the most materiall and remarkeable passages that hapned in the late well-formed (and as valiently defended) siege laid before the city of Glocester' (1643), in J. Washborn (ed.), *Bibliotheca Gloucestrensis* (Gloucester: J. Washborn, 1825), p. 212.

up the Rivers".[80] This is evidence of the beginning of the Royalist campaign of attrition, as favoured by Gustavus Adolphus (p. xvii) and, perhaps crucially, the Royalist Prince Rupert.

Dorney also records that "Captaine Lieutenant Harcus, assisted by Colonell Stevens' ensigne, at midnight issued forth of the south port, with a small party, beat the enemy from their trenches and brought away many of their shovels and pickaxes."[81] The account of the Royalists using shovels and pickaxes indicates that the men attacked were sappers, creating a sap, as Hexham has been seen describing (p. xviii) and in Figure 1. Hexham also illustrates the tools, including shovels and pickaxes as seen in Figure 9.

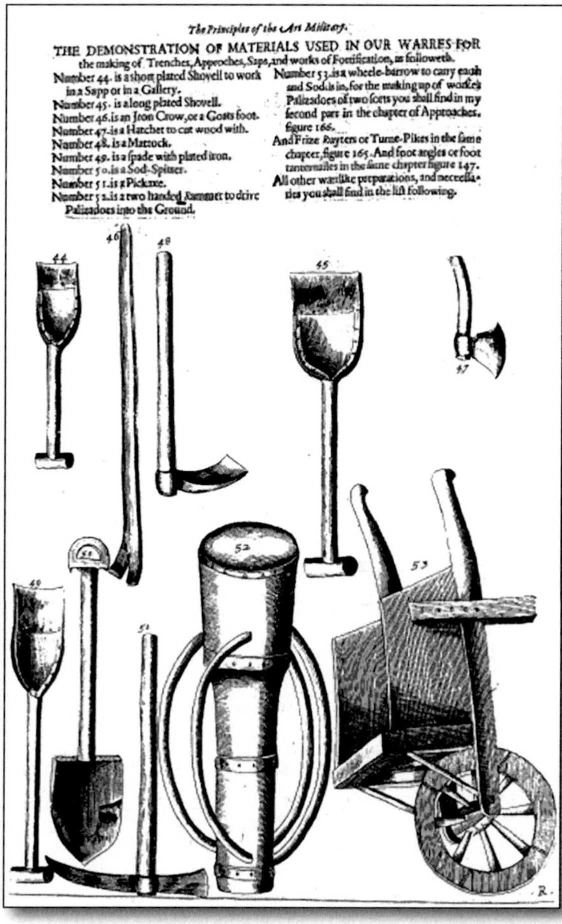

Figure 9 Illustration from Henry Hexham's The Third Part of the Principles of the Art Military (1643, opposite p. 75) showing the tools used to construct trenches, approaches, saps and fortifications. (Reproduced by permission of the University of Illinois (Urbana-Champaign Campus) Library. Image published with permission of ProQuest®. Further reproduction is prohibited without permission. Image produced by ProQuest® as part of Early English Books Online. www.proquest.com)

Interestingly, the archaeological excavations at Southgate Street revealed evidence of one of the saps: a 1m deep and 1m wide steep-sided, flat-bottomed feature was excavated, at approximately right angles, 20m away from the current street line.[82] The ditch had been cut from the previously determined 17th century level and did not align itself with medieval or later features. Because of how regular the cut was, it follows that the feature was not open for a significant period of time.[83] It is possible that this is the sap that Captain Lieutenant Harcus, Colonel Stevens and party assaulted during the siege on 11 August.

The suggested positions of the Royalists can be seen in Map 2, illustrating the predominant focus on the Roman/medieval wall and the East and South Gates. What can clearly be seen from this information is that the artillery ranges of the Royalist battery positions numbered one to three – containing two 24-pdrs (10.88kg; demi-cannon in Table 5), 15-pdrs (6.80kg; culverin in Table 5), 12-pdrs (5.44kg; demi-culverin in Table 5) and 6-pdrs (2.72kg; saker (ordinary) in Tables 1, 4 and 5) – should have been able to significantly damage and even breach the wall and gates.

It is known, however, that the Royalists only fired 17 rounds each day.[84] Examining the artillery available based on the three artillery positions between East Gate and South Gate on Map 2, with the data from the contemporary gunner William Eldred (pp. xxiv–xxv), two demi-cannons should be firing 20 shots per day. The two culverins could fire 24 rounds

80 Ward, *Animadversions of Warre*, p. 100.
81 Dorney, 'A briefe and exact relation of the most materiall…', p. 213.
82 Malcolm Atkin, *Trial Excavations on the Bank of England site, Southgate Street, Gloucester, 1988: An Interim Report* (Unpublished Report: Gloucester Excavations Unit, 1988), p. 11;
83 Atkin, 'Excavations in Gloucester, 1988', p. 10.
84 Lynch, *Bristol and the Civil War: For King and Parliament*, p. 71.

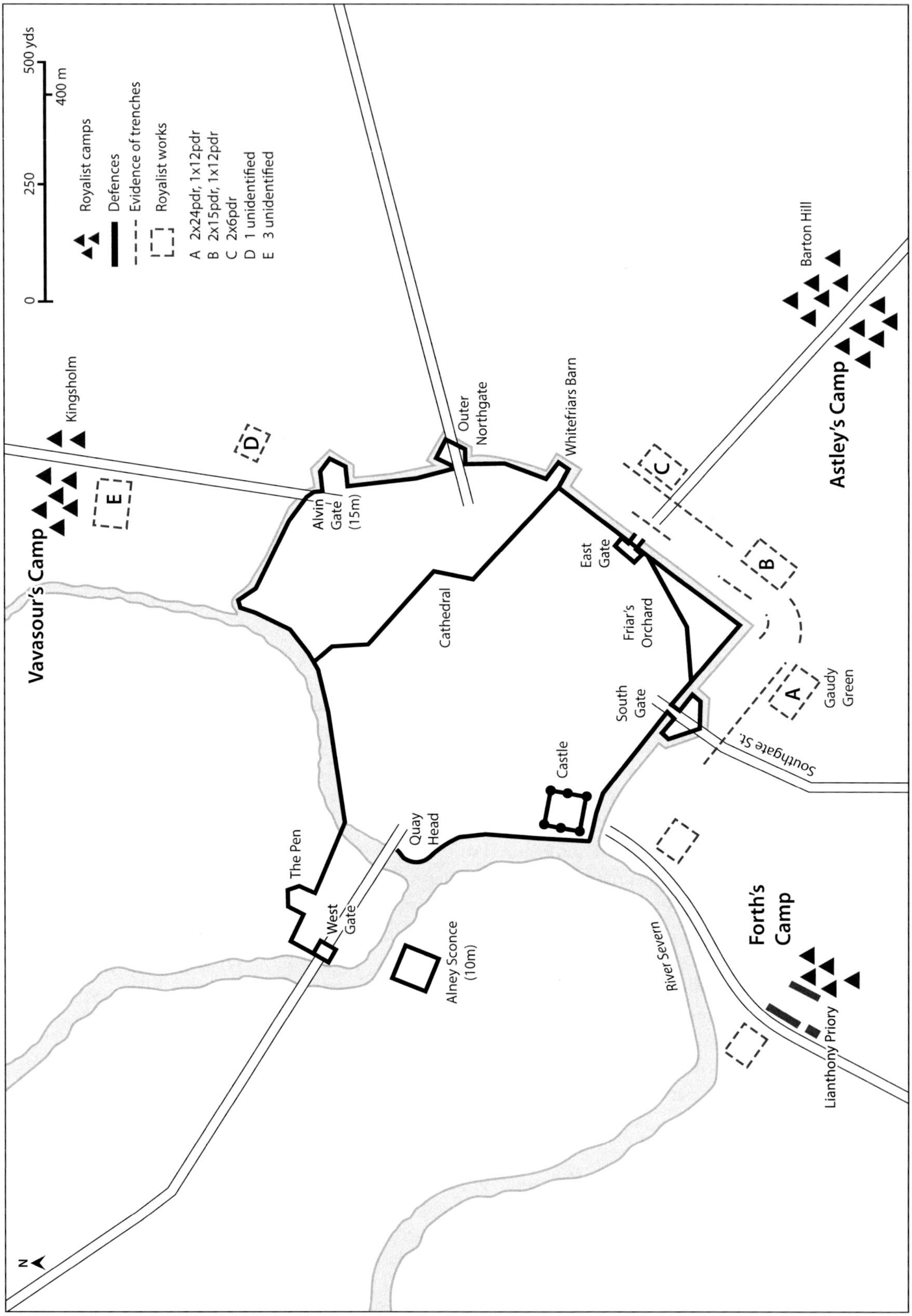

Map 2 Map showing the position of the Royalists' siegeworks in relation to some of the defences of Gloucester. (Reproduced by permission of Jon Day)

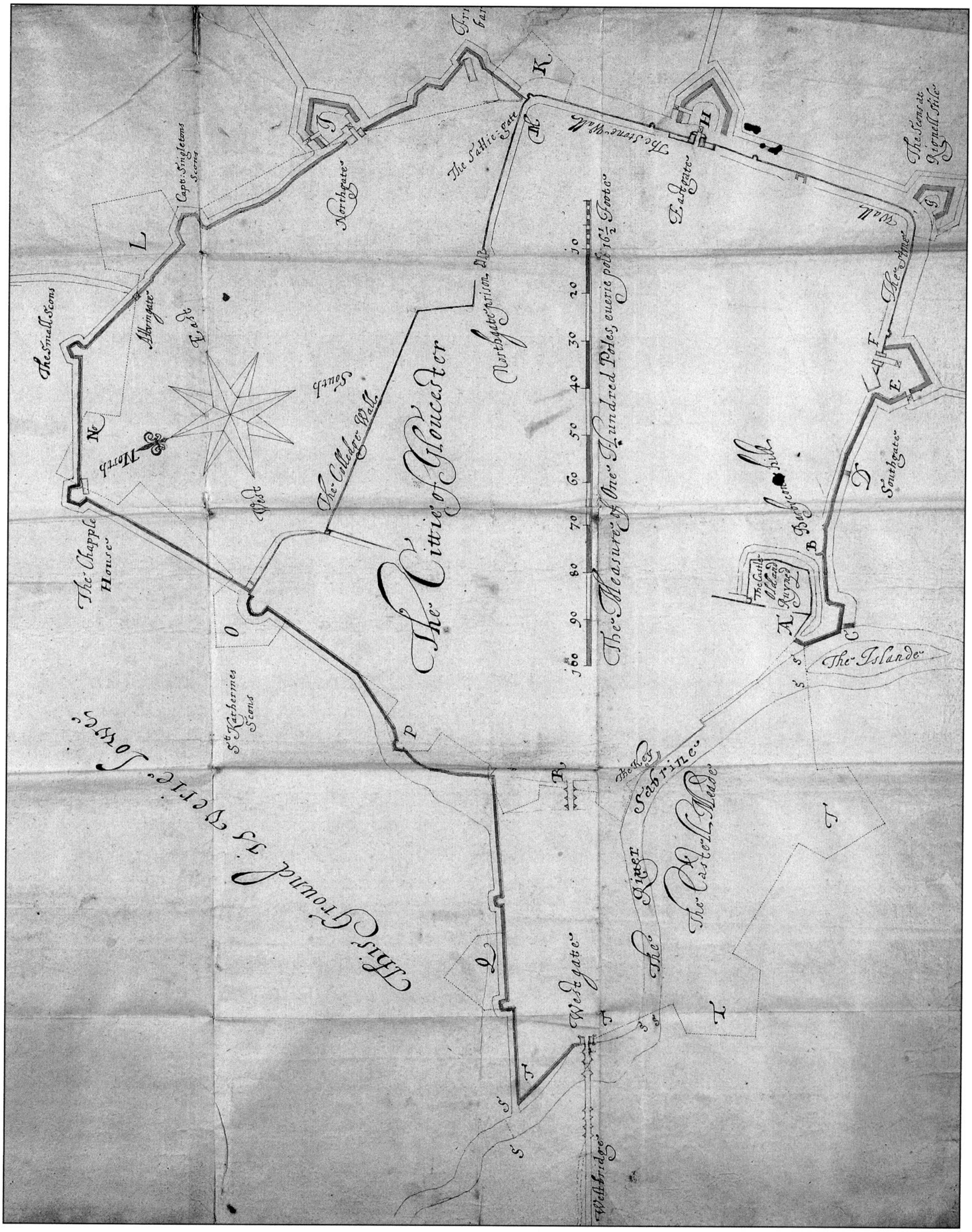

Map 3 Plan D 12862 illustrating the Civil War defences and plans of Gloucester. (Reproduced by permission of Gloucestershire Archives)

per day, while the two demi-culverins and pair of sakers should be firing 28 shots each. This means that this section of Gloucester could have been bombarded daily with 100 rounds. Therefore, over the 26 days of the siege between 10 August and 5 September, this section of the defences could have theoretically been bombarded with 2,600 shots. This information illustrates why the Royalists were unsuccessful in their siege of Gloucester, and why the historian Christopher Duffy noted the "tempo of the whole operation was far too slow".[85] Like the Parliamentarians at Bristol, their inability to use artillery effectively damaged the Royalists' progress in this siege.

The understanding of the defensive positions was enhanced with the discovery in 2012 of an important cartographic source – Plan D 12862 – which is held in Gloucestershire Archives (Map 3).[86]

The plan shows the series of fortifications and defences present during the siege, including the following:

A) The bastion under the castle

This feature is referenced by Corbet as the "breast-work upon Seavern side under the castle to defend an assault from those high grounds beyond the river".[87]

B) Barbican (Barbycon) Hill

Dorney recorded that cannon fired "from the Barbican" on Monday, 21 August.[88]

E) The South Gate

The medieval gate was repaired in 1642 using 500 tiles and required complete repair after the 1643 siege.[89] Archaeological excavations in 1983 at 106 Southgate Street revealed, when comparing the results to the cartographic source of John Speed's 1610 plan of the city, that medieval buildings were destroyed to make way for a defensive ditch. The ditch itself (context 366) was V-shaped, measuring 5.5m across and 2.3m in depth, with the east section containing a large section of ashlar masonry (context 385). The position of the masonry represented a series of steps, indicating possibly a gun emplacement. The masonry may have been reused from the destroyed church of St Owen. Some contexts contained burnt twigs and latticework or straw, suggesting the use of gabions at this location. The final fill of the ditch was a dense black silty clay layer and was waterlogged.[90] It is not clear whether the gabions were positioned around the besieged artillery and were subsequently destroyed in a bombardment or assault, or whether they were dumped in the ditch by the besiegers in an attempt to level the landscape and make the ditch easier to cross during an attack.

85 Christopher Duffy, *Siege Warfare: The Fortress in the Early Modern World 1494–1600* (London: Routledge & Kegan Paul Ltd, 1979), p. 153.

86 Rhodes, 'The Civil War Defences of Gloucester', p. 159.

87 Corbet, 'An Historicall relation of the military government of Gloucester', pp. 52–53.

88 Dorney, 'A briefe and exact relation of the most materiall…', pp. 218–19.

89 Rhodes, 'The Civil War Defences of Gloucester', p. 171.

90 Veronica Yuill, *Excavations at 106, Southgate Street, Gloucester* (Unpublished Report: Gloucester Excavation Unit, 1983), pp. 23–31.

Several medieval buildings have survived to the present day on Southgate Street. The first is St Mary de Crypt (Plate 3). During the siege, the building was used as an ammunition magazine.[91] The second is the medieval friary of Greyfriars, situated just off Southgate Street (Plate 4). For a short time, it was utilised as a command post, in addition to being Massey's quarters, and was hit by cannon fire.[92] The photograph of the modern Southgate Street (Plate 5), illustrates the compact nature of early medieval streets, which is an important aspect to bear in mind when analysing the impact of warfare on the populace inside, whilst illustrating what the Royalists and Parliamentarians were fighting over. Another surviving building is St Michael's Tower (Plate 6), which stands at The Cross, where the four main gate streets, and is an important illustration of the architecture present during the siege.

Plate 3 St Mary de Crypt, Gloucester (facing east). (Author's photo)

F) Stone wall

This wall was of Roman origin and survived the siege.[93] In front of the wall was an area of the city ditch called Gooseditch. This was subjected to archaeological excavations in the 1970s and 1980s, when it was discovered

91 Atkin and Laughlin, *Gloucester and the Civil War: a city under siege*, p. 159.

92 *Ibid.*

93 Rhodes, 'The Civil War Defences of Gloucester', p. 173.

Plate 4 Greyfriars, off Southgate Street, Gloucester (facing south-south-east). (Author's photo)

Plate 5 Modern Southgate Street, Gloucester (facing south-west). (Author's photo)

Plate 6 St Michael's Tower, Gloucester (facing south). (Author's photo)

that around 1640 the ditch was cut to drain it of water. The ditch was recut during the Civil War to prevent further flooding.[94] The decision to drain a ditch presents an interesting tactical and strategic issue. For example, Papillon states:

> "They have another smaller dike in the middest of these great dikes, if in case they be drie, called *La Cunette* ... this small dike is commonly full of water in all places; for the raine-water descending from the Rampiers, and the side of the great dike, fill it, although the ground be voyd of springs; this small dike is verie usefull, for it preserves the Garrison from being scaled, or suprized in the right time ... without noyse."[95]

Applying this statement to the decision to drain the city wall ditch presents a quandary. Papillon writes about the main ditch being dry, which in this case it was not until the cut was made, suggesting that 17th century military theory would have utilised a flooded ditch to the besieged's advantage as it prevented the besiegers from launching an undetected approach because they would be heard moving through the water. However, based on the archaeological evidence, the tactical decision in 1643 was for the ditch to be emptied of its water, at least in this section. This is despite Corbet describing the ditches as "narrow, but watered round". Interestingly, he also reports that the Royalists "had drawne the trench neer the moate, where they made a kind of mine to drain it, and sunk much of the water: and attempted to cast faggots into the moate, but were beaten off by our musketiers".[96]

G) The scons (bastion) at Rignell Stile

Dorney mentions Rignell Stile regarding activity on 12 August 1643, and that a "bridge of ladders over the moat" was made in order to attack the Royalists in their trenches at Gawdy Green.[97]

H) East Gate

Archaeological excavations between 38 and 44 Eastgate Street revealed evidence of bombardment during the Civil War, along with the targeting of a medieval tower. Specifically, context 11A3 revealed evidence of a culverin cannonball, along with lead, stone debris, tiles and window glass. Sections 305 and 320 revealed evidence of building debris from the 13th-century Eastgate Tower.[98] This evidence provides a tangible link to the reality of siege warfare, and how, despite the people of Gloucester attempting to secure the gate by having it "dammed up, and rammed with a thicknesse of earth

94 Carolyn Heighway, *The East and North Gates of Gloucester and Associated Sites Excavations 1974–81* (Bristol: Western Archaeological Trust, 1983), pp. 61, 255.

95 Papillon, *A practicall abstract of the arts of fortification*, p. 15.

96 Corbet, 'An Historicall relation of the military government of Gloucester', p. 47.

97 Dorney, 'A briefe and exact relation of the most materiall...', p. 213.

98 Heighway, *The East and North Gates of Gloucester and Associated Sites Excavations 1974–81*, pp. 9, 41, 60, 203, 255.

Plate 7 Remains of Eastgate Tower, Gloucester (facing south-south-west). (Author's photo)

cannon proofe",[99] it was still susceptible to an assault. This is a reminder of the ineffectiveness of using earth on medieval walls, as noted by the engineer Papillon, who wrote in 1645 that such walls could not be protected from cannon fire by lining them.[100] Part of the Eastgate Tower survives under Boots the Chemist (Plate 7).

K) The Sallie Gate

Also referred to as a Postern Gate, a section of the stone wall was discovered during excavations in 1971. The postern was repaired with hooks and hinges, along with elm boards, in 1642.[101]

K1) Friars' Barn

Corbet notes that a "sconce was built upon a rising ground that look into their trenches, where we could plant four piece of ordnance to cleare within the wals a ground called the Friar's orchard",[102] whilst Dorney states that Royalist trenches were within musket shot when a skirmish occurred on 16

99 Corbet, 'An Historicall relation of the military government of Gloucester', p. 46.
100 Papillon, *A practicall abstract of the arts of fortification*, pp. 11–12.
101 Rhodes, 'The Civil War Defences of Gloucester', p. 178.
102 Corbet, 'An Historicall relation of the military government of Gloucester', p. 52.

August.[103] Further additions included "lyning the Fryar's barne on the outside with earth for the preservation of our canon there" on 23 August,[104] although the inherent effectiveness of this strategy is questionable, as Papillon notes above.

K2) The North Gate (the Lower North Gate), lettered I

Whilst Corbet described the fortifications of North Gate as being a "slender work upon a low ground",[105] Captain Backhouse said that the fortification was one of "three sconces ... another before the north gate ... all of very great strength, but they are none of them as yet finished".[106] The archaeological record, however, revealed a significant ditch measuring 8m in width when excavations were conducted in 1982 for a relief road on Bruton Way.[107] Combining the historical and archaeological evidence of the defences, they suggest that a sconce-like feature was under construction, and that a significant ditch lay before it.

L) Captain Singleton's bastion

The bastion as illustrated on the plan lies underneath Nos 42–50 Worcester Street, built under the supervision of William Singleton, an Alderman and Member of Parliament for Gloucester.[108]

L1) Alvin Gate

Dorney records that the gate was besieged by Royalist artillery during the siege.[109]

N) Chapple House

A bastion was constructed here on the site that once housed the medieval chapel of St Thomas, and lies underneath 28 Dean's Walk and 7–15 Serlo Road.[110]

T) West Gate

To the north of this gate was an earthwork in Pen Meadow named 'The Pen'. It was completed before the siege and saw action between 10 August and 2 September 1643.[111] On one such engagement, Dorney noted that "Our canon ... from the pen upon the west-gate, discharged upon the body of horse in Walham."[112]

103 Dorney, 'A briefe and exact relation of the most materiall...', p. 215.

104 *Ibid.*, p. 219.

105 Corbet, 'An Historicall relation of the military government of Gloucester', p. 42.

106 Captain Backhouse, 'A true relation of a wicked plot intended and still on for against the city of Glocester to betray the same into the hands of the Cavaliers' (1644), in J. Washborn (ed.) *Bibliotheca Gloucestrensis* (Gloucester: J. Washborn, 1825), p. 308.

107 Anthony P. Garrod, *Inner Relief Road Bruton Way to London Road Junction Gloucester Site 23/1982* (Gloucester City Historic Environment Record Entry, 1982).

108 Rhodes, 'The Civil War Defences of Gloucester', p. 180.

109 Dorney, 'A briefe and exact relation of the most materiall...', p. 216.

110 Rhodes, 'The Civil War Defences of Gloucester', p. 181.

111 *Ibid.*, p. 184.

112 Dorney, 'A briefe and exact relation of the most materiall...', p. 211.

Plate 8 View of 26 Westgate Street, Gloucester (facing north). (Author's photo)

It is appropriate here to discuss the extant buildings along Westgate Street. No. 26 Westgate Street (Plate 8) was reportedly the headquarters of Massey, while 30 Westgate Street (Plate 9) belonged to Mr Commerline during the siege and was hit by shot on Friday, 25 August. Other buildings include the Folk Museum, which dates from the 16th century (Plate 10), and St Nicholas's Church (Plate 11), which sustained damage with the loss of the top of the spire that was present during the siege.[113]

113 Atkin and Laughlin, *Gloucester and the Civil War: a city under siege*, p. 158.

Plate 9 View of 30 Westgate Street, Gloucester (facing north-east). (Author's photo)

Plate 10 The Folk Museum on Westgate Street, Gloucester (facing south-south-west). (Author's photo)

Just off of Westgate Street, in the north-west of the city, are two important buildings. The first is St Mary's Gate (Plate 12), which like the Folk Museum and St Nicholas's Church is an important feature in the landscape and helps to contextualise the ground the armies were fighting over. The other, in St Mary's Square, is the church of St Mary de Lode (Plate 13), which was used as a prison for Royalist troops captured at Highnam in March 1643.[114]

T1) The Key

Corbet noted that "Upon the key head an halfe moon was raysed."[115] It is worthwhile remembering that Robert Ward, in his 1639 work *Animadversions of Warre; or, A militarie magazine of the truest rules, and ablest instructions, for the managing of warre*, illustrated the half-moon as a semi-circular/arrow point feature, which should have been part of a larger series of features.[116] The map also shows an important feature of the landscape, specifically to the north-east, noting that "This ground is verie lowe", highlighting again the importance of those involved in siege warfare having a critical understanding and appreciation of the landscape around them.

114 *Ibid.*, p. 159.

115 Corbet, 'An Historicall relation of the military government of Gloucester', p. 52.

116 Ward, *Animadversions of Warre*, p. 39.

Plate 11 St Nicholas's Church on Westgate Street, Gloucester (facing east-north-east). (Author's photo)

Plate 12 St Mary's Gate, Gloucester (facing south-east). (Author's photo)

Plate 13 St Mary de Lode, Gloucester (facing north). (Author's photo)

In an attempt to determine the positions and extent of the fortifications of the city, this study has examined and combined the results of cartographic data, historical documentation and archaeological evidence to present a clearer picture of what was extant at the time of the siege. The most notable evidence of all three sources is that revealed at East Gate, illustrating the reality of siege warfare.

The importance of the weather and the effect it had – and continues to have – on siege warfare was demonstrated during the siege at Gloucester. On 24 August 1643, torrential rain flooded the Royalists' trenches, and reportedly soaked King Charles I, who had intended to observe the first day of a new artillery bombardment from Robinshood's Hill. The bombardment had to be cancelled because of the weather conditions. Tactically, this was a further negative for the Royalists, as the mortar assault had been ineffective and sporadic the previous day.[117]

As has been seen, mining has been an essential siege tactic for centuries. A critical example in this siege was the Royalists' attempt to mine the East Gate. Countermines were dug in response by the Parliamentarians. However, the local geology affected both sides' use of this technique, as they each

117 Day, *Gloucester & Newbury 1643: The Turning Point of the Civil War*, p. 79.

encountered springs, forcing them to stop.[118] Archaeologically, a possible mine was discovered 115 yards (105m) from East Gate on Wellington Street. The mine measured at least 10½ yards (9.5m) in width and was supported by timber props.[119] Here can be seen the importance of geology, and how the landscape affects what siege techniques can be conducted in specific theatres of war. The use of mines appears to have been a tactical mistake by the Royalists. The siege was moving too slowly, and the Royalists were not taking advantage of the strategic position they found themselves in. They already had control of Shrewsbury, Worcester, Bridgnorth and Bristol; the taking of Gloucester would have meant that they would have controlled the entire Severn Valley region.

As the siege continued, the Royalists used grenades fired out of mortars.[120] The theologian and mathematician Doctor William Chillingworth provided for the besiegers a "great store of engines after the manner of the Romane Testudines cum Pluteis which they intended to have assaulted the parts of the city, betweene the south and west gates".[121] The reuse of Roman military theory and machines illustrates the great lengths the Royalists were attempting to go through to secure Gloucester for the king.

The defenders were stout in their resolve to hold Gloucester for Parliament. Dorney reported that under bombardment, the "maids and others wrought daily without the works in the little mead, in fetching turfe in the faces of our enemies".[122] The importance here of turf to support and hold the earthen fortifications should not be underestimated, as Ward noted when describing the *offensive* fortifications at the siege of Breda (p. xx). Corbet also noted that the defenders would use anything available to them, including "wooll-packs and cannon baskets",[123] to seal breaches made.

Despite artillery bombardment and the use of saps, mining, grenades and siege machines, which had had a devastating impact on the city, the Royalists were unsuccessful in their siege. The consequences of the siege are seen most vividly in the scarred remains of St Oswald's Priory (Plate 14). Despite the impact of the Dissolution of the Monasteries, the Priory was still intact in 1643, but it was destroyed during the siege.[124]

The signalling by two fires from Wainlode Hill on 4 September indicated that the city was about to be relieved by a force commanded by the Earl of Essex. The Royalists withdrew the following day, burning their huts as they abandoned their positions.[125]

Dorney reported that the Parliamentarians lost 50 men during the siege operations, but that the Royalists had suffered at least 1,000 – and possibly

118 Dorney, 'A briefe and exact relation of the most materiall…', p. 221; Corbet, 'An Historicall relation of the military government of Gloucester', p. 51.

119 Atkin and Howes, 'The use of archaeology and documentary sources…', p. 29.

120 Corbet, 'An Historicall relation of the military government of Gloucester', p. 47.

121 Dorney, 'A briefe and exact relation of the most materiall…', p. 225.

122 *Ibid.*, p. 227.

123 Corbet, 'An Historicall relation of the military government of Gloucester', p. 47.

124 Atkin and Laughlin, *Gloucester and the Civil War: a city under siege*, p. 159.

125 Robert Morris, *The Siege of Gloucester 1643* (Bristol: Stuart Press, 1993), pp. 9–10.

Plate 14 The ruins of St Oswald's Priory, Gloucester (facing north). (Author's photo)

1,500 – casualties in their ill-fated attempt to take Gloucester.[126] It is probable that if the Earl of Essex and his army had not arrived, the city would have surrendered the following week, as supplies were almost depleted and breaches were in place along the south wall and at East Gate.[127]

Ultimately, the failure of the Royalists to capture Gloucester was a clear tactical and strategic blow to the king's cause. The Royalists' ineffective use of mining and artillery is a clear reason as to why they were unsuccessful in their siege. This setback to the Royalist cause would have repercussions for the rest of 1643 and beyond.

126 Dorney, 'A briefe and exact relation of the most materiall…', p. 227.
127 Atkin and Laughlin, *Gloucester and the Civil War: a city under siege*, p. 115

Chapter 2

The Sieges of 1645

Despite the unsuccessful siege of Gloucester, and the inconclusive First Battle of Newbury on 20 September 1643, going into the winter of 1643–44, King Charles had control of two-thirds of England and Wales. However, by the spring of 1644, the strategic situation had changed. Following defeats for their forces at King's Lynn, Winceby, Chichester and Arundel, the Royalists also lost the Battle of Marston Moor on 2 July. Parliament, however, was unsuccessful in its attempt to capture Newark, while a lack of co-operation between Waller and Essex in the south forced Essex's withdraw from Lostwithiel in Cornwall. On 27 October 1644, the Second Battle of Newbury ended in a stalemate.[1] Moving into 1645, the Parliamentarians launched the next siege in the Severn Valley area against Shrewsbury.

The Parliamentarian Siege of Shrewsbury, 22 February 1645

The archaeologist Nigel Baker notes that the town of Shrewsbury lies within a loop of the River Severn. The loop surrounds an area of approximately 1km (0.62 miles) north to south and the same distance east to west. Topographically, the land inside the loop sits on two hills approximately 49m and 70–72m above sea level. The hills are divided by a central valley sloping to the west, between 60m and 65m above sea level. Near the higher northerly hill sits St Mary's Church, of Anglo-Saxon date; the land to the north-west and east falls towards the river. The high ground continues to the north-east towards a north-facing slope, upon which sits a Norman castle. The landscape between St Mary's Church and the Norman castle forms a small pass and cuts into the eastern escarpment. The southerly hill contains another Anglo-Saxon church, St Chad's. The surrounding landscape forms a wide ridge from the north-west to the south-east. This area and the northern hill are composed of natural sands, sandy silts and sandy clays. The caps of both hilltops consist of gravel, which is sporadic in places. Between the

1 Peter Gaunt, *The English Civil Wars 1642–51*, pp. 38, 40–44.

floodplain of the River Severn and the southern hill, the soil consists of sandy clays sitting on Keele Beds sandstone.[2]

Shrewsbury, along with nearby Bridgnorth and Ludlow, were all medieval town-walled sites that had developed via the positioning of castles, which utilised natural defensive positions on high ground and had a defensive system utilising the River Severn.[3] The river was the most important mode of transportation in and out of the county of Shropshire during the 17th century, connecting the area to the major ports of Gloucester and Bristol. Shrewsbury, along with Bridgnorth, was an important inland port.[4] Parliament restricted the Royalist use of the river by holding Bristol in December 1642. Although the Royalists captured Bristol in 1643, the Severn remained important to Parliament as Gloucester was under its control. Shrewsbury and Worcester were also at this time under the control of the Royalists. In April 1644, cannon shot and grenades were carried by the Royalists from Bridgnorth to Worcester so that they could be transferred to Oxford. A barge was used along the Severn for several days in September 1643, to transport turf which was cut from the surrounding fields of Shrewsbury to be used in the revetting of Shrewsbury's earthen fortifications.[5] Topographically, Shrewsbury Castle sits 49m above sea level, while the suburb of Frankwell is 62m above sea level,[6] with both sites situated on a bedrock of sandstone.

In 1642, the population of Shrewsbury was around 7,000.[7] The town was an important centre for the manufacture of weapons for the Royalist cause. This included the manufacture of swords, as by early 1643, 43 new swords were produced for just 6 shillings each. Between 1642 and 1644, wooden and iron components for gun carriages – including gunnery tools, which included rammers, sponges, budge barrels and gunpowder horns – were produced in the city too. Cartridges for gunpowder was also made using locally produced cloth.[8]

By 1350, the medieval defences of Shrewsbury, which included the castle, town walls and outworks, were approximately 1.98 miles (3.2km) in length. The town walls depicted on the Burghley Map of *c.* 1575 show that the defensive circuit was in good repair. In 1612, John Speed's map of the town revealed that although the early Stuart walls of Shrewsbury were not defensible, they were not generally in a ruinous state. The walls, such as the surviving Town Walls Tower (Plate 15), and the castle acted as an *enceinte* (main line of defence) for Shrewsbury at the outset of the war. To defend Shrewsbury, wooden turnpikes were built and utilised as portable barricades.

2 Nigel Baker, *Shrewsbury: An archaeological assessment of an English border town* (Oxford: Oxbow Books, 2010), pp. 23–24.

3 Jonathan Worton, *To Settle The Crown: Waging Civil War in Shropshire, 1642–1648* (Solihull: Helion & Company Limited, 2016), p. 216.

4 *Ibid.*, p.190.

5 *Ibid.*, pp. 190–91.

6 Memory Map Inc. © Crown Copyright Ordnance Survey 2008 Licence No: PU100034184 (Central England).

7 Jonathan Worton, '"The Strongest Works in England"?: The defences of Shrewsbury during the Civil Wars, 1642–1651', *Transactions of the Shropshire Archaeological Society*, Vol. 87 (2012), p. 95.

8 Worton, *To Settle The Crown*, p. 171.

Plate 15 The Town Walls Tower, Shrewsbury (facing south-south-west). (Author's photo)

Chains were added at various positions in 1644. During 1644 and 1645, the wealthier inhabitants of Shrewsbury were charged to pay for workmen in the construction of the fortifications throughout the town.[9] The turnpike was designed to stop people and horses at the entrance to the town. According to Nicholas Stone, in his manual *Enchiridion of Fortification or, A handfull of knowledge in martiall affaires*, a turnpike should have iron at both ends, and be between 12 and 13ft (3.65–3.9m) in length and half a foot (15cm) in width.[10] It is not surprising that we continue to see the effective use of wood in siege warfare, having seen it used throughout history, at the siege of Plataea in 429 BC and the siege of Alesia in 52 BC, to give but two examples.

By the early 1400s, Shrewsbury Castle had fallen into disrepair. However, whilst the castle was not in ruins in the 1630s, it was unable to accommodate a Royal visit in 1642 and house magazines of munitions.[11] To remedy this, the castle was modified. The works included accommodation and an ancillary building for a garrison, along with a stone barbican of loophole shape and a drawbridge to fortify the main entrance.[12] To repair the castle and town walls, stone was transported to Shrewsbury from several sources, including the quarry near Abbey Foregate and one at Emstree. Sandstone was quarried from Grinshill, while lime, widely available in Shropshire, was transported to Shrewsbury in 1643. Sand and water were taken from the River Severn so that clay could be softened and mortar mixed together.[13]

The *Mercurius Aulicus*, the Royalist propaganda newspaper, noted false intelligence about Shrewsbury in January 1645 (dated 1644) that had been received by Sir Francis Ottley, which stated that "the town is so weak and poor it is not able to maintain a troop of horse". Noting this, and having information of a "vulnerable point", it said a garrison from Wem marched towards Shrewsbury on 14 and 15 February, although it decided to turn back on a dark night with wet roads.[14]

An anonymous account titled *A true and full relation of the manner and taking of the towne and castle of Shrewsbury* recorded that:

> "Shrewsbury, which is a very strong Town, well Walled, and compassed about with a navigable River , in the form of an Horse-shooe; the neck of land at the opening of the Horse-shooe, being not a Bow shot over, in which stands (on the East-side on the top of an of an high Hill) a strong *Castle*, the River running directly along, close under the side of the hill: From the North-West side of the hill, there runs a strong Wall, and a great Ditch to the River, on that side."[15]

---

9 Worton, '"The Strongest Works in England"?', pp. 98, 100, 102; Jonathan Worton, 'The Royalist and Parliamentarian War Effort in Shropshire during the First and Second Civil Wars, 1642–1648' (PhD Thesis, University of Chester, 2015), pp. 190, 192.

10 Nicholas Stone, *Enchiridion of Fortification or, A handfull of knowledge in martiall affaires* (London: Richard Royston, 1645), pp. 36–37.

11 Worton, '"The Strongest Works in England"?', p. 100.

12 Worton, 'The Royalist and Parliamentarian', p. 190.

13 Worton, '"The Strongest Works in England"?', p. 107.

14 Anonymous, *The Garrisons of Shropshire, During the Civil War, 1642–48* (Shrewsbury: Leake and Evans, 1867), p. 74.

15 Anonymous, *A true and full relation of the manner and taking of the towne and castle of Shrewsbury* (London, 1644), p. 4.

The castle is described in this account as strong, thereby noting the additions and repairs made to it in 1642. The medieval wall appears to be intact and now defensible. The strong wall on the north-west could actually be the Roushill Wall (discussed below in more detail). Overall, analysis of this source suggests a strongly fortified town.

Lord Capel took command of the region around Shrewsbury for the Royalists sometime around 20 March 1643. His plan was to conduct the digging of trenches and use the subsequent spoil to create ramparts designed to, in part, protect the eastern suburb of Coleham and Abbey Foregate. Additional methods included the use of natural obstacles in the landscape and connecting buildings.[16] Jonathan Worton noted that for several years, from 1643 until 1645, significant areas of Shrewsbury were under development. A contemporary, Richard Gough, was reported as stating that several houses were destroyed below the castle to make a clear, unobstructed field of fire. Wood for defences came from Lythwood, and sawpits at Coleham provided large supplies of timber. As previously mentioned, turf was also gathered from pastoral fields.[17] The use of turf is an important tool when constructing a fortification; as has been seen, Robert Ward discussed its continued significance in *Animadversions of Warre; or, A militarie magazine of the truest rules, and ablest instructions, for the managing of warre* (p. xx). In addition, Richard Norwood, in his 1639 manual *Fortification or Military Architecture*, along with Nicholas Stone both discuss cutting turf into wedges to place on top of the ramparts.[18]

Construction of a trench towards Frankwell in August 1643, and a rampart system, was superseded by the construction of a large fortification. The exact position of this fortification, or sconce, at Frankwell is unknown; however, a ridge spur would most likely be its location, as that utilised the high ground (62m above sea level) and was separate from the main defences of the town. The area is known as 'The Mount' – a reference to 17th century terminology for that feature.[19] Jonathan Worton discusses this feature, utilising Richard Norwood and his work *Fortification or Military Architecture*. Norwood noted that a four-sided sconce – that is, a fortification composed of four bastions, and based on a Dutch design – would be 24ft (7.31m) in width, 4ft (1.21m) in height, contain a parapet 6ft (1.82m) high and have a ditch that was 6ft (1.82m) deep and 30ft (9.14m) in width.[20] Such a construction does not even account for Norwood's suggestion of using wooden palisades (which, as has been seen, would have been available), or the fact that in July 1644 a work gang spent between them 79 days refurbishing the fortification.[21] It is

16 Worton, '"The Strongest Works in England"?', p. 104.

17 *Ibid.*, pp. 97, 107.

18 Richard Norwood, *Fortification or Military Architecture* (London: Andrew Crooke, 1639), pp. 92–93; Stone, *Enchiridion of Fortification*, p. 35.

19 Worton, 'The Royalist and Parliamentarian', p. 191; Worton, '"The Strongest Works in England"?', pp. 97, 104.

20 Worton, '"The Strongest Works in England"?', p. 105; Norwood, *Fortification or Military Architecture*, pp. 143–44.

21 Norwood, *Fortification or Military Architecture*, p. 145; Worton, '"The Strongest Works in England"?', p. 105.

known, however, that by 1644, the fortification was able to successfully repel an exchange of musketry fire.[22]

The construction of a stone wall at Roushill in 1643 was to protect the riverside defences between the medieval fortifications upstream and the Welsh Bridge.[23] The Shrewsbury Corporation accounts recorded stone being carried to the area from the town walls on 13 May 1643.[24] A redoubt was also constructed between the Welsh Bridge and medieval outwork, to fortify this section of the defences. Near this location, a timber watchtower was also constructed to, no doubt, observe movements along the River Severn. Beyond the suburb of the Castle Foregate, earthwork fortifications would be constructed on open land. These would be constructed of earth, timber and turf.[25] The riverside wall from Garewald's Tower was also extended to the Welsh Bridge during the Civil War.[26] It is unfortunate that no surviving contemporary plan of the Civil War fortifications exists.[27]

A map that aids the analysis of the defences of Shrewsbury during the siege is the *Prospect of the Town of Shrewsbury as it appeared in the Great Frost, 1739* (Map 4). Despite this plan being produced nearly 100 years after the Civil War, it contains some important information. Firstly, it helps in the understanding and appreciation of the topography of the landscape, and why Shrewsbury Castle commanded the landscape (although this is also seen in John Speed's 1612 plan of the city). Secondly, and given the frost, the importance of the River Severn to Shrewsbury is stressed. The map also shows the survival and good condition a century later of the medieval wall and Town Walls Tower, which has survived to this day (see Plate 15). Finally, and perhaps most importantly, the map provides cartographic evidence of the Roushill Wall, in the top left of the image and annotated by the letter 'D'. This is important evidence, as it is an independent source, rather than biased towards the Royalist or Parliamentarian side, relating to the wall that work was commenced on in May 1643 (at least according to the Shrewsbury Corporation). In spite of any artistic licence, it must still have been a significant stone feature in the landscape.

Having combined the cartographic evidence with the historical evidence, particularly that of the Shrewsbury Corporation, archaeology can also be turned to for further illumination of this feature. Excavations for the construction of the Riverside Medical Centre at the junction of Smithfield Road and Roushill in February 1987 revealed evidence of the town wall known as the Roushill Wall. This is believed to have been constructed during the Civil War, either by the Royalists in 1643 or by the Parliamentarians in 1645, although the wall was not completed until 1651. It was approximately 158 yards (145m) in length. The reason for the construction of a wall during the war, and at this section, was that from Gilbert's Tower to the old Welsh

22 Worton, *To Settle The Crown*, pp. 208–09.
23 Worton, '"The Strongest Works in England"?', p. 105.
24 Philip A. Barker, 'Excavations on the Town Wall, Roushill, Shrewsbury', *Medieval Archaeology*, Vol. 5 (1961), p. 204.
25 Worton, '"The Strongest Works in England"?', p. 105.
26 Baker, *Shrewsbury*, p. 134.
27 Worton, '"The Strongest Works in England"?', p .97.

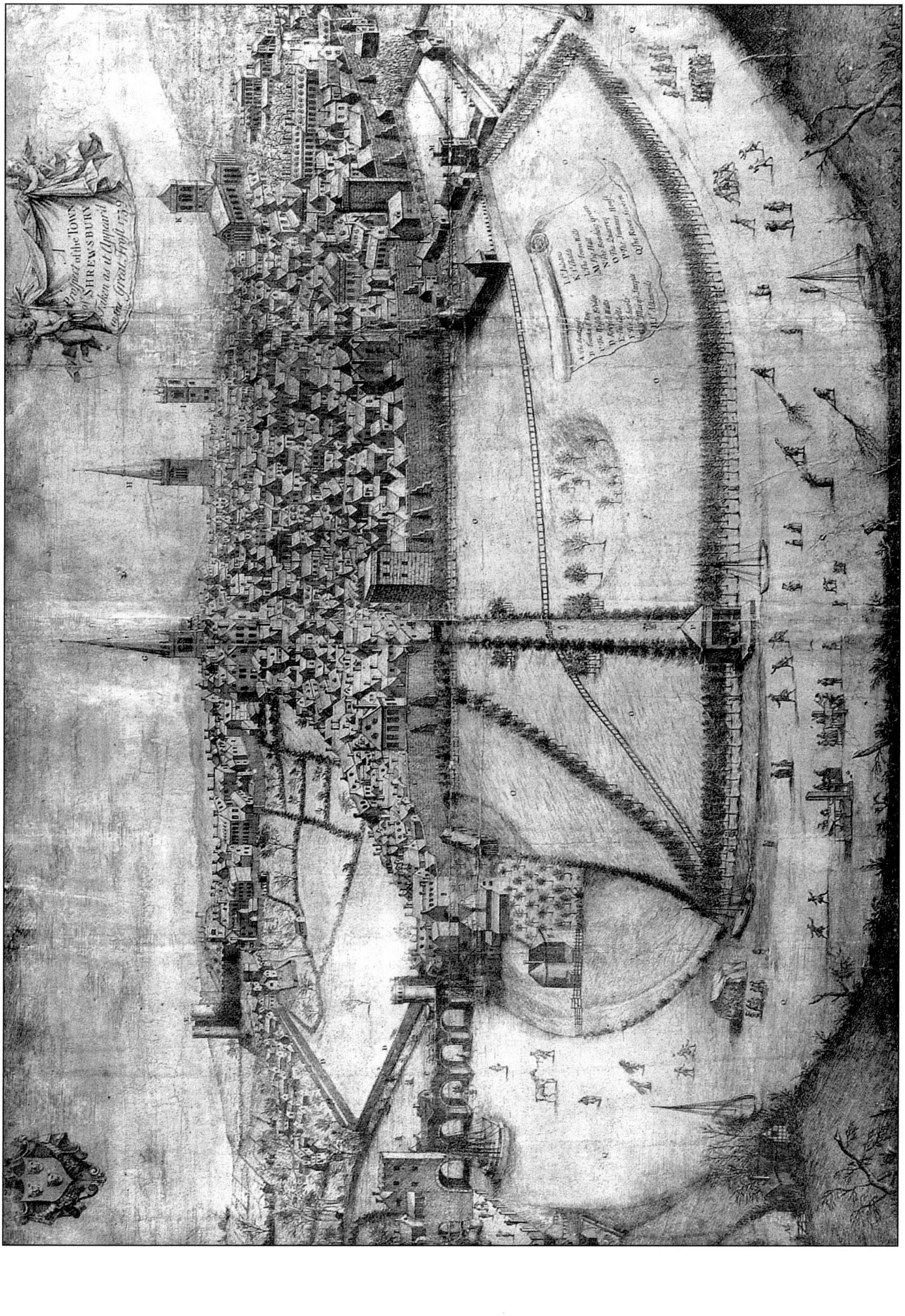

Map 4 A plan of Shrewsbury titled *Prospect of the Town of Shrewsbury as it appeared in the Great Frost, 1739* (Reference: PH.5.13.5.22.219). (Reproduced by permission of Shropshire Archives and the Museum Curator)

Bridge, it was believed that the wet marshland of Raven Meadows was satisfactory to perform a defensive role. Of the exposed section of wall – some 14¾ yards (13.5m) – it was uniformly 5½ft (1.65m) in width and was made mostly of red sandstone and bonded together with a lime mortar. The outer faces of the wall had regular-sized stones, well dressed in a rubble core, which contain a few pieces of white sandstone. It was aligned in a south-west/ north-east direction. The high quality of construction suggests that the wall was built between 1645 and 1651, as the lack of quality in the repairs on other sections of the medieval town wall indicate earlier, more hurried work before the 1645 siege.[28] This archaeological evidence appears to combine well with the cartographic depiction of the wall in *Prospect of the Town of Shrewsbury as it appeared in the Great Frost, 1739*, thereby suggesting that the evidence of both sources is reliable. It is important to remember that any views would have needed to be amended if the evidence presented contradicted the currently held beliefs; For it is evidence, and evidence alone, that must guide knowledge and understanding.

Further archaeological evidence in the form of a 2009 watching brief did not reveal anything specifically relating to the Civil War, despite an indication in a desk-based assessment that the town ditch was back-filled, although this cannot be precisely dated to this period. Excavations conducted in 2012 on Smithfield Road, some 100m north-east of a 1961 observation, revealed no evidence of Gilbert's Tower or the Roushill Wall, suggesting that the defences ran between the River Severn and the site of the excavations.[29]

The Parliamentarians launched the siege on 22 February 1645. Lieutenant Colonel William Reinking, a mercenary who was of German or Dutch descent,[30] was with the Parliamentarian forces during the siege. His account of events is analysed below.

Reinking states that the Parliamentarians twice attempted to approach the castle via the river using a boat, although with difficulty going upstream, this plan was abandoned, as the boat was discovered by two sentinels. Instead, carpenters with axes approached the palisades by the outworks of the castle. It took the carpenters 15 minutes to cut down one palisade. The sentinels were made aware of this, and the alarm was raised in both the town and the castle. With one palisade cut down, a group of men were able to run towards a low place in front of a stone wall near the council house, and utilising a scaling ladder approximately 8ft (2.43m) long, scaled the wall. The Parliamentarians were then able to get into the main street (St Mary's Water Lane, Plate 16) near the castle. A small skirmish occurred, with one of Reinking's men being injured by a rapier. Reinking gave a command for Major Fenwick to open the castle gate so that the musketeers and horsemen could enter (via Water

28 T.M. Brown and Michael. D. Watson, 'The Civil War Roushill Wall, Shrewsbury', *Transactions of the Shropshire Archaeological and Historical Society*, Vol. 66 (1989), pp. 85–89.

29 Adam Lee, *Archaeological Watching Brief of Sainsbury's Supermarket, The Smithfield, Bridgnorth, Shropshire* (Unpublished Report: Worcestershire County Council, 2009); Hal Dalwood, *Desk-Based Assessment of Sainsbury's Supermarket Site, The Smithfield, Bridgnorth, Shropshire* (Unpublished Report: Worcestershire County Council, 2007), p. 8; Laurence Hayes, *Premier Inn Shrewsbury Archaeological Excavation Report* (Unpublished Report: SLR, 2012), pp. 1, 3, 31.

30 Worton, *To Settle The Crown*, p. 87.

Plate 16 St Mary's Water Lane, Shrewsbury (facing west). (Author's photo)

Lane). A further skirmish occurred between up to 12 men. Reinking found no opposition at the stone bridge; he then marched towards the castle. The Frankwell sconce was also surrendered.[31]

An important piece of information to analyse from this account is the fact that it took a quarter of an hour for the carpenters to cut through one palisade. This suggests that despite the weakness in the fortifications at this point, if the Royalists were fully aware of the approach, they would have been able to make the task much more difficult. This evidence demonstrates how the use of palisades, whilst not ultimately effective in this case, did still slow down the besieging men significantly, especially when time was of the essence. The use of carpenters also highlights the number of occupations required when conducting siege warfare, rather than only fighting men taking part. Indeed, as Jonathan Worton notes, numerous pieces of timber were brought into Shrewsbury between August and September 1643, to prepare gun platforms at the castle and fortification at Frankwell.[32]

31 William Reinking, *A more exact and particular relation of the taking of Shrewsbury, then hath hitherto been published. With the manner and performance thereof by Lieutenant Collonel William Reinking commander in chief in that designe* (London: Published by Authority, 1645), pp. 4–6.

32 Worton, '"The Strongest Works in England"?', p.106.

Another account titled *A true and full relation of the manner and taking of the towne and castle of Shrewsbury* notes that the town was well fortified and palisaded. It describes how eight Parliamentarian carpenters attempted to proceed by boat to land within the defenders' breastworks underneath Castle Hill on the east side. Breaking through the palisade, musketeers ran near Sir William Owen's House (the Council House) and entered the town. Opening the gates, 350 foot soldiers entered the town. Having taken control of the streets, some troops proceeded towards the market place; after an exchange of fire, the Parliamentarians captured the main Court of Guard there. The rest of the troops moved towards the Castle's forward-gate (North Gates), which was opened within 15 minutes. The castle and the sconce at Frankwell held out until 12:00 p.m.[33] This account highlights a further 15-minute delay (in addition to the delay below the castle near the river). This suggests that not only did the North Gates hold, but that it was fortunate for the Parliamentarians that this delay did not cause them further problems.

The Parliamentary propaganda newspaper *Burning Bush Not Consumed* described the taking of Shrewsbury by Colonel 'Mitton' (Mytton).[34] The following description was given:

> "Upon the 22nd of this month of February, we drew out our Garrisons of Wem, Moreton and Stoke, 250 horse, and the like number of foot; so William Brereton having sent us 250 foot and 350 horse, which party by our order was commanded by Lieutenant Colonel Rinkling (who in the marshalling and managing of this design deserves much honour) and Captain Willyer, together with Mr. Huson, a minister, who also most bravely and valiantly led on the firelocks with 50 troopers dismounted under the command of Lieutenant Bendebne, who led on their men with unsorted resolution; after whom followed also 350 foot more, which by Severn side stormed the town, near unto the Castle wall, and marched into the Market house, and there surprized the main guard, and then sent a party to secure the Castle Forehead Gate, which was effected without much difficulty; and after a quarter of an hour, the drawbridge was let down, and the gate opened, where valiant Colonel Mytton, Colonel Boyer, and all the gentlemen of this Committee, with the horse entered; and after the Castle was surrendered upon quarter, for all but the Irish to march to Ludlow and then enemy delivered up a strong work in Frankwell, upon bear quarter for their lives; by twelve o'clock at noon wee became absolute masters of the Castle and the Town, wherein were taken many considerable prisoners, good store ammunition, and great store of ordnance. The Committee of Wem took as much care as possibly could be that the well affected in the town might not in any measures suffer, or be plundered, and therefore the officers kept off their souldiers from plundering the time that we the Committee might see right done, but and not but malignants only to suffer … We also tooke fifteen pieces of ordnance, many hundreds of armes, diver barrels of powder, all Prince Maurice his Magazine, divers carriages, bagge, baggage of the Prince; we lost only two men. And was not this a most rare and remarkable mercy and famous victory …

33 Anonymous, *A true and full relation*, pp. 4–6.

34 Anonymous, *The Garrisons of Shropshire, During the Civil War, 1642–48*, p. 74.

> "The invading party had divided, one ran up the bank of the Council House Garden, which is nearest to the castle, and scaling the wall with light ladders reached the North or Castle Gate; the other took the path by the river side, under the Council House, then the residence of Sir William Owen, and notwithstanding that a Fort existed on each side the Water Gate, they entered the town unmolested, being plainly indebted to treachery for their success."[35]

Examination of this source reveals that Colonel Mytton had 250 horse and William Brereton another 350, thereby totalling 600 cavalry approaching Shrewsbury. Given the use of turnpikes and palisades, any approach using horse would have been made more difficult, in the same way as a cavalry charge into pikemen on a battlefield. There is a reference to a 15-minute wait outside Castle Forehead Gate and how the sconce at Frankwell and the castle held out until midday. This continues to illustrate the importance of modern earthworks when facing cavalry and musketry. Of particular interest is a reference to 15 artillery pieces being captured, but unfortunately it is not known whether these pieces were demi-culverins, minions and/or falcons, as further analysis of their potential effectiveness could have been discussed. The use of scaling ladders for the assault demonstrates how the siege techniques, and pre-planning for such assaults as used during the Roman and medieval eras, continued to affect warfare at this time. Curiously, there is no reference made to the fortification (redoubt) at Roushill, suggesting that it was ineffective.

Despite some differences between the four published Parliamentarian accounts, such as, Reinking and Mytton disputing who deserved credit for capturing Shrewsbury, analysis by the historian Jonathan Worton has maintained that a Parliamentarian force of 1,200 troops approached the town in the early morning of Saturday, 22 February 1645, having information of a weak point in the riverside defences. Some broke through the fortifications beneath the castle, moved up the river cliff slope and used scaling ladders at a low section of the town wall, near the Council House, occupied by Sir William Owen, who later came under suspicion for being a Parliamentarian sympathiser. From here, they entered the town, with some skirmishes with the Royalist garrison. The main body of Parliamentary forces entered through the northern town gates and had secured the town by 9:00 a.m. Worton adds that the castle and surrounding fortifications held out until noon.[36]

According to Worton, the approach of some of the infantry with matchlock muskets, some having lit their match cord under the command of Reinking, was criticised by Colonel Mytton, as the light could have given away their position.[37] Terry Bracher and Roger Emmett claim that a group of eight carpenters arrived underneath the castle via boat and started to remove the palisade. A breach was made in the defences before the Royalists knew what was happening, and Captain Benbow scaled the walls and moved towards an

35 *Ibid.*, pp. 75–76.

36 Worton, '"The Strongest Works in England"?', pp. 96, 110; Terry Bracher and Roger Emmett, *Shropshire in the Civil War* (Shrewsbury: Shropshire Books, 2000), p. 36.

37 Worton, 'The Royalist and Parliamentarian', p. 202; Worton, *To Settle The Crown*, p. 227.

area north of the castle gates. Lieutenant Colonel Reinking and his troops then entered through the gates via Water Lane.[38] Worton also states that it appears that two defectors gave the Parliamentarians information on where the fortifications were at their weakest along the river before the assault.[39]

Interestingly, some modern analyses of events at Shrewsbury have suggested that the taking of the town could not be classified as a siege, because very little fighting had occurred; indeed, the town escaped any serious damage during the Civil War, with only the destruction of houses outside the Castle Gates to make a better defensive perimeter in 1643. However, Stephen Porter notes the removal of buildings at Frankwell to the west of the town, and at Abbey Foregate to the east. W.A. Champion and B. Coulton, along with H.R. Hannaford, note that a "fort" near Cadogan's Chapel was constructed to monitor the roads from a westerly direction. The fort, known as Cadogan's Tower, was connected to a defensive ditch running from the windmill at Frankwell to the River Severn, with an additional ditch dug between Coleham and Abbey Foregate. The town wall was extended by the meadow at Roushill. Evidence of what were potentially three musket loops, cut into the wall, can be seen in the town wall at Wyle Cop, which, if dating to the Civil War, would have given enfilading fire along the wall behind Dogpole.[40]

The fort near Cadogan's Chapel seems to be a reference to the sconce at Frankwell. Despite the removal of buildings in the suburb of Frankwell, it appears that this was a strategic and tactical success, as the fortification was able to withstand an assault for several hours, demonstrating the effectiveness of modern artillery earthwork features, albeit against musketry fire rather than an artillery barrage.

On the eve of 22 February 1645, according to Jonathan Worton and as depicted in Map 5, it appears that Shrewsbury had fortifications – that included designs based on the contemporary military manuals of the period – which were made of earth and had prevailing ditches along with timber palisades which acted as emplacements for the artillery.[41] The earthworks constructed by the Royalists to defend Shrewsbury Castle were of such standard that the Parliamentary assault team required carpenters, who moved in with soldiers who were wielding sledgehammers. The detached fortification at the suburb of Frankwell, designed to defend the westerly approach to the town, was surrendered on separate terms, thereby indicating its importance. In addition, towers and drawbridges defended both bridges, which originally formed part of the town's medieval defensive circuit.[42]

---

38 Bracher and Emmett, *Shropshire in the Civil War*, p. 36.

39 Worton, 'The Royalist and Parliamentarian', p. 220.

40 Stephen Porter, *The Blast of War: Destruction in the English Civil Wars* (Stroud: The History Press, 2011), p. 23; W.A. Champion, and B. Coulton, with contributions by J. Lawson, 'Shrewsbury 1640–1780', in W.A. Champion and A.T. Thacker (eds), *The Victoria History of the Counties of England. A History of Shropshire Volume VI, Part I* (Woodbridge: The Boydell Press, 2014), pp. 181, 216; H.R. Hannaford, *Shrewsbury Town Walls: A Conservation Management Plan* (Unpublished Report: Shropshire Council, 2015), pp. 6, 49.

41 Worton, 'The Royalist and Parliamentarian', p. 190.

42 Worton, *To Settle The Crown*, pp. 217, 220.

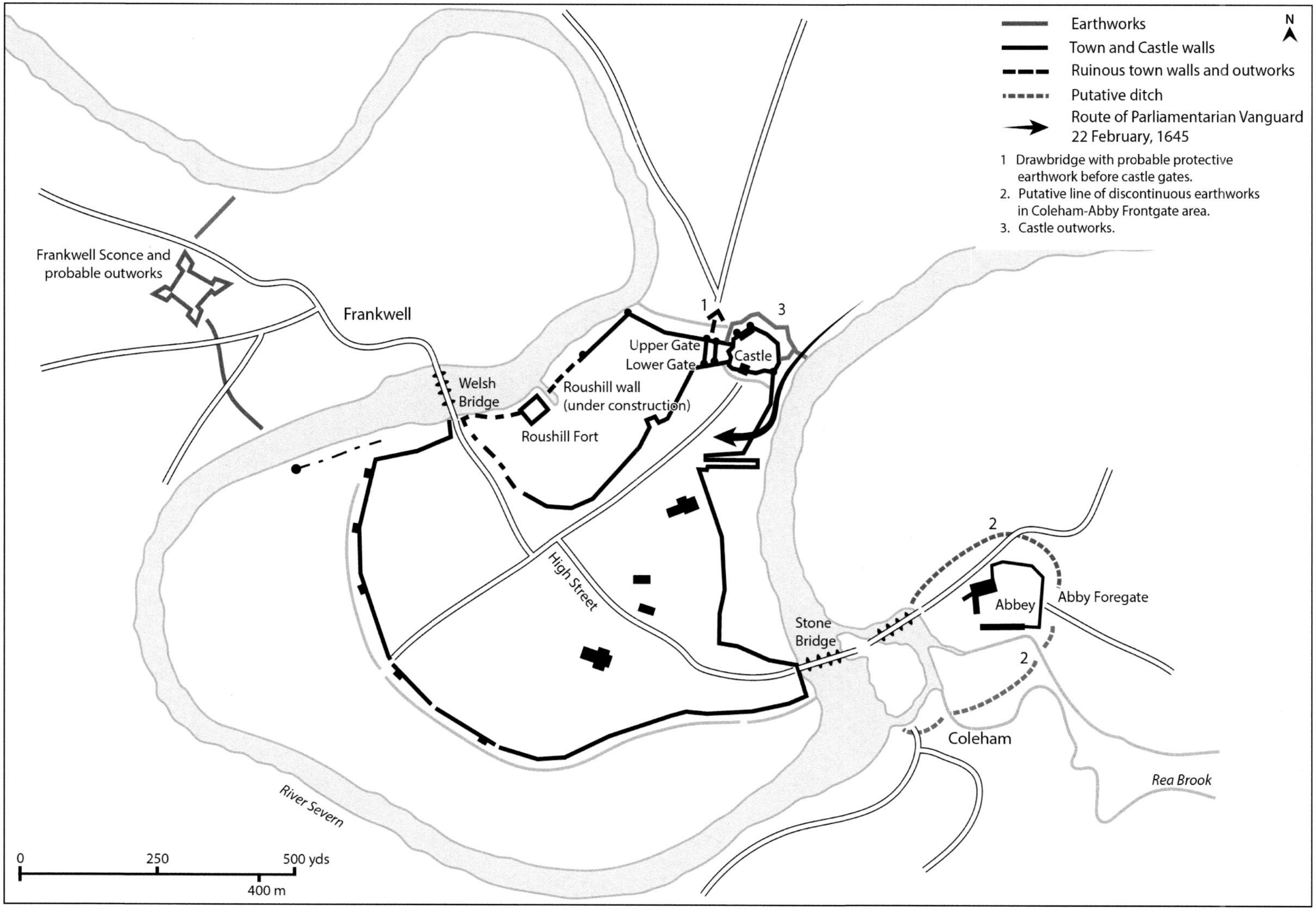

Map 5 A plan of the fortifications of Shrewsbury in 1644. (Reproduced by permission of Dr Jonathan Worton and Shropshire Archaeological and Historical Society — Figure 1 Plan reconstruction of Shrewsbury's Civil War fortifications as they may have appeared at their fullest extent, in the autumn of 1644 under Royalist occupation. Researched and drawn by Dr Jonathan Worton (University of Chester), based on the mapping in Nigel Baker's Shrewsbury: an Archaeological Assessment of an English Border Town, and Bill Champion's Everyday Life in Tudor Shrewsbury at page 103)

Overall, by examining the evidence, it can be seen how easily – despite the construction of significant fortifications like the sconce at Frankwell and the wall at Roushill, along with additions and repairs made to Shrewsbury Castle – a town can be captured. Despite the Royalist defenders having utilised modern earthworks containing palisades, ditches, turnpikes and chains across the river, along with the natural barrier of the River Severn itself, the existing medieval town walls, towers, the castle and the destruction of the suburbs of Frankwell and Abbey Foregate in an attempt to strengthen the defensive line, it was ultimately in vain. For the Parliamentarians, capturing the town was a relatively easy and brief campaign.

Topographically, the sconce at Frankwell was placed in an ideal and commanding location, being 62m above sea level. It and Shrewsbury Castle (49m above sea level) were both on a sandstone bedrock, which does not appear to have caused the working gang any difficulty, given the 79 days working on the sconce – persistence had paid off. The strength of these two features in the landscape is demonstrated by the fact that they held out the longest in the face of the Parliamentary army.

The combination of historical, cartographic information – namely *Prospect of the Town of Shrewsbury as it appeared in the Great Frost, 1739* – and archaeological evidence presents a tangible link to the events at Shrewsbury, rather than something that is simply recorded in the history books. The cartographic evidence has suggested that the wall would have been a significant barrier to the approaching Parliamentarians, while the archaeological evidence has demonstrated that the Roushill Wall was made predominately of red sandstone, bonded together with lime mortar and dressed in a rubble core. Combining this with the historical record of the Shrewsbury Corporation, it is possible to suggest a date for construction of the wall commencing in May 1643. This clearly demonstrates the importance of using all the available evidence, and what can be achieved when combining historical, cartographical and archaeological information.

The fortifications constructed at Shrewsbury are an important example of how Civil War era features compare to the military manuals of the period. It has been seen how relatable the construction of the sconce at Frankwell was to Richard Norwood's 1639 manual *Fortification or Military Architecture*, in addition to Nicholas Stone's *Enchiridion of Fortification or, A handfull of knowledge in martiall affaires*, especially regarding the importance of turf in fortifications. This continues to demonstrate how, despite using the most up-to-date ideas and techniques for fortification construction and design, and despite complex and necessary preparations, these features can be tactically lost in a relatively short amount of time, in this instance thanks largely due to a group of carpenters and 15 minutes' work at a palisade.

The capture of Shrewsbury is a testament to how much can be lost in war so quickly. This fact is even more important when it is considered how vital the town was to the Royalist cause in providing it with swords, cartridges, gunpowder and numerous other items. For the loss of very few men in combat, the Parliamentarians were able to take an important town in Shropshire.

As Jonathan Worton argues, the capture of Shrewsbury by Parliament in 1645 was the turning point in the First Civil War in Shropshire. Shrewsbury, along with Bridgnorth, controlled the strategically important bridges across the Severn.[43] The war was turning in Parliament's favour, and their focus next turned upon Bristol.

The Parliamentarian Siege of Bristol, 21 August–11 September 1645

The importance of Bristol to the Royalist cause was paramount. Soon after its capture in 1643, a mint was established as there was a great need for money. In addition, paperwork for the military and civil jurisdictions began production, with *Mercurius Hibernicus* – a propaganda pamphlet – being published in the city. Raising money from taxation, particularly custom dues from the port, continued. The city also acted as a hospital base for the region. Of perhaps greatest importance was the city's ability to produce weapons. By May 1645, Bristol was able to manufacture 15,000 muskets and 5,000 pikes per annum.[44]

Just as Bristol was increasing its role and relevance in the Royalist war machine, things were changing for Parliament. Its army was reorganised into the New Model Army of 22,000 troops, consisting of one regiment of dragoons, 11 of cavalry and 12 of infantry. Of this new force, 2,000 infantry under the command of Henry Ireton approached Bristol on 21 August 1645.[45]

The approach of part of the New Model Army meant that Prince Rupert was only able to burn the outlying villages of Clifton and Bedminster to prevent their use by the Parliamentarians. To stop villages to the north being attacked, Ireton, along with 500 infantry, dragoons and five regiments of horse, was dispatched to the area.[46] Rupert was attempting a scorched earth policy, which would have had several effects. The first would have been a clear field of fire, meaning that the Parliamentary forces would have had no cover during their approach to the city. As seen in 1643, because of the geology of Bristol, sapping and mining methodologies were unable to be employed. Rupert's scorched earth policy would have also limited the defensive perimeter required. This was especially important at Bristol because of the hills to the north and the fortifications positioned there, and the general terrain of the surrounding landscape. Creating a smaller defensive line, as had been the case at Gloucester, would have been beneficial considering the amount of artillery and number of men required to defend a large perimeter, in this case 3 miles (4.82km) in length. Finally, the destruction of the surrounding villages would have deprived the besiegers of any resources the

43 Worton, *To Settle The Crown*, p. 216.

44 John Lynch, *Bristol and the Civil War: For King and Parliament* (Stroud: The History Press, 2009), pp. 124–26, 129; Patrick McGrath, *Bristol and the Civil War* (Bristol: Bristol Branch of the Historical Association, 1981), p. 36; John Barratt, *Sieges of the English Civil War*, p. 39.

45 Lynch, *Bristol and the Civil War: For King and Parliament,* p. 138.

46 McGrath, *Bristol and the Civil War*, p. 36; Lynch, *Bristol and the Civil War: For King and Parliament,* p. 145; Barratt, *Sieges of the English Civil War*, p. 39.

villagers may have had, in addition to accommodation for the troops and the accompanying train. Both strategically and tactically, this approach would have been useful to the Royalists, and Parliament was fortunate to stop it.

On 22 August, the Parliamentarian troops of Sir Thomas Fairfax that were positioned by the southern section of the River Avon were attacked. The attack was repelled, but over the following two days, Parliamentarian troops from Somerset crossed at Keynsham. Meanwhile, east of Bristol, Thomas Rainsborough's Brigade positioned itself on Durdham Down, having its flank protected by Ireton's horse. Between the Rivers Avon and Frome was the brigade of Edward Mountagu. Fairfax, along with Oliver Cromwell, moved his headquarters to Stapleton on 23 August.[47]

On the same day, Joshua Sprigg, Fairfax's chaplain, noted that "the enemy's cannon played from the great fort and Prior's fort, but hurt none but one dragoon, who had had his thigh shot off."[48] It appears that Royalist artillery gunners at Royal Fort and Prior's Hill Fort were not that accurate in their shooting. This is an example of the reality of war, as theoretically, the artillery should have had a greater impact on a regiment of dragoons. It also illustrates the impact of war on a personal level, as if the soldier survived, his injuries were life-changing.

The Royalists besieged in Bristol – who had around 2,500 soldiers, 1,000 cavalry and between 800 and 1,000 members of Trained Bands and auxiliaries[49] – continued to execute sallies. This included one at 4:00 a.m. on 24 August, from a sally port near Prior's Hill Fort, towards Colonel Welden's Brigade.[50] These attacks were continued because in addition to stopping the besiegers from completing their preparations for an assault, it also gave the Royalists an opportunity to observe the numbers and strength of the army outside the city, as the Parliamentary line was spread pretty thin.[51] The weakness of the line was acknowledged by Sprigg, who stated that "[T]he army was in a great strait, the whole strength thereof being but sufficient, and scarce that, for its present undertaking before Bristol."[52]

At around midday on 1 September, Prince Rupert, along with 1,000 cavalry and 600 infantry, launched another attack from the Royal Fort. This was unsuccessful.[53] The following day, the Parliamentarian leaders planned their final attack on the city. The approach can be seen in Map 6. Colonel Welden with four regiments would attack the southern section of the defences, while Lawford's Gate would be stormed from both sides by forces under the command of Colonel Montague. Colonel Rainsborough along with five regiments were tasked with taking Prior's Hill Fort and the defensive line

47 Lynch, *Bristol and the Civil War: For King and Parliament*, p. 145; Barratt, *Sieges of the English Civil War*, p. 39.

48 Joshua Sprigg, *Anglia Rediviva; Englands Recovery: being the history of the motions, actions, and successes of the army under the immediate conduct of his excellency Sir Thomas Fairfax, KT* (Oxford: Oxford University Press, Forgotten Books 2012 Reprint, 1647), p. 100.

49 Barratt, *Sieges of the English Civil War*, p. 38.

50 Sprigg, *Anglia Rediviva*, pp. 100–01.

51 Lynch, *Bristol and the Civil War: For King and Parliament*, p. 149.

52 Sprigg, *Anglia Rediviva*, p. 103.

53 Lynch, *Bristol and the Civil War: For King and Parliament*, p. 148.

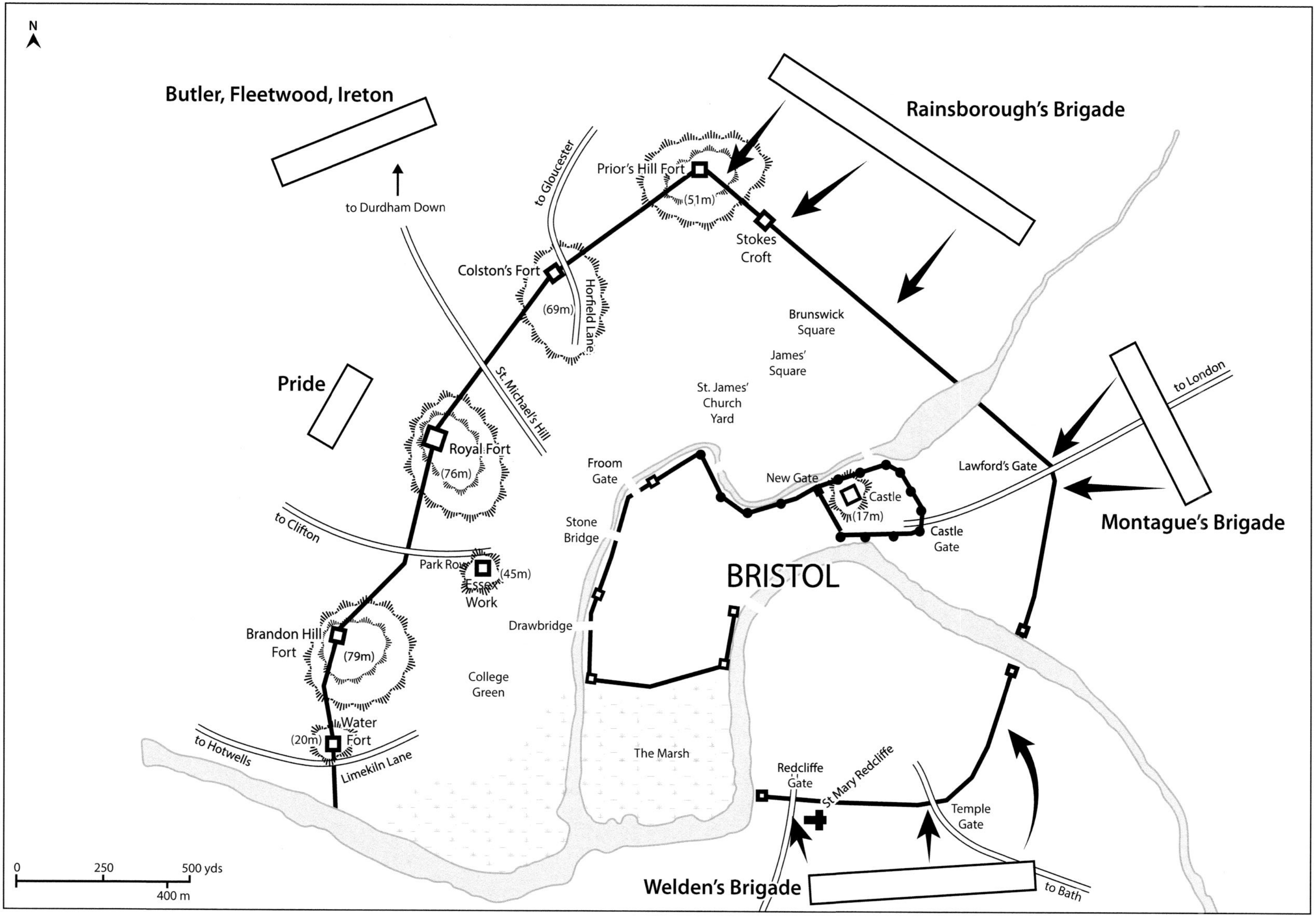

Map 6 The Parliamentarian approach on Bristol on 10 September 1645. (Redrawn from Patrick McGrath's *Bristol and the Civil War* (1981), p. 39.)

between that fortification and the River Frome. Plans were also drawn up for 200 soldiers to assist seamen in an attack on the Water Fort. A regiment of horse and foot would move around the Royal Fort in a diversionary action. Two regiments of horse, with a regiment of dragoons, would carry ladders with them in an attempt to take Washington's Breach for a second time, the section of the defences having been stormed by the Royalists in 1643.[54]

Bernard de Gomme, who was now Engineer General for the Royalists, and John Mansfield, another engineer, described the Royalists' defences at this stage of the siege as follows:

> "The Line generally was three foot thicke. The height of it five foot where it was highest. The graffe commonly six foot broad, and where it was widest but seven. The depth in most parts foure foot, and five where deepest.
>
> "Between Pryor-hill-Fort, Stokes Croft-gate, and beyond the little River towards Laffords-gate, in which places the Enemy entered, not five foot high. The graffe five foot broad, and all that part of the line much decayed.
>
> "The ditch of the great Fort on the right hand the gate before the face of the Bulwork, was not foure foot deep, and eighteen foot broad, so that horses did go up and down into it. The highest work of the Fort was not twelve foot high, and the curtens but ten.
>
> "Within one hundred foot of the Fort, there was a deepe hollow way, where the enemy might lodge what numbers bee pleased, and might be in the graffe the first night, and in that part the Fort was minable.
>
> "Brandon-hill Fort, was about twelve foot about the levell of the great Fort and that being not able to make any long resistance, the Enemy gaining it, would command the other.
>
> "The Hedges and Ditches without the Line were neither ther cut, nor levelled, so that they lodged their men securely near our workes, at their first approach."[55]

Bearing in mind the nature of the source, and who it was written for, it can still be seen what the Parliamentarians were facing when they approached the city. De Gomme describes the defensive curtain line as 3ft (0.91m) thick and 5ft (1.52m) in height. The ditch (graffe) was 6ft (1.82m), sometimes 7ft (2.13m) wide, and 4ft (1.21m), occasionally 5ft (1.52m) in depth. Horses can jump more than 6–7ft (1.82–2.13m), although the height of the curtain wall could have been problematic for dragoon or horse regiments to storm over the curtain line. Nevertheless, on balance, it appears that the line and ditch would be insufficient to stop a cavalry assault.

The defensive line between Prior's Hill Fort, Stokes Croft Gate, the River Frome ('little River') and Lawford's Gate was, at most, 5ft (1.52m) in height, with the same distance for the width of the ditch. Along with the main defensive line, this section appears to have been in a worse condition than

54 Sprigg, *Anglia Rediviva*, pp. 104–06; McGrath, *Bristol and the Civil War*, pp. 37–38.

55 Bernard de Gomme (1645), 'The State and condition of the Line of fortifications about the City of Bristoll, as likewise of the great Fort (as appeares by the subscriptions of the Engineers, who had taken an exact survey of them were) as followes', in *A Declaration Of His Highnesse Prince RUPERT* (1645), pp. 9–10.

it was in 1643. De Gomme does not mention any additions made to defend that sector, such as storm poles.

It appears that the great or Royal Fort was not completed to a sufficient standard. De Gomme describes the measurements of the ditch as "not" 4ft (1.21m) in depth and 18ft (5.48m) in width, and suggests that the cavalry could function in it. This implies that de Gomme was unhappy with the dimensions of the fortification at this section, possibly suggesting that it was unfinished. The dimensions differ to those discussed in the literature of the period, when examining the manuals of Richard Norwood and Robert Ward, for example.[56]

De Gomme continues to write about the inadequate state of the Royal Fort, noting that what is either a bastion or rampart is only 10ft (3.04m) in height. The Engineer General would have probably been well aware of the recommended dimensions, such as Robert Ward's and David Papillon's suggestion that a curtain wall should be 30ft (9.14m) in height, a difference of some 20ft (6.09m) against what it actually was.[57]

De Gomme was aware of the tactical weaknesses of the Royal Fort, noting that there was a hollow way within 100ft (30.48m) of it. This demonstrates his personal understanding of how the landscape and the terrain affected tactical decisions. Conversely, when examining the landscape as a whole, it can be seen from Plate 17 and the view of the city of Bristol from St Michael's

Plate 17 View from St Michael's Hill near the Royal Fort facing the city of Bristol (facing south-east). (Author's photo)

56 Norwood, *Fortification or Military Architecture*, p. 112; Ward, *Animadversions of Warre*, p. 60.
57 Ward, *Animadversions of Warre*, p. 61; Papillon, *A practicall abstract of the arts of fortification*, p. 16.

Hill why the Royal Fort was sited where it was – because it had a commanding view of the city below.

This is where archaeology plays a role. Excavations in 2011 revealed interesting results. Prior to the Civil War, the site was utilised as a quarry. No evidence of Windmill Hill Fort was recovered, but cut 160 revealed evidence of the eastern ditch of the Royal Fort. The ditch ran in a north-west to south-east direction and was 55 yards (50m) in length. Flanks were present at each end of the ditch. Beyond the limits of the excavation, the northern flank extended a further 5½ yards (5m). The south-eastern bastion had two flanks. One headed in a northerly direction for 5m, whilst a sharp flank headed east for 13 yards (12m). The earlier quarrying affected the bastion, as the surrounding landscape was 'made up' with numerous contexts of clay, stones and buff-coloured mortar. The northern section of the ditch was cut 1.8m into the natural geology, Quartzitic Sandstone (Brandon Hill Grit). As the landscape was undulating, the southern section of the ditch was cut to a depth of 2.5m when natural bedrock was reached. The outer section of the ditch followed a gradual curve and was not cut to mirror the flanks. At the bastions, the ditch was 6½–7½ yards (6–7m) in width, whilst in the centre this increased to 12–13 yards (11–12m).[58] The archaeologist Andy King has interpreted this as a counterscarp and scarp.[59]

Interpreting the evidence, the 5m flank appears to be a flank of the bastion, rather than the bastion face itself. The 12m flank appears to be the bastion face. When comparing this to the literature of the period – for example Richard Norwood's *Fortification or Military Architecture* – the bastion for a five-sided bastion fortification should be 93¼ yards (85.3m), with the length of the flank being about 33⅓ yards (30.48m).[60] The lengths of both the flanks and the bastions are significantly shorter than what the literature suggests. It is possible that insufficient men and resources were employed for the task of completing the fort. Yet this in turn poses another question – why, as Andy King suggests, would de Gomme have completed a scarp and counterscarp if the fort overall was not complete? Perhaps the scarp and counterscarp relate to the 1650s work on the fortification, or perhaps de Gomme decided to consolidate one section of the fortification? It is possible that the answers to such questions may never be known. In the Introduction to this study (p. xix), Robert Ward notes that the bottom width of a ditch of a battery was 11.58m. It appears that the archaeological evidence of the Royal Fort ditch, in the centre at least, conforms to the standards indicated in the literature. As the archaeological record differs from de Gomme's own account, his reliability as a source has to be questioned. A possible explanation could be that de Gomme was focusing on purely uncompleted areas. What also has to be considered is that if de Gomme was writing for Prince Rupert, perhaps he

58 Andy King, *Archaeological Excavation at the site of the Royal Fort, St Michael's Hill for University of Bristol* (Unpublished Report No. 2142/2012: Bristol and Region Archaeological Services, 2012), pp. 1, 6–7.

59 Andy King, '"Not fullye so loftye": excavations at the Royal Fort, St Michael's Hill, Bristol', *Post-Medieval Archaeology*, Vol. 48 (1) (2014), pp. 1–44.

60 Norwood, *Fortification or Military Architecture*, table between pp. 36–37.

was 'covering his own back' if the Parliamentarians stormed the fortification and took it over. One final point of interest is to note that the Parliamentarian Iremaine in 1645 described the Royal Fort as "one of the bravest Citadels in England, in it foure and twenty pieces mounted upon five Bastions, Powder in quantity, Victuals in abundance of all forts, fourscore or an hundred tunne of Bread sufficient to serve almost one hundred thousand men a day".[61]

Cut through clay, the steepness of the ditch was between 35 and 45 degrees, and near vertical when cut through the natural geology. The base of the ditch was 74m above sea level at the southern section, whilst the bastion was 76.3m above sea level. This suggests that the rampart could have been 5m in height from the base of the ditch. The southern bastion may have had a concrete footing sealed by clay, rubble deposits and mortar. This further suggests the possibility of a revetted stone bastion.[62] However, the stone bastion would not date to 1645, as the antiquarians William Barratt and Samuel Seyer both state that the Royal Fort bastions were revetted in 1650.[63] Earlier excavations in 2007 revealed evidence of rubble and flecks of white mortar, suggesting the demolition of the fortification.[64] This evidence indicates that at least part of the fortification was revetted. During the First Civil War, a fortification built of stone would have been almost unique; the historian Peter Harrington notes that the majority of the fortifications would have built of earth and turf, with brick and stone only added to earthworks in a small number of cases.[65]

Inside the limits of the fortification was a feature called 'The Long Building' (recorded as context 465). This measured 28 yards (26m) in length and 6½ yards (6m) in width, and was parallel with the ditch. The building had two rooms, the smallest of which was located at the north-east end. The walls of the building consisted of rubble of various sizes, between 0.55m and 0.72m in width, and were bonded together with buff-coloured lime mortar. Seven muskets balls were found in deposit 241. One possible use of the building would be as a masonry barrack block, so that black powder and munitions could be kept dry.[66]

To the north-west of 'The Long Building' was a square feature (context 420) that measured 7.6m in width, 4.3m in depth and had stone walls 2m in height. The walls were made of stone and bonded together with the same buff-coloured mortar discovered in 'The Long Building'. Crucially, there was no evidence of water inside the feature. Because of all of these factors, the feature was interpreted as a magazine store.[67]

---

61 S. Iremaine, *An Exact relation of Prince Rupert His marching out of Bristoll* (London: 1645), p. 2.

62 King, *Archaeological Excavation at the site of the Royal Fort*, pp. 7–9.

63 William Barratt, *The history and antiquities of the city of Bristol* (Bristol: William Pine, 1789), p. 691; Samuel Seyer, *Memoirs Historical and Topographical of Bristol and its neighbourhood from the earliest period down to the present time Vol. 2* (Bristol: John Mathew Gutch, 1823), p. 303.

64 Kevin Potter, *Archaeological Watching Brief during geotechnical trenching at the proposed Maths & Biosciences Building, Tyndall Avenue, Bristol* (Unpublished Report No. 1871/2007: Bristol and Region Archaeological Services, 2007), p. 5.

65 Peter Harrington, *English Civil War Fortifications 1642–51* (Oxford: Osprey Publishing Ltd, 2003), p. 17.

66 King, *Archaeological Excavation at the site of the Royal Fort*, pp. 8–9.

67 *Ibid.*, p. 9.

A well was also discovered, measuring to a depth of 5m, but the full depth was unable to be established. It was 3m in diameter and cut into the natural geology. Unfortunately, no evidence recovered could date the feature to the Civil War.[68] If the well did date to the Civil War, it illustrates that having a water supply could have helped to maintain a healthy fighting force, in addition to having water for cooking and for horses to drink.

Finally, context 199, at the base of the ditch, discovered a cannonball which measured 10.3cm in diameter and weighed 4.2kg. The size and weight of the cannonball indicates that it would have been used in a demi-culverin artillery piece.[69] In Samuel Fawcett's survey of 1643, he does not record Windmill Hill Fort as having this weapon available. This suggests two things – either the Royalists added an additional number of pieces to the fortification in the two years it was under their control, or that it was fired by the Parliamentarians during the 1645 siege. It appears more probable that the shot was fired towards the fortification, as it is unlikely that cannon balls were left on the ramparts to fall into the ditch.

The earliest plan of the Royal Fort, dating from 1669, is by the mathematician Philip Staynred. He produced a drawing of the fortification, describing it as "an Irregular Fort, containing 5 Bastions; being the platform of the Royal Fort sometimes on St. Michael's Hill, on the North West Side of the City of Bristol".[70] Nicholas Stone, in his 1645 work *Enchiridion of Fortification or, A handfull of knowledge in martiall affaires* (Figure 10), illustrates a fortification containing five bastions, describing it as "*Figura Irregularis*".[71] The use of the word 'irregular' by both Stone and Staynred suggests that the construction of a fortification like the Royal Fort would have been highly unusual. Figure 10 also illustrates palisades and gabions – essential features of a complete and fully functioning fortification.

Returning to de Gomme's description, he notes that Brandon Hill is the highest point in the series of northern fortifications. No further information is given on the size of the fortification, and what changes – if any – were made since 1643. Importantly, what de Gomme appears to have been suggesting is that if either Brandon Hill Fort or the Royal Fort was captured by the enemy, it would mean that the other fortification would not be able to withstand an artillery bombardment from there.

Today, the fortifications at Brandon Hill sit in a park and are designated a Scheduled Monument (Plate 18). However, what appears on the face of it to be a stone-faced bastion dating to the English Civil War is not what it seems.

By way of a brief background, in the modern landscape, 200m north of the Water Fort, the ditch of a small curtain wall meets a small spur – an artillery platform of triangular shape (Plate 19). These features were constructed in

68 *Ibid.*, p. 10.

69 *Ibid.*, p.19.

70 Philip Staynred, *A compendium of fortification, both geometrically and instrumentally, by a scale: the making whereof is shewed by the tables, and their use, both of the tables and the scale, for speedy protracting of any fort consisting of 8 bulwarks, whose bastion-angles shall not exceed 90 degrees, and so the like for bastion-angles of 12 bulwarks* (London: Printed by E. Cotes, 1669), p. 9.

71 Nicholas Stone, *Enchiridion of Fortification or, A handfull of knowledge in martiall affaires* (London: Richard Royston, 1645), Plate 8, p. 33.

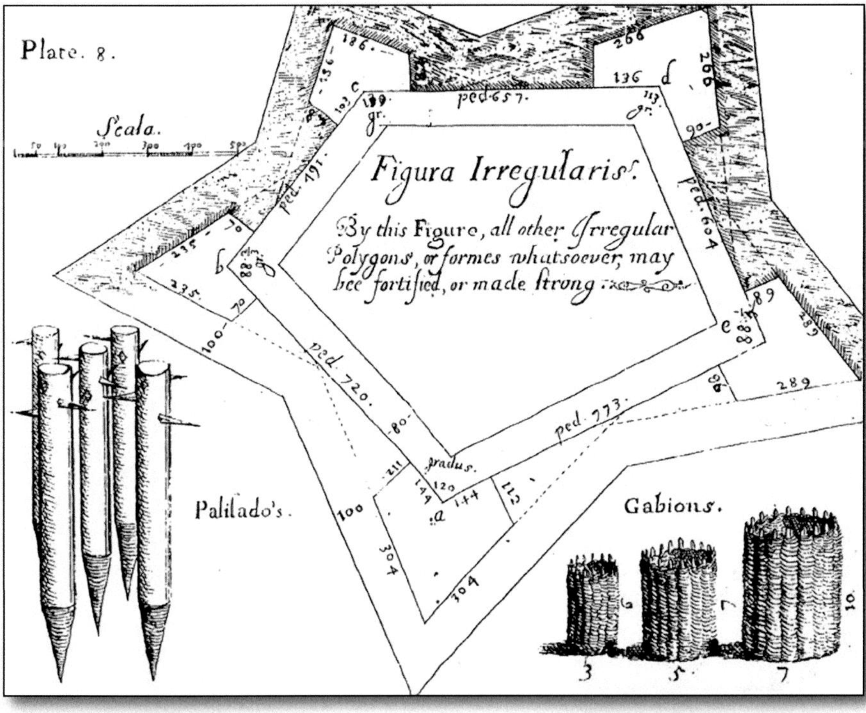

Figure 10 Illustration from Nicholas Stone's Enchiridion of Fortification (1645, p. 33, Plate 8) showing an irregular fortification containing five bastions, along with palisades and gabions. (Reproduced by permission of the University of Illinois (Urbana-Champaign Campus) Library. Image published with permission of ProQuest®. Further reproduction is prohibited without permission. Image produced by ProQuest® as part of Early English Books Online. www.proquest.com)

Plate 18 The stone-faced bastion of Brandon Hill, Bristol (facing east-south-east). (Author's photo)

Plate 19 The spur of the defences of Brandon Hill fortification, Bristol (facing south-south-west). (Author's photo)

1643 by the Parliamentarians. West of the spur is an outwork of bastion shape, which was probably constructed by the Royalists in 1644. It appears that the outwork was revetted in stone of Quartzitic Sandstone of nearly 1m thickness, which was bonded together with a white mortar containing black flecks. Further north, a small stone revetment, some curtain wall, is extant. There is a gap of 50m until the wall reappears. It rises in height by 2.5m and is adjacent to a ditch that is 5.5m in width and 1.1m in depth. At a height of 3m, the wall ends at a stone bastion, which is surrounded by a ditch and an internal platform that is 3.5m in width. This is the bastion connected to Brandon Hill Fort.[72]

During the 2011 excavations, 'Trench One' analysed the ditch. The evidence revealed that it was similar in form to a Civil War ditch excavated in 2002 at the Old Market suburb in Bristol. The width of the ditch was 5.4m at its upper section. None of the finds dated to the Civil War period. However, importantly, the ditch was recut in the late 19th century or early 20th century.[73]

As previously discussed, the width of the ditch falls short of that suggested by the literature of the period (p. xix); however, this can be explained by the geology of the site affecting how far it could be adequately excavated, considering the 3-mile (4.82km) defensive perimeter both sides had to

72 James Russell, *The Civil War Defences of Bristol: Their Archaeology & Topography* (Bristol: Author, 2003), pp. 13–14.

73 Andy King, *Archaeological Evaluation at Brandon Hill, Bristol for Bristol City Council* (Unpublished Report No. 2515/2011: Bristol and Region Archaeological Services, 2011), pp. 5–6.

defend. But 5.4m is sufficient to not make it easy for the enemy to storm this position; they would need to get over the obstacle by throwing faggots and/or gabions into the ditch or using scaling ladders.

'Trench Two' examined the bastion itself. A retaining wall (context 209) was constructed directly onto the bedrock and was made of Brandon Hill Grit, and crucially, it was bonded together with an off-white charcoal speckled mortar. This mortar in Bristol dates to between the late 18th century and the early 19th century. The wall was thus thought to resemble a garden wall rather than a fortification.[74]

Analysing the evidence overall, it indicates that only the shape of the ditch bears some similarity to the Old Market ditch excavated in 2002. The wall and earthen bank are a replica of a Civil War fortification. The bastion most likely dates from the Georgian era (18th century), and is possibly a garden wall representing a folly. It was the antiquarian Samuel Seyer who first connected this feature to the Civil War.[75]

This archaeological evidence is an important reminder not to take long-held assumptions as historical fact. It is possible that Samuel Seyer made a mistake in suggesting that the bastion he observed and discussed in his 1823 memoirs dated to the Civil War. Based on the archaeological evidence, he was almost certainly examining a folly. This also brings into question the Scheduled Monument status of the feature. Because it is a Scheduled Monument, special permission rightly has to be obtained from the Secretary of State to conduct any ground-penetrating investigations on such a site. Without this archaeological evidence, it is possible that historians would have continued to date the current extant feature to the Civil War, whereas the actual evidence indicates otherwise.

Excavations were also conducted at 30 Gloucester Lane, which was near Lawford's Gate. The ditch (context 231) was L-shaped and was seen to extend for 7.3m east–west and 9.2m north–south. Four sondages (small test pits) were excavated. The first sondage revealed that the ditch was 2.1m in depth, and was angled at 35 degrees from the vertical. The primary fill consisted of a waterlogged silt of a blackish-grey consistency. The second sondage indicated that the ditch was a gradual slope at this point, with an angle of 50 degrees. The third sondage focused on the east–west profile of the ditch. It revealed that the angle of the ditch here was steep, being 35 degrees. The top of the ditch had a width of 6.2m, with the north-facing section revealing that the ditch would have been around 2.2m in depth, with a flat base around 1.8m in width. No useful evidence was recovered in the fourth sondage. The material and structural evidence indicates that the ditch was part of the Royalists' defences constructed between 1643 and 1645.[76]

The archaeological evidence is in contrast to de Gomme's account of the defences, as he indicates that that section of the defensive line was "much decayed". This unfortunately leads one to question de Gomme as a trustworthy

74 *Ibid.*, p. 6.

75 *Ibid.*, p. 11.

76 Andy King, *Archaeological Excavations at 30 Gloucester Lane, Old Market, Bristol* (Unpublished Report No. 1084/2003: Bristol and Region Archaeological Services, 2003), pp. 4–5.

source, considering the physical evidence. The steep angle of the ditch (35 degrees) would have presented itself as a problem, considering the nature of warfare, when approaching the enemy under musketry and cannon fire.

Returning to de Gomme's description of the state of the defences in 1645 (p. 86), he states that the hedges and surrounding ditches were not maintained. If de Gomme's account is to be believed, this suggests that the Royalists did not operate a scorched-earth policy in the immediate vicinity of the fortifications, despite burning the villages of Clifton and Bedminster. This, as de Gomme rightly notes, was a tactical error on the Royalists' part, as it meant that the advancing Parliamentarians could hide behind these features.

Despite de Gomme's description of the defences, fortifications such as the Royal Fort had 22 cannon, whilst Prior's Hill Fort had 13. By August 1645, a total of 151 cannons were positioned around the city.[77]

Returning to the account of the siege, Joshua Sprigg (whose writing the historian Patrick McGrath notes is the "best account of the attack on Bristol in 1645")[78] recounts that men and horses died on Thursday, 4 September, because of the extreme wet weather.[79] This illustrates the graphic consequences of conducting siege warfare during the autumn months during the 17th century.

After having their offer to surrender rejected, the Parliamentarians decided to storm the city. At this time, the New Model Army had around 7,000 soldiers surrounding Bristol, along with between 800 and 900 officers. At around 2:00 a.m. on 10 September, the attack began with the firing of four cannons against Prior's Hill Fort. Colonels Mountagu and Pickering with their regiments then attacked Lawford's Gate, taking it relatively quickly and capturing 22 artillery pieces. It appears that the ditch at Gloucester Lane was unable to hold back the approach of the Parliamentarian forces. By lowering the bridge, Major Desborough moved into the city, with both cavalry and infantry following.[80] The infantry regiments of Fairfax and Hardress Waller were able to easily break through between Lawford's Gate and the River Frome, encircling the area to cut off the defenders at the gate – the "decayed" line described by de Gomme giving the attackers no problems.[81] The regiments of Birch and Skippon attacked to the north of the River Frome, capturing the Royalists' guns and turning their pieces against them. Major Bethel, with accompanying cavalry – including part of Greave's force and the regiments of Whalley and Rich – after using pioneers to break through the line, caused the Royalist defenders to retreat to Colston's Fort and the Royal Fort.[82]

---

77 Barratt, *Sieges of the English Civil War*, p. 38.

78 McGrath, *Bristol and the Civil War*, p. 48.

79 Sprigg, *Anglia Rediviva*, p. 108.

80 *Ibid.*, p. 116; Lynch, *Bristol and the Civil War: For King and Parliament*, p. 154; McGrath, *Bristol and the Civil War*, p. 40.

81 Sprigg, *Anglia Rediviva*, p. 116; Lynch, *Bristol and the Civil War: For King and Parliament*, p. 157; McGrath, *Bristol and the Civil War*, p. 40.

82 Sprigg, *Anglia Rediviva*, pp. 116–17; Barratt, *Sieges of the English Civil War*, p. 42; Lynch, *Bristol and the Civil War: For King and Parliament*, p. 157.

The key section of the Royalist defences was Prior's Hill Fort, which was attacked by the regiments of Rainsborough and Hammond.[83] Despite de Gomme not referencing the fort in his description of the defences, it appears to have been modified. Sprigg described the work as a "high work", with the scaling ladders provided to storm the fortification being "too short".[84]

After several hours of fierce hand-to-hand fighting, and the Royalists firing case shot from their cannon, it was only when dawn began to break that the Royalists surrendered Prior's Hill Fort. By this point many of the outer fortifications were in Parliamentary hands.[85] Sprigg noted that if "the enemy had daylight when we first entered, we could not have stood upon any ground".[86] The troops attacking the southern section of the city's defences (the Portwall) were unsuccessful – a repeat of the events of 1643 – with Bristol Castle continuing to fire, narrowly missing Cromwell and Fairfax, who were stood on Prior's Hill Fort. Fires had spread throughout the city, and whilst fire-fighting was underway, Prince Rupert offered to surrender the city at 09:00 a.m.[87]

Terms were agreed, and the next day, 11 September, Prince Rupert – "clad in Scarlet, very richly laid with silver Lace, mounted upon a very gallant black Barbary Horse"[88] – left Bristol through the Royal Fort (Plate 20). The Royalists had lost Bristol for very similar reasons to those that had cost the city for the Parliamentarians in 1643.[89]

A final analysis of the tactics employed at Bristol shows that the Royalists only partially employed a scorched-earth policy. By only burning the villages of Clifton and Bedminster, having been cut off by the Parliamentarians whilst attempting to set light to villages to the north of Bristol, and by not removing hedges, the Royalists were at a significant disadvantage. The attack on the villages conducted by the Royalists, whilst tactically sensible because the New Model Army's line was stretched so thin, was in reality unsuccessful.

The storming of the city by the Parliamentarians was well organised; attacking very early in the morning, and not at dawn, gave them a tactical advantage. However, just like had happened in 1643, they failed to breach the southern section of the defences. The use of scaling ladders is an old-fashioned and common tactic in siege warfare, although it appears that the Parliamentarians were unprepared for the height of the walls of Prior's Hill Fort.

Like the Parliamentarians in 1643, the Royalists in 1645 could not hold onto Bristol. Despite commanders and morale being key factors in both events, the question needs to be asked whether Bristol could ever have been successfully held. The topography of Bristol, and the need to utilise the hills to the north, created a 3-mile (4.82km) perimeter. It would have

83 Sprigg, *Anglia Rediviva*, p. 116.
84 *Ibid*., p. 117.
85 *Ibid*., p. 126; Barratt, *Sieges of the English Civil War*, p. 43.
86 Sprigg, *Anglia Rediviva*, p. 118.
87 Barratt, *Sieges of the English Civil War*, p. 43; Russell, *The Civil War Defences of Bristol*, p. 12.
88 Iremaine, *An Exact relation of Prince Rupert His marching out of Bristoll*, p. 2.
89 Barratt, *Sieges of the English Civil War*, p. 44.

Plate 20 The modified gatehouse of the Royal Fort, Bristol (facing west). (Author's photo)

taken a significant number of men and resources to construct the necessary fortifications and complete a continuous defensive line and ditches, and it appears that neither side was either willing or able to put in the necessary money, time and resources to hold the city, despite Bristol being "England's second city".[90]

90 Mark Kishlansky, *A Monarchy Transformed: Britain 1603–1714* (London: Penguin Books Ltd, 1996), p. 154.

Chapter 3

The Sieges of 1646

The successful sieges of Shrewsbury and Bristol meant that Parliament was in control of affairs in the Severn Valley going into 1646. The first siege of that year began at Bridgnorth in late March.

The Parliamentarian Siege of Bridgnorth, 31 March–26 April 1646

The River Severn divides the historic High and Low Towns of Bridgnorth. Topographically, the town sits between about 30m and 60m above sea level, with the High Town positioned on the west bank of the river and the Low Town on the eastern bank. Geologically, the town sits on Permian Bridgnorth Sandstone, with the High Town located on a promontory which overlooks the river. The soils are unclassified, but are brown sands which are well draining.[1]

In 1886, an interesting account of the topography of Bridgnorth was published, using the papers made by the Reverend Richard Cornes in 1739.[2] Cornes was surveying and making notes on Bridgnorth less than 100 years after the Civil War, and therefore this source is an important tool to understand and appreciate the landscape of Bridgnorth around the time of the siege.

Cornes states that the town is divided into two parts, which are unequal, by the River Severn, with a stone bridge connecting the two. The Low Town is small and contains just two streets, while the High Town situated on the west bank of the Severn rises in height and contains six streets. Cornes recounts that the church of St Leonard and most of the High Town were burnt down during the Civil War. He adds that the town contained a castle positioned at the south end of the High Street.[3] It is clear from Cornes' description

1 Victoria Buteux, with contributions by Derek Hurst, Richard Morriss, Elizabeth Pearson and Paul Stamper, *Archaeological assessment of Bridgnorth, Shropshire* (Extensive Urban Survey – The Central Marches Historic Towns Survey 1992–6, 1996), pp. 1–2.

2 Richard Cornes, 'A short topographical account of Bridgnorth in the county of Salop', *Transactions of the Shropshire Archaeological and Natural History Society*, Vol. 9 (1886), pp. 193–210.

3 Cornes, 'A short topographical account of Bridgnorth', pp. 195, 198, 201.

of Bridgnorth that it was tiny. The River Severn, and the medieval castle, dominated the town. It is evident that the reason for the importance of control of the town during the Civil War lay in the need to control the river and the castle, which would have been the most significant features in the landscape.

The castle at Bridgnorth was constructed on a steep spur, and it was from there that the early 12th century town expanded to the north. The borough developed inside the outer bailey of the castle, now contained within East Castle Street and West Castle Street.[4] By the 1630s, the population of Bridgnorth was around 2,200.[5] William Hardwicke noted that there were numerous entrances into the town – Bridge Gatehouse, Cowgate, Cripple Gate, Barrier Gate, Listley Gate, Tainter Wall, West or Hungary Gate, Whitburn Gate and North Gate. This was, in addition, a half-moon battery, which was levelled during the siege to stop Parliamentary troops using it to their advantage.[6] The North Gate survives to the present day (Plate 21).

By the 17th century, Bridgnorth was of strategic importance due to its position on the River Severn and its road networks to the larger centres of Shrewsbury and Worcester.[7] Bridgnorth Castle was described by the antiquarian John Leland in the reign of Henry VIII as sturdily walled but ruinous.[8]

In 1642, bullets were produced in Bridgnorth, and along with other towns, it was an important centre of animal husbandry.[9] As control of the River Severn was vital, the Royalist garrison had chains fitted across the bridge by the Low Town in 1642. To finance the construction of fortifications in August 1642, the Corporation of Bridgnorth had levied £20 to improve the town defences. In contrast, the Corporation of Shrewsbury imposed a rate of £250: which had amounted to at least £2,800 by late 1644. Orders were also given in May 1643 to fortify the fords in the area.[10]

Further enhancements to the town's defences commenced in December 1643; however, dissatisfied with the works by 1 May 1645, the Royalists ordered more additions. This included the re-cutting of the town ditch and the construction of earthworks at the North Gate, in addition to works near the churchyard at St Leonard's. As part of the construction of the fortifications at the churchyard, a schoolhouse and gardens were destroyed. The wealthier

4 Jeremy Haslam, 'The articulation of burgages and streets in early medieval towns, part 1: the case of Bridgnorth, Shropshire', *Landscape History*, Vol. 37 (1) (2016), p. 52.

5 Terry Bracher and Roger Emmett, *Shropshire in the Civil War* (Shrewsbury: Shropshire Books, 2000), p. 74.

6 Williams Hardwicke, 'Collections for a History of Bridgnorth, Salop', a MS by William Hardwicke; annotated by Wilfred Watkins-Pitchford, *Transactions of the Shropshire Archaeological Society*, Vol. 49 (2) (1938), pp. 199–203.

7 Bracher and Emmett, *Shropshire in the Civil War*, p. 74.

8 Anonymous, *The Garrisons of Shropshire, During the Civil War, 1642–48* (Shrewsbury: Leake and Evans, 1867), p. 80.

9 Jonathan Worton, *To Settle The Crown: Waging Civil War in Shropshire, 1642–1648* (Solihull: Helion & Company Limited, 2016), pp. 171, 180.

10 Jonathan Worton, 'The Royalist and Parliamentarian War Effort in Shropshire during the First and Second Civil Wars, 1642–1648' (PhD Thesis, University of Chester, 2015), p. 194; Worton, *To Settle The Crown*, pp. 137, 221.

Plate 21 The surviving North Gate, Bridgnorth (facing north-north-west). (Author's photo)

inhabitants, rather than build the fortifications themselves, were charged a fee of 6d a day, which increased to 11d in winter.[11] In 1644, buildings near the castle, town wall and ditch were cleared or utilised for fortifications. In March 1645, the governor, Sir Lewis Kirke, ordered the reduction in height of the tower of St Leonard's Church. In May, both the old and new town halls were dismantled and the timbers stored in the church. To create a clear field of fire, the buildings beyond the defences of the North Gate were ordered to be taken down. Even the town cross was removed so that the besiegers could not utilise it for cover, observation or indeed as a firing position towards the castle.[12] In 1991, an archaeological evaluation report of St Mary's Rectory suggested evidence of the re-cutting of the inner bailey ditch of the castle during the conflict, no doubt by the Royalists, to reinforce the defences.[13]

The destruction of this property provided the defenders with several advantages. The first was that it gave them a clear field of fire from which to attack the besiegers, as it required the attackers to run towards the town's fortifications through open ground. Leaving these buildings in position would have provided the besiegers with cover in order to get closer to the fortifications. This was the case when the Parliamentarians captured Malmesbury in 1644, as they used the still standing houses to get within pistol shot of the defenders' positions. The compromising of the effectiveness of the besieging forces' positions from which to fire impacted not only short-range fire but also the use of artillery against the defences of Bridgnorth. The Parliamentarians' ability to construct batteries, ditches, communication trenches and mines were all compromised because they were unable to use buildings and walls as shelter on their approach. A further advantage for the besieged forces was that the lack of buildings and houses outside of the town's fortifications meant that the besiegers were deprived of accommodation. Not only did this include the soldiers conducting the siege, but also any relief forces which were positioned in reserve to bring supplies to the front line. This meant that any relief army and/or camp followers may have had to camp in huts or tents or find alternative accommodation further from the town.[14]

As Stephen Porter had noted, an effective governor would have removed any nearby woodland and other materials, to force the besiegers to waste time and energy in attempting to locate and transport supplies from further afield. An important, and sometimes overlooked, caveat of sieges is how much of the surrounding suburbs and the town itself were destroyed, in order to create the fields of fire necessary to defend what remained. Indeed, this is an important issue to examine when looking at the Frankwell and Abbey Foregate suburbs of Shrewsbury and the Foregate suburb of Worcester.[15]

Regardless of the success, or lack of it, in preparing Bridgnorth for a potential siege, the town was quickly captured by Parliamentary troops on 31

11 Worton, 'The Royalist and Parliamentarian', pp. 190, 192; Worton, *To Settle The Crown*, p. 218.

12 John Frederick Arthur Mason, *The Borough of Bridgnorth, 1157–1957* (Bridgnorth: Bridgnorth Borough Council, 1957), p. 24; Worton, 'The Royalist and Parliamentarian', pp. 196–97; Worton, *To Settle The Crown*, p. 223.

13 Buteux *et al.*, *Archaeological assessment of Bridgnorth*, p. 13.

14 Stephen Porter, *The Blast of War*, pp. 20–21.

15 *Ibid.*, pp. 21–23.

March 1646. The garrison refused to surrender, and some 400 men withdrew to the castle under the command of Colonel Billingsley. The colonel, however, was killed in the withdrawal. The lack of a stone wall near St Leonard's Church was blamed as being one of the reasons for the Parliamentarians breaking through that position, with a battle taking place in the churchyard. After Parliamentarian success, the north aisle of the church was used to store ammunition.[16] The number of Parliamentarian troops besieging Bridgnorth Castle in April 1646 was said to be 700.

The *Burning Bush Not Consumed*, a Parliamentary propaganda publication, provided the following detail about events at Bridgnorth:

> "Mar. 30 1646. Much about the aforesaid time we were certainly informed that this most active and gallon Committee of Shrewsbury, not resting after they had taken in High Aicell, sent out a party of horse and foot upon a designe against Bridgenorth, but the length of the march, and the weariness the souldiers hindered them, and as the towne took the alarme before they could refresh themselves a little and go on in designe, as was intended, notwithstanding the next day they re-commenced it. Colonel Billingsley who commanded in chiefe the towne, would give no answer to the summonses; Colonel Howard who commanded the Castle, gave a flat denial, whereupon in the afternoone having set out three forts the brave Salopians resolve to storme. One fort was assigned to Colonel Gaulden, another to Major Braine, and the third to Major Hickson, who at the warning given fell all three on with such a courageous, undaunted resolution, that they stormed the towne, killed Colonel Billingsley in the heat of the storm, together with some others, and took divers prisoners; the rest of the gentry fled into the Castle. The North Gate fort stood also somewhat dispute but we likewise gained it, and so all the towne taken wholly into their possession, and in its proper place we shall certifie the taking in of the Castle also, which yet awhile stands out very obstinately against them."[17]

This account records that the Parliamentarian commanders Colonel Gaulden, Major Braine and Major Hickson each stormed a fort, and that the Royalists withdrew to the castle, but not before a skirmish at the North Gate. It appears that none of the other gates into the town, as cited by William Hardwicke, were able to hold out for a significant period of time – this may simply illustrate that these gates were not effectively manned. The Royalists retreated rather quickly to the relative safety of the castle.

Another Parliamentary account, this time in *A Perfect Diurnal* dated 9 April 1646, noted:

> "We had the intelligence of two most cruell and barbarous acts of the enemy, the one is frying Bridgenorth thus certified. That our forces in towne setting a summons to the Castle, it was accepted, and a treaty was to follow; but in the interim the Governor sent out warrants to the Towne to bring a month's provisions

16 Mason, *The Borough of Bridgnorth*, p. 24.

17 Anonymous, *The Garrisons of Shropshire, During the Civil War, 1642–48*, pp. 36–37.

> into the Castle, which they being in the capacity to do, our forces being quartered in the towne."[18]

The 'frying' of Bridgnorth relates to the afternoon of 7 April, when a red-hot cannonball or grenade was fired from the castle and hit St Leonard's Church, where the Parliamentarians had stored their ammunition. The church caught fire, and with the aid of a north-easterly wind, buildings to the west and south of the churchyard caught fire. The fire then moved towards the High Street, which had already suffered some destruction due to incendiaries fired from the castle. Whilst properties outside the town walls, down the hill and across the River Severn over the bridge in the Low Town, along with houses inside the inner bailey of the castle, had survived, damage to the town was estimated to be around £90,000.[19] It is interesting to note here that the North Gate was the main stumbling block in the Parliamentarians' assault of the town. This was undoubtedly due to the new earthworks that were constructed at the site from May 1645, although it is disappointing that there is no exact description of the earthworks' appearance, nor information of whether or not they followed the designs of the military manuals of the period.

The account in *The Garrisons of Shropshire, During the Civil War, 1642–48* continues:

> "... and the possession of the town giving the Rebels great advantage in carrying on the siege of the Castle, the latter sent the town on fire. The first house that was burnt was near the northern postern of the Castle, and from thence the fire spread to the High Street, where it was extinguished by the Parliamentary troops. The Garrison of the Castle made another, more successful attempt to fire the town, on Easter Tuesday; the wind being high the flames spread rapidly in all directions, and houses and property to the amount of £60,000 were destroyed. The misery of the inhabitants described as being most severe, rich and poor, old and young, were left houseless, and sought shelter in the fields around the town, in woods and under rocks. Meanwhile the Parliamentary army continued for three weeks to bombard the Castle from a battery they had erected on the opposite hill, but without affecting a breach, and at length and attempt was made to lay a mine under St. Mary's Church, which stood within the walls of the Castle, where the Garrison had stored their ammunition. Colonel Howard then being aware of the total destruction of the Castle and its inhabitants, that must ensue if the mine was sprung, surrendered; and a few months after it was seized by the Parliament, who entirely demolished it, and gradually remove the ruins; and all that now remains of this stately Castle, which had received within its walls at different periods at least six of its royal masters, is a fragment of one tower.
>
> "The Church of St. Leonard had been converted into a powder magazine by the enemy, in consequence of which Sir Lewis Kirke, the Governor of the Castle,

18 *Ibid.*, p. 37.

19 Malcolm Wanklyn, 'Urban Revival in Early Modern England: Bridgnorth and the River Trade, 1660–1800', *Midland History*, Vol. 18 (1993), p. 38.

> before the appointed appointment of Colonel Howard, had bombarded it from a tower of the Castle, and it was burnt with the rest of the High Town."[20]

The historian Malcolm Wanklyn records that damage to the town was £90,000, rather than the £60,000 as recorded in *A Perfect Diurnal*. Whatever the figure, the fact remains that the majority of the town was destroyed. The aforementioned historical account is supported by later accounts, such as those by Watkins-Pitchford, who noted that a Puritan vicar recorded some significant activity near the North Gate Fort at the commencement of the siege on 31 March. He also records that the castle had fired on St Leonard's Tower and College House, setting both structures on fire by using flaming torches, with the majority of the High Town being burnt the following day and the gatehouse being destroyed.[21]

It is important to note that St Leonard's Church was destroyed, having been converted to store the Parliamentarians' powder. It was vital to have powder kept dry, and the stone-built structure would have been ideal. This may offer one explanation as to why Sir Lewis Kirke ordered the reduction in height of the tower of St Leonard's Church in March 1645. However, it is more likely that Kirke was concerned about the Parliamentarians using the tower as an observation or lookout position. Any suggestion that the church itself would have been a potential artillery position, and indeed whether the besieged had used a demi-cannon on the second floor of Ethelfleda's Tower (a tower of the castle as referenced in *A Perfect Diurnal*, dated 9 April 1646), is questionable for a variety of factors.[22] The first involves the weight of the cannon. Using the demi-cannon as an example, according to the manuals examined earlier, such as Table 5 (pp. xxiv–xxv), taken from Nye's *The Art of Gunnery* (1670), the gun would have weighed 6,000lb (2,721.55kg). Would it have been possible to manoeuvre a cannon, probably via a system of winches and pullies, to either the second floor of a 12th century castle or a church tower dating to the same period? Even if it is accepted that it was possible, there is then the second question of firing the artillery pieces, and the subsequent recoil. Robert Ward notes in *Animadversions of Warre; or, A militarie magazine of the truest rules, and ablest instructions, for the managing of warre*, when discussing the siege of Breda (1624–25), that planks were required for the recoil and repositioning of cannons.[23] It is for these two reasons that it can now be confidently stated that neither St Leonard's Church nor Ethelfleda's Tower in Bridgnorth Castle were used as artillery positions during the siege.

So, in April 1646, after the majority of the High Town was destroyed during two days of fighting that began on 31 March as the Royalists responded to Parliament's advance, the Parliamentarians began positioning their artillery to lay siege to the castle. It was the recent destruction of property that led

20 Anonymous, *The Garrisons of Shropshire, During the Civil War, 1642–48*, pp. 37–38.

21 Wilfred Watkins-Pitchford, 'A visit to Bridgnorth', *Transactions of the Shropshire Archaeological Society*, Vol. 52, 1947–1948 (1948), p. 154.

22 *Ibid*., p. 173.

23 Ward, *Animadversions of Warre*, p. 95.

to Parliament being able to site its approaches and entrenchments near the castle.[24]

It is at this point that cartography helps in understanding why the Parliamentarians decided to utilise the positions of Panpudding Hill, the site of an earthen ringwork and bailey castle dating to the 12th century, and a mound to the south, as artillery emplacements, which were separated from the town and castle by a valley.[25] By 10 April, a battery, including at least one mortar, was ready to bombard the castle.[26] Figure 11 illustrates, albeit rather abstractly, a mortar firing upon a castle.

Figure 11 Illustration from Henry Hexham's The Third Part of the Principles of the Art Military (1643, opposite p. 30) showing a mortar firing upon a castle. (Reproduced by permission of the University of Illinois (Urbana-Champaign Campus) Library. Image published with permission of ProQuest®. Further reproduction is prohibited without permission. Image produced by ProQuest® as part of Early English Books Online. www.proquest.com)

The map source is titled *A copy of an Old Map of the Borough of Bridgenorth in possession of the Corporation* (Map 7), with a pencil mark dating the map to *c.* 1660,[27] although the authors Terry Bracher and Roger Emmett, in addition to the archaeologist Hal Dalwood, date the source to *c.* 1610.[28]

The map depicts a hillside, with some trees, referred to as 'Old Castell Hill'. This is no doubt the site of the 12th century castle at the position of Panpudding Hill, and a further mound to the south. The hillside is important as it illustrates the change in local topography, not to mention the fact that

24 Worton, 'The Royalist and Parliamentarian', p. 205; Worton, *To Settle The Crown*, p. 229.

25 George Bellett, *The Antiquities of Bridgnorth* (Bridgnorth: W.J. Rowley, 1856), p. 171; Worton, 'The Royalist and Parliamentarian', p. 205; Worton, *To Settle The Crown*, p. 229.

26 Worton, *To Settle The Crown*, p. 229.

27 Shropshire Archives, *A copy of an Old Map of the Borough of Bridgenorth in possession of the Corporation*, Reference: SRO P40.V.2.5, *c.* 1660.

28 Bracher and Emmett, *Shropshire in the Civil War*, p. 74; Hal Dalwood, *Desk-Based Assessment of Sainsbury's Supermarket Site, The Smithfield, Bridgnorth, Shropshire* (Unpublished Report: Worcestershire County Council, 2007), Figure 5.

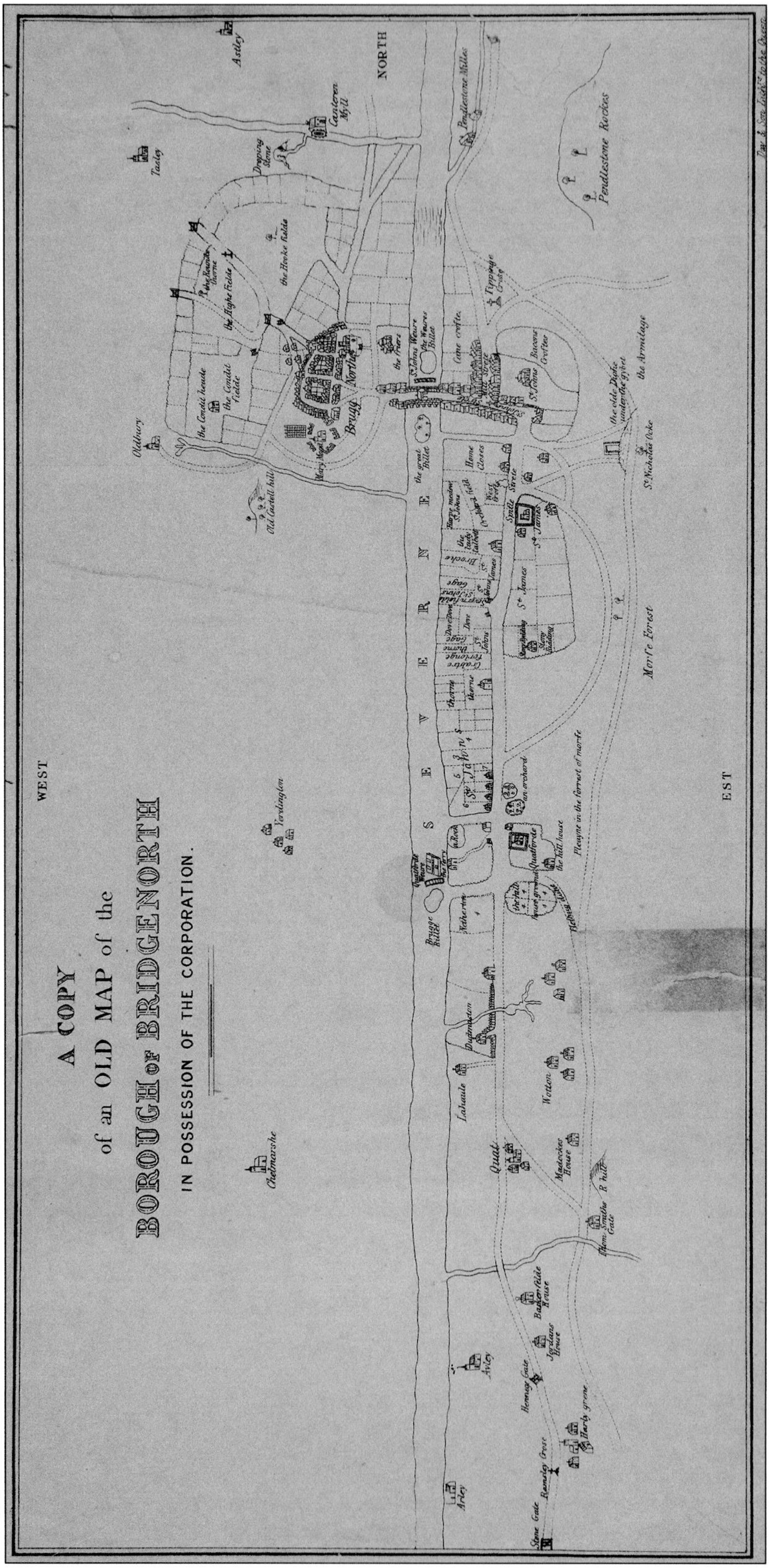

Map 7 A plan of Bridgnorth titled *A copy of an Old Map of the Borough of Bridgenorth in possession of the Corporation c.* 1660 (Reference: SRO P40.V.2.5).
(Reproduced by permission of Shropshire Archives)

the site of an earlier castle at Bridgnorth is known through the study of toponymy (the study of place names). It is, however, the topography that demonstrates why these positions were chosen. Panpudding Hill has an elevation of 56m above sea level[29] and is approximately 250m south-west of Bridgnorth Castle, which has an elevation of 63m above sea level.[30]

Fortunately, archaeological investigations have been conducted in the area around Bridgnorth. In 1983, excavations by the Birmingham University Field Archaeology Unit revealed that the mound immediately south of the ringwork and bailey castle of Panpudding Hill (as Plate 22 illustrates the landscape near Panpudding Hill), with its long gentler slopes to the south and west, and steep drops on the north and east, had archaeological evidence dating to the Civil War. The top of the mound contained a depression, which suggested raised banks on each side. The unit's second and fourth trenches revealed evidence of gravel and packed stones, which was interpreted as evidence of the supporting or fortifying of the north and east sections of the site. The pottery discovered there dates to the Civil War, and there is no evidence of medieval activity.[31]

Plate 22 View of the landscape near Panpudding Hill, Bridgnorth (facing north). (Author's photo)

29 Memory Map Inc. © Crown Copyright Ordnance Survey 2008 Licence No: PU100034184 (Central England).

30 *Ibid.*

31 Annette Roe, 'Bridgnorth (Panpudding Hill)', *West Midlands Archaeology*, Vol. 26 (1983), p. 87.

Combining this evidence with the historical accounts, it is clear that the mound south of Panpudding Hill was utilised during the siege. It appears that time was taken to secure the battery position, as indicated by the use of gravel and pack stones. The battery position appears to have followed the general designs referenced by Robert Ward, such as raised earthen banks, thus demonstrating that the Parliamentarians utilised the local geology to good effect, albeit without any palisades or wooden stakes. Its location in the landscape – being only approximately 250m away from the castle – combined with its relative topographical height makes it an ideal position for a battery.

Having identified that the potential battery sites are approximately 250m away from the castle, it is useful to refer back to the tables of artillery mentioned earlier. Firstly, examining Smith's work *The Art of Gunnery* (Table 1) (p. xxi), it can be seen that if a demi-culverin was positioned at Panpudding Hill or the southern mound, it would have been able to effectively bombard the castle, as its point-blank range was 289.56m for an artillery piece weighing 3,000lb firing a shot of 11.75lb (5.01kg). The same also applies when examining the demi-culverin in Norton's *The Gunner* (Table 2) (p. xxii), as the point-blank range for that piece is 265.17m. It is interesting to note that the saker, minion, falcon and falconet pieces are unable to successfully hit a target at point-blank range that is 250m away. If a culverin (ordinary whole) was available to the besiegers, then according to Nye's *The Art of Gunnery* (Table 5) (pp. xxiv–xxv), that artillery piece would have been able to hit the castle, as the point-blank range was 365.7m, with the maximum range being 731.5m.

What appears to be evident is that the artillery deployed at these sites was extremely ineffective. This can be explained by a variety of reasons. Firstly, the large amount of ammunition that was stored in St Leonard's Church and subsequently destroyed meant that the Parliamentarians lacked the volume of shot to regularly bombard the castle. This may explain the ineffectiveness of the mortar piece. Secondly, the gunners firing the artillery could have been poor and/or inexperienced, meaning they were unable to use the artillery effectively and hit their target. Thirdly, the actual artillery may have been smaller field pieces, and therefore only able to sporadically hit targets at their maximum range. A fourth and final issue may have been a logistical one: getting the necessary supplies to the battery positions. Map 8 illustrates the artillery position of Panpudding Hill, in relation to Bridgnorth Castle, along with Colonel Lavington's tunnel (discussed below).

Returning to Map 7, and regardless of the actual date, the source shows the importance of the River Severn cutting through the landscape. Starting at Bridgnorth Bridge, a small gatehouse can be seen in the centre. Positioned to the north (direction indicated on the plan) and in the river is 'St. Johns Weure', with nearby a small island known as 'The Weares Billet'. To the south of the bridge is another island known as 'the great Billet'. This evidence clearly indicates the importance of the River Severn and trade and transportation along the river.

On the west bank of the River Severn sits the High Town, with a series of houses adjoining the road on either side. Examining the map in a clockwise direction, it moves along the modern B4363, Underhill Street (and the

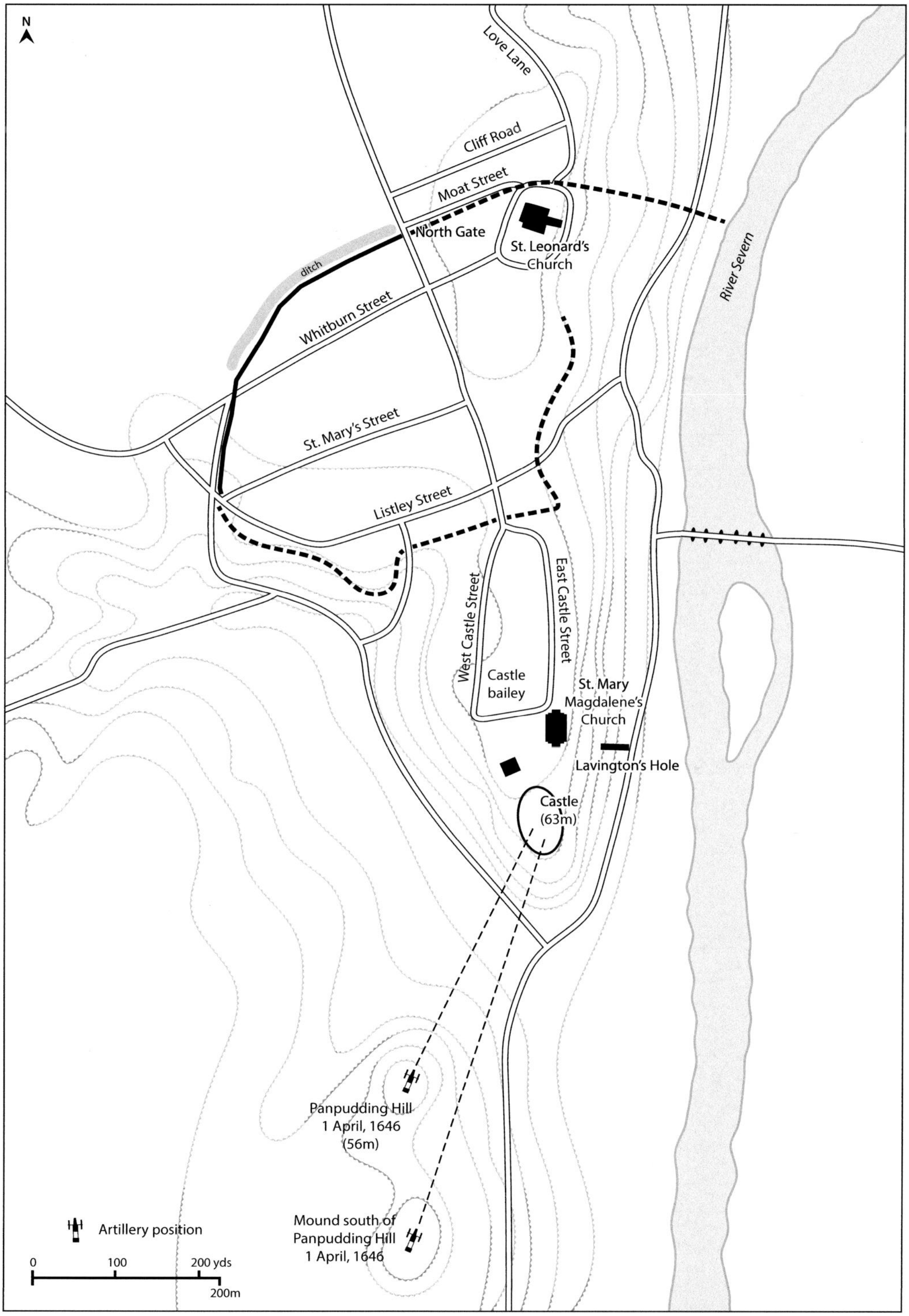

Map 8 Plan of Bridgnorth showing the besiegers' artillery positions of Panpudding Hill and the mound south of Panpudding Hill, along with Lavington's Tunnel, in relation to Bridgnorth Castle. (Base image from Figure 2, 'Bridgnorth, to the west of the River Severn (north to top)' in article by Jeremy Haslam titled 'The articulation of burgages and streets in early medieval towns, part 1: the case of Bridgnorth, Shropshire', Landscape History, Vol. 37 (1) (2016), pp. 51–68, © 2016 Society for Landscape Studies, reprinted by permission of Taylor & Francis Ltd, http://www.tandfonline.com on behalf of Society for Landscape Studies.)

remains of 'Lavington's Hole') and East Castle Street towards the now-destroyed site of 'Mary Magd', denoting the old site of the church of St Mary Magdalene and tower. As the historian John Mason notes, the church that held the Royalist gunpowder was that of St Mary.[32] What is of most interest is that Bridgnorth Castle is not referenced, or if it is depicted, it is not a prominent feature in the townscape. From this position, the map depicts a tributary to the south running in an east–west direction towards Oldbury.

Continuing in a clockwise direction, the map illustrates the road network from Bridgnorth to Oldbury. Following the road north and back into Bridgnorth, a series of field systems are depicted to the west of the main town, with a house and field known as 'Condit'. To the north-west of Bridgnorth, there are further trackways and field systems. The 'Highe Fields' not only indicate more agricultural land, but denote a change in the topography of landscape and show how, in parts, Bridgnorth sits surrounded by high ground. The importance of high ground cannot be underestimated when assessing positions to build batteries when attempting to besiege a town such as Bridgnorth.

The field system to the north of Bridgnorth is depicted as a series of enclosed fields to the north of the town. Entrance into the town at this position is through a gatehouse. Coming full circle, to the south-east of the main road north, there is depicted what appears to be St Leonard's Church and a semi-circular churchyard. As discussed earlier, whilst the church itself would not have been a position from which to fire artillery, the site could have been useful to the besiegers. This is because topographically, the church sits at 74.37m above sea level,[33] which means that the site is some 18m higher than Panpudding Hill and 11m higher than Bridgnorth Castle. In addition, the distance between these sites is only some 558m.[34] It would be surprising that the site was not utilised as an artillery position during the siege, although this has been explained by the fact that the church was destroyed and the site was unusable. When examining Smith's *The Art of Gunnery* (Table 1) (p. xxi), the evidence demonstrates that theoretically, the demi-culverin, saker (ordinary) and minion artillery pieces could hit targets at a distance of 1,371.6m, 1,143m and 1,066.8m respectively at maximum range, despite David Blackmore suggesting that the demi-culverin would have been ineffective for siege warfare.

Returning to the map, to the east there is a building named 'the Fraers', which appears to be the Friary on the bank of the River Severn. Looking at the High Town itself, the map seems to depict a series of small, cramped houses, all drawn in a similar fashion by the cartographer. Moving across Bridgnorth Bridge and the River Severn, there is the smaller Low Town. The main road of St Johns Street has a series of houses along either side, which continue along Mill Street. Along the bank of the River Severn are a series of field systems, along with an orchard field, with the lack of development at this period in history denoting the importance of the High Town over the Low.

---

32 Mason, *The Borough of Bridgnorth*, p. 25.

33 Tegan Daly, *St Leonard's Church Bridgnorth, Shropshire Archaeological Watching Brief* (Unpublished Report: Headland Archaeology Ltd, 2012), p. 1.

34 Memory Map Inc. © Crown Copyright Ordnance Survey 2008.

Returning to the siege and the castle in particular, Wilfred Watkins-Pitchford has noted that it has been local tradition that a wall of Bridgnorth Castle had six or seven iron hooks, rectangular in shape, which were used to hold a large mattress of wool to protect the wall from artillery bombardment.[35] Whether or not this is true, the effectiveness of a mattress of wool against artillery shot is doubtful, although as has been seen, woolsacks were used at Bristol in 1643.

It is unfortunate that little archaeological research has been conducted on the site. Archaeological excavations were conducted around Bridgnorth Castle by *Time Team* in 2000, although the results have not been published. The results of geophysical prospection, namely eight resistivity surveys at East Castle Street, Rectory Garden, St Mary Magdalene, Castle Grounds, Castle Hill Gardens and Castle Grounds, are available; however, on their own, they provide little information.[36]

To the south of the High Town and east of the castle area, an archaeological evaluation was conducted on land at the rear of a plot known as The Habit in 2014. Two deposits (denoted 117 and 118) that were excavated consisted of silty sand 1.3m above the natural sand, and may indicate deliberate levelling. Artefactual material consisted of flecks of charcoal and clay pipe fragments. The combination of this evidence and the close proximity of the north-eastern section of Bridgnorth Castle means that it may date to the Civil War.[37] The evidence may suggest the construction of defences to assist in holding the castle, or it could have been the construction of a platform or battery to assist the Parliamentarians with their artillery barrage. Whatever the case, this is some of the only archaeological evidence that is available relating to the Siege of Bridgnorth. This highlights an issue of English Civil War archaeology, as it is ephemeral and difficult to locate, in part because of subsequent urban development during the intervening centuries. It does, however, illustrate that there is still more to be discovered.

Returning to the conduct of the siege, the castle was bombarded for 26 days; however, very little was damaged. The Parliamentarians, under the command of the engineer Colonel Lavington (or Lavingstone), then began tunnelling into the east side of Castle Hill, approximately due west from a cave opposite the current 42 Underhill Street (see Map 8). The purpose of the mine (known as 'Lavington's Hole', Plates 23 and 24) was to target St Mary's Church (Castle Chapel), where the Royalists held their ammunition. Destroying the church and the ammunition would have provided an entry way into the castle grounds, whilst obviously depleting the garrison's ammunition supplies. The mine that was dug has always been deemed insufficient. This is because the angle of ascent was not steep enough and in

35 Wilfred Watkins-Pitchford, 'Bridgnorth Castle and Ethelfleda's Tower', *Transactions of the Shropshire Archaeological and Natural History Society*, Vol. 46 (1) (1931), p. 5.

36 GSB Prospection, *Bridgnorth, Shropshire: geophysical survey* (Unpublished Report: 2000/109 Bridgnorth Shropshire, 2000), pp. 1–3.

37 Tim Malim, *The Habit, Bridgnorth Archaeological Evaluation* (Unpublished Report: SLR, 2014), pp. 2, 19.

fact had only reached as far as the outer section of Castle Walk, in addition to being 34ft (10.36m) below the surface. However, it appears that this 'bluff' of mining was, in part, responsible for the Royalists' capitulation on 26 April, when Colonel Sir Robert Howard surrendered to Colonel Andrew Lloyd, a Parliamentarian commander who had been given command of a Regiment of Foot in Shropshire in 1645.[38] What the excavation of the mine illustrates is the importance and appreciation of geology. The geology of the area is sandstone, and it is therefore soft enough to excavate and tunnel through. It is also important to remember that the conditions inside the mine would have no doubt been difficult. Working by candlelight, it would have been hot and dark.

Plate 23 Lavington's Hole, Bridgnorth (facing west). (Author's photo)

In terms of siege warfare techniques, the use of mines dated back to the siege of Plataea in 429 BC, and was a tried-and-tested method of achieving its aim. Despite the mine at Bridgnorth not being effective as a mine *per se*, psychologically the threat of it contributed to the Royalists surrendering the

38 Watkins-Pitchford, 'Bridgnorth Castle and Ethelfleda's Tower', pp. 11–12; Watkins–Pitchford, 'A visit to Bridgnorth', p. 174; Mason, *The Borough of Bridgnorth*, p. 25. Worton, *To Settle The Crown*, p. 124.

Plate 24 Lavington's Hole, Bridgnorth sign. (Author's photo)

castle and concluding the siege. As seen in Plate 25, the surviving elements of the castle, following its slighting, lean 17 degrees to the east.[39]

Ultimately, the siege of Bridgnorth was one of attrition. Despite the failure of the artillery to successfully bombard and breach the 12th century castle, it was only a matter of time before the 400 or so soldiers of the garrison would surrender to the Parliamentarians, although they could not have foreseen that outcome at the time. The burning of the town, whether by accident or by design, limited the need for numerous batteries by the besieging army. The evidence appears to demonstrate that the presence or fear of a mine cutting through to St Mary's Church, and the Royalists' ammunition store, meant that this siege concluded successfully for Parliament, despite the lack of clinical strikes by their artillery.

It appears that the Royalists who occupied Bridgnorth Castle were fighting a lost cause. Help was not approaching, and it was only a matter of time before the troops inside the castle either starved to death or surrendered. Following the conclusion of events at Bridgnorth, the final siege of the Civil War in the Severn Valley occurred at Worcester, beginning in late May 1646.

39 Watkins-Pitchford, 'Bridgnorth Castle and Ethelfleda's Tower', p. 5; Mason, *The Borough of Bridgnorth*, p. 25.

Plate 25 The slighted remains of Bridgnorth Castle (facing south-south-west). (Author's photo)

The Parliamentarian Siege of Worcester, 20 May–23 July 1646

Almost three full years after Henry Townshend (p. 34) had described the people of Worcester picking up spades and shovels and working to level the landscape to prepare the defences of the city, war was at the city gates once again.

At the beginning of the 1646 siege, the population of the city was, according to the governor, Colonel Henry Washington, 5,676.[40] Townshend had recorded that the Royalist garrison of the city comprised 1,507 men. The city itself had this number at 1,600. This figure excludes the Worcester Town Regiment, which numbered around 400 men, with the garrison consisting of three mainly foot regiments, along with a small force of 224 cavalry. These were under the command of Colonel Washington, William Russell and Samuel Sandys, although Major Moore had control of Sandys' regiment during the siege. However, the regiments were not complete, with Sandys' consisting of only 272 men and officers. The city had 28 artillery pieces, including six light drakes,[41] which would not have been particularly powerful.

After Townshend's earlier comments in 1643, further work was conducted on the defences of the city, with the *Chamber Order Book* on 10 July 1643 noting that "every one of the chamber and every able commoner shall send a man to worke at the Foregate in the towne ditch for Tewsday and Wednesday next to make reddie the said worke against the queens majesties coming into this cittie."[42] We begin to see a different approach to defence, with the recutting of the city ditch outside of Foregate, in addition to the fact that the queen was due to stay in Worcester, thus symbolically illustrating the importance of the town to the Royalist cause.

Along with the earlier evidence of the removal of the suburbs, the *Chamber Order Book* records the removal of houses, in what can only be determined as long-term preparation of the defences. The record states that discussions occurred on 30 October 1643 to take down houses near Sidbury Gate, and also that by 20 November 1643 the houses of Mr Street had been removed.[43] The *Chamber Order Book* continues that a significant sum of money, £150, was spent on 17 November 1643 to construct fortifications and drawbridges throughout the city.[44] The implication here is that drawbridges were constructed to block the entrances to the gates into the city in response to the attempted storming of St Martin's Gate in the 1643 siege.

Records for strengthening of Worcester's defences continue through 1643, 1644 and 1645, with the *Chamber Order Book* recording on 19 February

---

40 John Barratt, *Sieges of the English Civil War*, p. 98.

41 Malcolm Atkin, *The Civil War in Worcestershire* (Stroud: Alan Sutton Publishing Ltd, 1995), p. 107; Malcolm Atkin, *Worcestershire under Arms: an English County During the Civil Wars* (Barnsley: Pen & Sword Ltd, 2004), p. 128; Barratt, *Sieges of the English Civil War*, pp. 99–100.

42 Shelagh Bond (ed.), *The Chamber Order Book of Worcester 1602–1650* (Leeds: The Worcestershire Historical Society, 1974), p. 368.

43 Bond, *The Chamber Order Book of Worcester 1602–1650*, pp. 374–75.

44 *Ibid.*, p. 374.

1643/4 that Prince Rupert ordered 300 workmen to continue construction of the fortifications.[45] Similar work was carried out under the supervision of Colonel Martin Sandys, within the city walls,[46] suggesting continued clearance and preparation for an assault. The Chamber record notes that on 22 August 1645, Mr Gatten was paid £10 for his engineering work in relation to the fortifications in the gardens of the Blackfriars, Dolday and Froggate areas of the city.[47] Whilst it is known from these accounts that preparation of the city's defences took place in specific locations, it is unfortunate that the historical record alone does not provide further details regarding what type of fortifications were constructed, and the rationale behind those decisions. Nevertheless, the *Chamber Order Book* demonstrates the evolution of expenditure, resources and fortifications, illustrating the impact of the Civil War on the city.

Whilst there is no extant map or plan of the fortifications dating to the Civil War, there is a document titled *An Exact Ground Plot of the City of Worcester, As It Stood Fortified 3. Sep: 1651*, which was published in 1660 (Map 9). Although the plan relates to how the fortifications could have appeared at the later Battle of Worcester in 1651, factoring in artistic licence, it can confidently be asserted that the majority of these fortifications were present at the siege in 1646, being *in situ* by 1645, as noted by Malcolm Atkin.[48] Interestingly, Warwick Louth suggests that this plan demonstrates that one engineer had control of the defences constructed on the eastern part of the city, whilst another designed the western fortifications.[49] Whilst this premise might be accepted, this author's bias as a landscape archaeologist leads him to believe that if the landscape was truly understood, then any sensible engineer (or engineers) would use the natural topography and an understanding of geology to their advantage, and that the fortifications would naturally follow the extant landscape in front of them, utilising high ground wherever practicable.

Focusing on only specific sections of this source, it can be seen that the first fortification begins over the River Severn, north-west of the city, at a site known as 'the Causeway Bastion'. Stylistically different to a standard four-sided bastion (two flanks and two bastion faces), the bastion is depicted as having six bastion faces all of equal length. However, as Robert Ward illustrates, designs for 'sexagon' (six-sided) fortifications were produced, if not regularly constructed.[50]

Continuing on the plan moving east, there is a sconce at St Clements. The sconce is attached to a medieval tower, depicted as being three storeys in height. The tower is no doubt one that Nehemiah Wharton described in his writings from Worcester on 30 September 1642.

45 *Ibid.*, p. 377.

46 Ibid., p. 382.

47 *Ibid.*, pp. 398–99.

48 Atkin, *The Civil War in Worcestershire*, p. 56.

49 Warwick Louth, *The Arte Militaire: The Application of 17th Century Military Manuals to Conflict Archaeology* (Solihull: Helion & Company Ltd, 2016), p. 72.

50 Ward, *Animadversions of Warre*, p. 39.

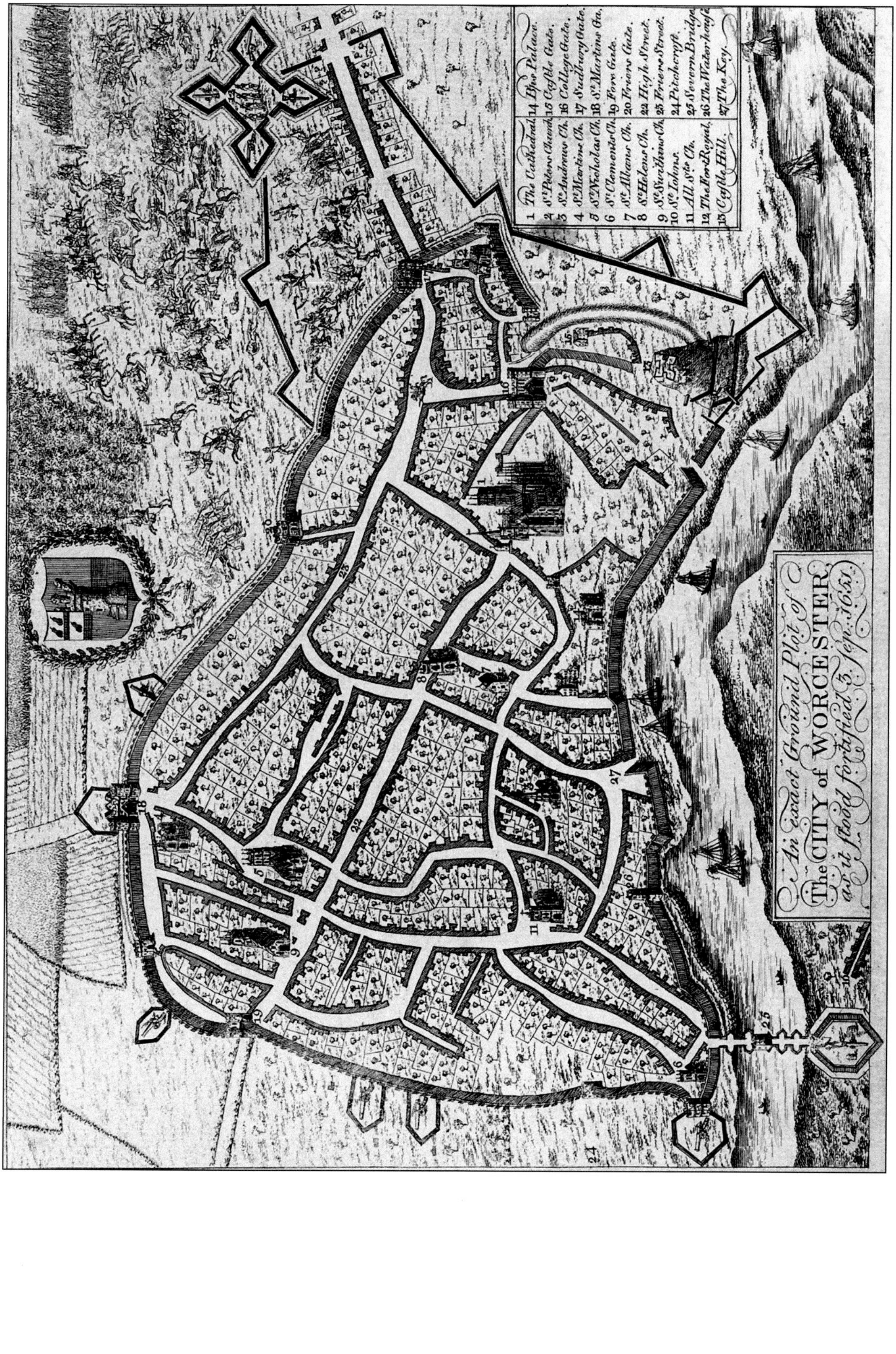

Map 9 A plan of the Civil War defences titled *An Exact Ground Plot of the City of Worcester, As It Stood Fortified 3. Sep: 1651*, drawn in 1660 (Reference: 899:41 BA510). (Reproduced by permission of Archive Enquiry Team, Worcestershire Archive and Archaeology Service, Worcestershire County Council)

Moving along the medieval wall, there are two bastions shown positioned in close proximity to one another: 'The Butts Bastion' and the 'bastion at The Butts/Farrier Street'. These two bastions are attached via flanks directly to the city wall. Strategically, these fortifications hold important ground, albeit immediately to the east of The Butts Bastion is the 20m contour line. Tactically, these fortifications are approximately, flank to flank, 30m from each other. This suggests a tactical weakness at this position, with the contemporary engineer David Papillon having proposed that in order to be tactically advantageous, bastions should be 250 yards (228.6m) from one another, so that the enfilading fire range (for musketry) can be at its maximum.[51]

Based on their topographical positions and an understanding of the tactical philosophy of the mid-17th century, both these bastions had their tactical ability compromised by being constructed too close to one another. This is curious. It appears that the bastions were constructed at these positions, in part, as an attempt to monitor any enemy advance from the north, but with the understanding that they were tactically compromised. The evidence suggests that the Royalists thus knowingly made a tactical mistake in constructing two bastions when in fact, only one bastion, utilising high ground near the city wall, would have been effective in this location. For the besiegers targeting these bastions, it meant that their artillery barrage did not need to be as accurate, as hitting either target could theoretically provide the desired result.

Archaeologically, excavations at The Butts in 1992 produced evidence of a significant ditch in what were recorded as contexts 111 and 207. The evidence revealed that the ditch, which had medieval origins, had minimum dimensions of 3.5m deep and 16m wide, followed an east–west alignment, was bowl-shaped and ran parallel to the city wall. The ditch profile was different to that at the east of city, where it had a flat (rather than concave) bottom. The ditch and the wall were separated by a gap of 5.5m; however, the medieval wall was truncated, probably due to the events of the Civil War.[52] The archaeological evidence suggests that the defenders were aware of the tactical inefficiencies of the bastions, hence why it was necessary to excavate a ditch that was 16m in width. Indeed, this ditch is larger than the dimensions given for a battery as discussed by Robert Ward, in his manual (pp. xxix–xx).

Continuing to St Martin's Gate, the plan shows a fortification facing east. Being mindful of the accuracy of cartographic sources, and the artistic licence of the artist, the sconce takes the appearance of a bastion, but adjoined to what appears to be an impressive gatehouse, flanked either side by two three-storey towers.

Archaeological excavations conducted in 2010 and 2011 on Worcester's Lowesmoor Trading Estate revealed important evidence for the ditch of the St Martin's sconce. The last dateable post-medieval layer related to the

51 Malcolm Atkin, 'David Papillon and the Civil War Defences of Gloucester', *Transactions of the Bristol and Gloucestershire Archaeological Society*, Vol. 111 (1993), p. 152.

52 Robin Jackson, *Evaluation at The Butts, Worcester* (Unpublished Report: Hereford and Worcester County Council, 1992), pp.1, 4, 6–7, 9–10.

backfilling of the ditch, which contained a significant number of tiles. This evidence suggests that the ditch and sconce were constructed on a site that once was a tilehouse, along with pottery assemblages revealing domestic ware and there being evidence of industry in metalworking. This illuminates the historical record, which shows that houses in this area, outside the city wall, were destroyed to create a field of fire. Recovery of stakes dated the ditch to the Civil War. Stratigraphy suggested that the ditch was waterlogged and susceptible to flooding. Environmental evidence of plant remains suggested that the ditch was freshly dug. Pollen data revealed evidence of grass, thereby suggesting meadowland, along with small quantities of oak, birch and willow. Evidence of oats, wheat and carrots suggests that the ditch was used to dump unsuitable crops. The base of the ditch was 18.24m above sea level; at its maximum, the ditch was 9m in width and 3m in depth, with an east–west alignment and a significant turn to the south. On the north side, evidence of postholes indicates that another structure may have been supported externally, potentially with a glacis.[53]

The evidence of stakes, in addition to the significant ditch, suggests that in this locus the defences were formidable. It appears that they conformed to the modern standards of the period, as indicated by Robert Ward when discussing the besieger's rather than the besieged's fortifications (pp. xxix–xx). This illustrates how the techniques of warfare are transferable so that either side can effectively adapt theory into reality. The use of stakes would have primarily stopped a cavalry charge at this section of the defences, acting like pikes on the open battlefield.

The cartographic representation of the Fort Royal appears to reflect the general sconce design of the period, as demonstrated by Robert Ward (see Figure 5 on p. 29). It is important here to recall that the Fort Royal was rebuilt in 1651.[54] The existing view of Worcester (Plate 26) explains why the high ground was chosen for the construction of the fortification.

From the south-west-facing rampart, the fortifications in the plan continue with an apparent break for London Road, with a demi-bastion and flank towards the city wall, which surrounds St Peter's Church and a tower. This section of the defences is termed 'Civil War entrenchment, Sidbury (south)'. Another entrenchment feature of Severn Street/Diglis appears in the form of a bank and ditch system. The Severn Street Bastion appears in design to be a spur feature.

Focusing on Castle Hill, where Worcester Castle once stood, there appears from the plan to be evidence of a mound, probably the remains of the original Norman motte, with a small four-sided sconce at its peak. A series of bank and ditch systems containing a combination of artillery positions and storm poles are also present on the mound.

This area has been investigated archaeologically. In 1966, Philip Barker conducted excavations at King's School Grounds, which found a large U–

53 Simon Woodiwiss, *Assessment and Updated Project Design for a programme of archaeological mitigation at St Martin's Quarter, Worcester* (Unpublished Report: Worcestershire Archaeology, 2014), pp. 1, 4, 10, 36–37, 42–43, 45–47, 60).

54 Atkin, *The Civil War in Worcestershire*, p. 56.

Plate 26 The view from a surviving bastion of Fort Royal towards Worcester Cathedral and the city itself (facing west-north-west). (Author's photo)

shaped ditch, 25ft (7.62m) in width, and 8ft (2.43m) in depth. The primary silt revealed fragments of tyg (a ceramic drinking vessel), which provided a *terminus post quem* (Latin for 'limit after which'), thereby dating the ditch to the 17th century. A palisaded trench and postholes dating to the same period were also discovered.[55] The palisades supporting a bank have been interpreted as being an outer 'glacis' bank, along with stakes (storm poles), as seen in Figure 12. The archaeological evidence supports and collaborates the cartographic source, which illustrates stakes (storm poles) and ditches in this section.

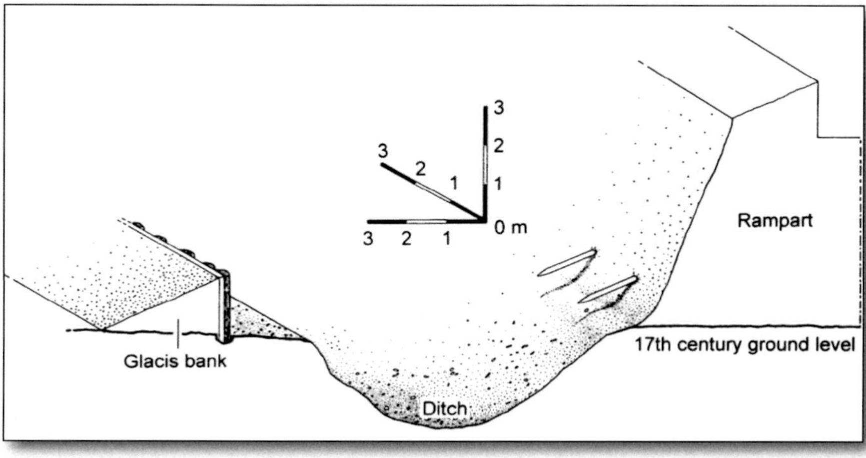

Figure 12 Illustration from Malcolm Atkin's The Civil War in Worcestershire (1995, p. 61) showing an interpretation of the excavations at King's School on Severn Street illustrating a significant ditch, stakes and a palisade supporting a glacis bank. (Reproduced by permission of Malcolm Atkin/Worcestershire Archive and Archaeology Service)

The siege of Worcester began on 21 May 1646, when a force of between 2,500 and 5,000 soldiers of the New Model Army approached the city under the command of Colonel Whalley, settling on the north side of the city and camping at Wheeler's Hill (the modern Rainbow Hill).[56] As for the size of the defending force, the *Chamber Order Book* recorded on 23 May 1646 that the city should provide enough money to maintain a garrison of 1,600 men.[57] Henry Townshend recorded on 24 May: "About 7 at night a strong sally, with 50 horse, fell on their foot that lined the hedges and were stationed about Roger's Hill, beat their guard there back and killed and hurt at least 40. 2 of ours killed and 3 hurt, 3 taken."[58] Further Parliamentarian activity was witnessed by Townshend on 26 May: "The enemy began to draw a line round about the House at Roger's Hill with Sconces, redoubts, etc., and to cross the lane towards Wheeler's Hill and so round again for their security to lodge in and to draw nearer the city."[59]

What can be seen from these sources is, firstly, confirmation of the garrison that was stationed in the city, namely approximately 1,600, against a significantly larger force of the drilled Parliamentarian New Model

55 Philip Barker, 'The Origins of Worcester', *Transactions of the Worcestershire Archaeological Society*, Vol. 2 (1968/1969), p. 99.

56 Atkin, *The Civil War in Worcestershire*, p. 107; Atkin, *Worcestershire Under Arms*, p. 125.

57 Bond, *The Chamber Order Book of Worcester 1602–1650*, p. 410.

58 John William Willis Bund (ed.), *Diary of Henry Townshend of Elmley Lovett 1640–1663* (London: The Worcestershire Historical Society, 1915), p. 114.

59 *Ibid.*

Army. Secondly, Townshend gives important information of the position of Parliamentarian siegeworks, by confirming two northern positions at Wheeler's Hill and Roger's Hill (itself north of Wheeler's Hill near Landsdowne Road).[60] Given these two positions occupy high ground, there can be seen, perhaps, an explanation of why two bastions were constructed at The Butts and at The Butts/Farrier Street. Townshend also reveals that the Parliamentarians began construction of fortifications, namely sconces and redoubts, and what appears to have been siege lines between Wheeler's Hill and Roger's Hill. This illustrates the beginning of a line of circumvallation, presumably with the intention of encircling the north, east and south of Worcester, with the River Severn a natural barrier at the west.

On 25 May, Whalley demanded the surrender of the city. Washington refused to do so, and took advantage of the lull in events to gather more supplies, leaving the city by the south.[61] On 2 June, a culverin positioned at St Martin's Gate exploded and killed a cannoneer – reportedly the best in the city – along with a 'Montross' (17th century spelling of matross, part of the crew required to fire an artillery piece), and injured another.[62] Nathaniel Nye's research (see Table 5 on pp. xxiv–xxv) has shown that a culverin can fire a maximum of 800 yards (731.5m). It appears that, as Malcolm Atkin notes, too much pressure had been put on the weapon in attempting to fire it further, leading to it exploding.[63] This may have been the result of a Parliamentarian drake positioned at Roger's Hill firing a shot that hit a drummer boy in the city, causing his "thigh [to] burst to pieces".[64]

Townshend recorded that on 3 June, the Parliamentarians began further siegeworks designed to enclose the city and complete the circumvallation (minus of course the River Severn): "The enemy drew down to Barbon 9 whole columns of foot and 8 of red, and set workmen to draw a line in Windmill field from the end of the village slope towards the river."[65] This evidence shows that the siege lines stretched from the Barbourne ('Barbon', north of the city) along the east side of the city down to Windmill Hill (now Green Hill on Bath Road) to the south, encapsulating the high ground to the River Severn, and using soldiers to complete the task.[66]

The situation deteriorated inside the city, with Townshend recording on 4 June that many of the foot soldiers left the city because they were not getting paid.[67] Further Parliamentarian troops then arrived, with approximately 1,500 horse and foot near a field close to Henwick's Hill (west of the River Severn). Some tried to capture the suburb of St John's, itself west of the River Severn, but were unsuccessful.[68]

Sporadic fighting continued, with Townshend recording on 11 June that:

---

60 Atkin, *The Civil War in Worcestershire*, p. 107.
61 *Ibid.*
62 Willis Bund (ed.), *Diary of Henry Townshend of Elmley Lovett 1640–1663*, p. 117.
63 Atkin, *The Civil War in Worcestershire*, p. 109.
64 Willis Bund (ed.), *Diary of Henry Townshend of Elmley Lovett 1640–1663*, p. 117.
65 *Ibid.*
66 Atkin, *Worcestershire Under Arms*, p. 125.
67 Willis Bund (ed.), *Diary of Henry Townshend of Elmley Lovett 1640–1663*, p. 119.
68 *Ibid*, p. 121.

> "This day in the morn was the first that the enemy shot his great ordinance. They gave 4 shots, and in the afternoon 8 more. No hurt to man nor house, only passed through. The first or second shot hit one end of the Bishop's wood building and so into his pantry and there fell. The bullet weighed 17 pounds and a half. There were other bullets of 19, 24, and one I saw weighed of 31 lbs. and a half, and one of those bullets went two foot into the mud wall at St Martin's Sconce. A boy of the City shot at the Butts gathering of peascods, dead. In the afternoon we shot our ordinance from St Martin's Blockhouse, but did no hurt at their ordinance to dismount them. Some of our Horse about Henwick's Hill and a few foot pickered with the enemy, and some of their horse and foot shot."[69]

The above account records that new artillery pieces have arrived for the siege, firing a total of 12 shots per day. If we relate this evidence to what Eldred (p. xxii) records, then cannon, demi-cannon and culverins could have been available, amongst other pieces. Using the shot weight, a 17lb 5oz (7.85kg) shot could have been fired from a culverin (ordinary whole), as illustrated in Nye's *The Art of Gunnery* (1670) (Table 5) (pp. xxiv–xxv). A shot of 19lb (8.61kg) and 24lb (10.88kg) could have been fired from a demi-cannon, with the shot of 31½lb (14.28kg) also being fired from a demi-cannon or cannon, which as Table 5 illustrates, could theoretically handle a shot of up to 58lb (26.30kg). The evidence of Townshend's testimony also indicates that the sconce at St Martin's was made of earth and was effective in stopping the shot, although its impact was significant in being able to go through 2ft (0.60m) of earth. The recording of the death of a boy reveals that shots were fired into The Butts area of the city. Finally, it can be seen that the Blockhouse (Friar's Gate) had artillery, but it was ineffective when targeting the besiegers.

On 14 June, St Martin's was again targeted by the besiegers, along with the Cornmarket, with damage caused to property. The Parliamentarians completed a bridge of boats (as illustrated in Figure 13) across the River Severn and took control of the Pitchcroft area to the north of the city, outside of the city walls, but closer than Barbourne, by constructing a half-moon.[70] It is instructive to recall that Robert Ward, in his 1639 work *Animadversions of Warre; or, A militarie magazine of the truest rules, and ablest instructions, for the managing of warre*, described the half-moon as semi-circular/arrow point, an important feature that theoretically should have been part of the large series of fortifications and placed in front of two bastions.[71]

On 16 June, Townshend recorded that around 7:00 p.m., after an uneventful day, the Parliamentarians, using two drakes and three cannons, fired shot from Roger's Hill. There was also musketry fire from Barbourne and the half-moon covering the bridge of boats and river, while bonfires were lit at Wheeler's Hill and St John's.[72] The latter was an attempt by the Parliamentarians to psychologically subdue the Royalists and townsfolk of Worcester and persuade them to surrender by indicating that Oxford – the Royalist capital during the

69 *Ibid*, p. 124.

70 *Ibid*, pp. 125–26.

71 Ward, *Animadversions of Warre*, p. 39.

72 *Ibid*, p. 127.

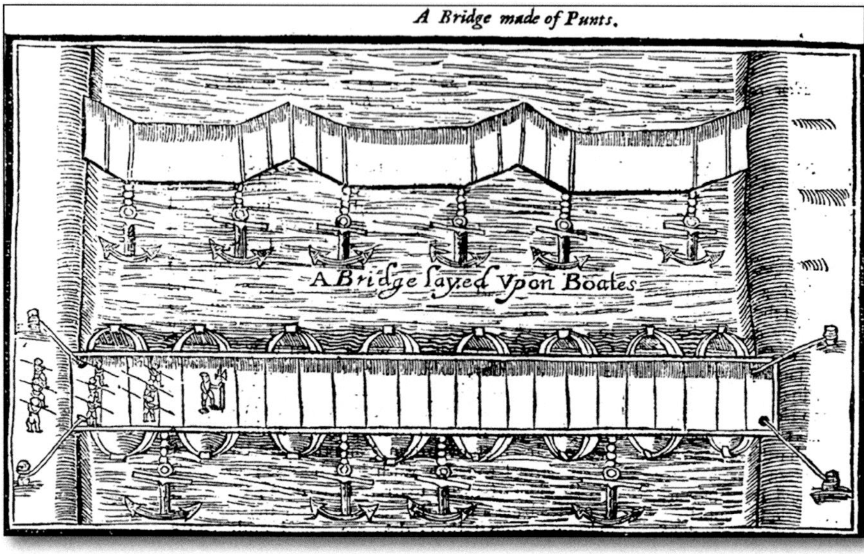

Figure 13 Illustration from Robert Ward's Anima'dversions of Warre showing a Bridge of Boats (1639, p. 376). (Reproduced by permission of Beinecke Rare Book and Manuscript Library, Yale University. Image published with permission of ProQuest®. Further reproduction is prohibited without permission. Image produced by ProQuest® as part of Early English Books Online. www.proquest.com)

war – had been captured. The taking of Oxford did not actually occur until four days later, with the city receiving the news on 25 June.[73]

The siege was beginning to have drastic effects on the population inside the city, both psychologically and with regard to munitions and food supplies, so much so that Townshend reported that Smith the Baker was to be thrown "over the walls if he baked not presently".[74]

On what appears to have been 22 June, rather than Malcolm Atkin's suggestion of 23 July,[75] Townshend records the construction by the defenders of a blind between Foregate and St Clements. The blind was described as a series of poles and rafters, criss-crossed together, some 15ft (4.57m) high, compacted with horse dung and earth, and the whole construction being some 30 yards (27.43m) in length. The purpose of the blind was to stop the Parliamentarian assault from St John's. Amongst the numerous things that Townshend said "should have been done at times of leisure, and not to shift off to the last hour of necessity",[76] he states that the defences between the Foregate and the blind itself should have been lined with at least 15ft (4.57m) of earth, if not 20ft (6.09m) at the top, with the bottom of the wall only having 6ft (1.82m) of lining. Townshend appears to suggest that the poor condition of the wall meant that it would have not survived an artillery barrage, even with earth support.[77] Regardless of the correct date, this evidence demonstrates that the city defences were still not completely ready for the siege, even if engineers like Papillon (p. 32) would not have suggested lining the medieval walls with earth.

Archaeological evidence of a defensive ditch located at Blackfriars in 1985 by Charles Mundy has led to Malcolm Atkin suggesting that the alignment of

73 Atkin, *The Civil War in Worcestershire*, p. 111; Atkin, *Worcestershire Under Arms*, p. 126.
74 Willis Bund (ed.), *Diary of Henry Townshend of Elmley Lovett 1640–1663*, p. 133.
75 *Ibid*, pp. 133–34; Atkin, *The Civil War in Worcestershire*, p. 62.
76 Willis Bund (ed.), *Diary of Henry Townshend of Elmley Lovett 1640–1663*, p. 134.
77 *Ibid*.

the blind was north–south, rather than east–west as Townshend recorded.[78] Evidence of this "last ditch"[79] of defence was located in 'Trench Two' (context 132), which ran east–west, measured 6m in width and had a maximum depth of 1.6m. 'Trench Three' located the same trench, with the bank in the east section rising to 1.7m in height. It was composed of gravel, redeposited marl, sand and silt, with a layer of pebbles forming the base.[80] To perhaps complicate matters further, Mundy states that his documentary research revealed the date for construction of the ditch (and presumably the blind) to be either 12 or 13 June 1646.[81]

Following the fall of Oxford, a truce was declared on 27 June, with an army of 10,000 infantry and 5,000 cavalry approaching Worcester. However, the truce did not last, and by 30 June, the siege had restarted, with Colonel Washington firing artillery from Foregate towards Pitchcroft and from Castle Hill to St John's, while a culverin fired towards Roger's Hill. The Royalists returned fire, firing nine shots.[82]

The siege continued, and on 2 July, Townshend recorded that an 18lb shot which hit Bishop's House had not exploded and was subsequently returned to the Parliamentarians via a Royalist cannon.[83] According to Nye's *The Art of Gunnery* (Table 5) (pp. xxiv–xxv), an 18lb shot could have been fired from a culverin, three varieties of demi-cannon or a full cannon piece. Given the approximate weight of the shot, it is likely that a culverin (ordinary whole) returned it to the Parliamentarians, as Malcolm Atkin has suggested.[84]

On 9 July, Rainsborough took command of the Parliamentarian forces, replacing Whalley. The following day, construction of new siegeworks began at Perry Wood Hill (Plate 27) along towards Red Hill Cross, with an additional two sakers being sited in these positions.[85] Townshend recorded that the new sakers had an immediate impact, being able to hit targets "a long mile from their works or Battery".[86] This evidence is supported by the data taken from Smith's *The Art of Gunnery* (Table 1) (p. xxi), which shows that an ordinary saker had a maximum range of 1,143m, thereby validating the accuracy of the statements made by Townshend when assessing how much credibility can be given to him as a source of accurate information about events during the siege.

Regarding the new siegeworks at Perry Wood Hill and Red Hill Cross, it can be seen that the geology did not affect their construction (the additional men arriving would have assisted in this work) and that the positions were chosen for their strategic and tactical superiority; namely the higher ground

78 Atkin, *The Civil War in Worcestershire*, p. 62.

79 *Ibid*, p. 63.

80 Charles Mundy, *Trial excavations in Worcester 1985* (Unpublished Report: Hereford and Worcester County Council, 1985), pp. 3, 5, 7.

81 Charles Mundy, *Worcester Archaeological Project 1985/86* (Unpublished Report: Hereford and Worcester County Council, 1986).

82 Willis Bund (ed.), *Diary of Henry Townshend of Elmley Lovett 1640–1663*, pp. 142, 155; Atkin, *The Civil War in Worcestershire*, pp. 112–13.

83 Willis Bund (ed.), *Diary of Henry Townshend of Elmley Lovett 1640–1663*, p. 159.

84 Atkin, *The Civil War in Worcestershire*, p. 113.

85 Willis Bund (ed.), *Diary of Henry Townshend of Elmley Lovett 1640–1663*, pp. 169–70.

86 Ibid., p. 170.

Plate 27 Perry Wood Hill (left of photograph) towards Worcester Cathedral and the city below (facing west-north-west). (Author's photo)

located outside of the city (thereby also explaining why the fortifications were constructed on Fort Royal Hill). Whilst it was unclear for several years whether or not the artillery emplacement of Tamar Close (Plate 28), located off Ronkswood Crescent and Newtown Road and measuring some 73m by 82m, dated to the 1646 siege or the 1651 Battle of Worcester,[87] it appears that the debate has been settled by the research of James Dinn, the Archaeological Officer of Worcester City Council. His research indicates that the site was used by Nathaniel Nye in 1646, not only as a siegework but also as one of two stations (the other near Wyld's Lane) to measure distances and angles to features within the city that could be targeted with artillery.[88] The survival of such a site in the landscape deserves further examination, as it represents an important source of information relating to Civil War archaeology, and means that a total of seven siegeworks were constructed around Worcester during the 1646 siege. Map 10 illustrates the position of the siegeworks in relation to the defences.

Inside the city, Townshend recalls that further work on the defences took place on 11 July, including additions to the fortification at Castle Hill and the removal of buildings in the southern portion of Sidbury. The Parliamentarians

87 Malcolm Atkin, *Worcester 1651* (Barnsley: Pen and Sword Books Ltd, 2008), pp. 55, 60.

88 James Dinn, 'News from City', *Worcestershire Recorder* (Newsletter of the Worcestershire Archaeological Society, Edition 86, Autumn, 2012), p. 5.

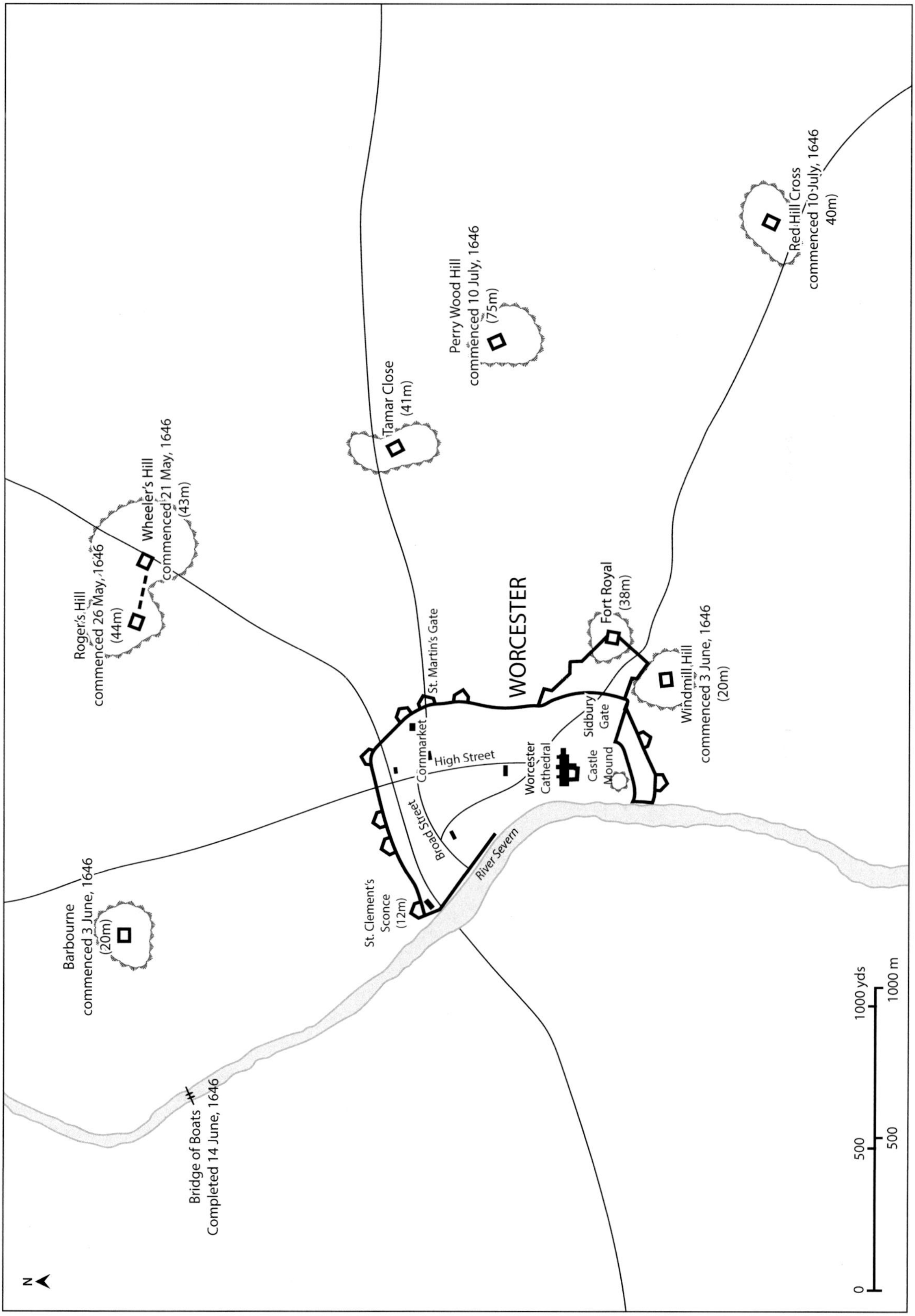

Map 10 The Parliamentarian siegeworks in relation to the defences of Worcester in 1646.

Plate 28 The Parliamentarian artillery emplacement at Tamar Close, Worcester (facing south-south-east). (Author's photo)

meanwhile continued building huts and firing artillery from Perry Wood Hill and Roger's Hill.[89]

The siege then continued, until Rainsborough offered his final terms on 18 July.[90] Townshend recalled: "The City began to grow so mutinous that many gave out, they will throw the soldiers over the walls or club them if they should oppose this Treaty."[91] Finally, on 23 July, the garrison walked out of the city and held a surrender ceremony on Roger's Hill. At 5:00 p.m., Rainsborough marched into the city with his troops, and consequently the last major act of the First Civil War drew to a close.[92]

Examining the cartographic and archaeological evidence alongside historical accounts, the siege techniques employed by the Parliamentarians at Worcester appeared to favour the earlier techniques of Maurice of Nassau (p. xvii). This is evident in the relatively slow approach towards the city by constructing several siegeworks and siege lines from which to bombard the city – the circumvallation technique (albeit incomplete). This method was most famously used by Julius Caesar at the siege of Alesia in 52 BC. The use of

89 Willis Bund (ed.), *Diary of Henry Townshend of Elmley Lovett 1640–1663*, p. 172.

90 Atkin, *The Civil War in Worcestershire*, p. 115.

91 Willis Bund (ed.), *Diary of Henry Townshend of Elmley Lovett 1640–1663*, p. 190.

92 Atkin, *The Civil War in Worcestershire*, p. 116; Atkin, *Worcestershire Under Arms*, p. 126.

a bridge of boats, meanwhile, illustrates the importance of the River Severn regarding any assault on the city from the west, whereas the Parliamentarians' understanding and appreciation of the local topography demonstrates the significance of landscape in siege warfare.

The historical accounts of the difficulties caused by unrest inside the city – illustrated vividly with the destruction of houses and property, and the threat to throw a baker over the city walls – show the impact of siege warfare as it slowly tightened its grip on the city. This was despite the preparations made by the city, in The Butts, the ditch and stakes of St Martin's Sconce and the sophisticated ditch, stakes and potential glacis at King's School Grounds, all discovered through archaeological research.

In the following chapter, the various Royalist and Parliamentarian siege techniques of the First Civil War in the Severn Valley are compared and contrasted, to determine why some sieges were successful while others were not, and where mistakes were made.

Chapter 4

Royalist Sieges versus Parliamentarian Sieges

This chapter will bring together the evidence that has been examined, to see how the sieges in the Severn Valley compare with one another, and whether there were any subsequent changes in the approach to warfare, its impact on the individual and the Severn Valley region as a whole.

The Sieges of 1643

The first siege examined, that of Worcester in 1643, was a Parliamentarian failure. This is in some respects surprising considering that Waller attacked the city with 3,000 men and eight cannons. Although this was not a large artillery train, the best historical information that is available records that a series of small works were made on a hill south-east of Worcester (now known as Fort Royal Hill), with money given for the construction of the defences, but that the city's main defences were the medieval ditch and wall with earthen banks along the latter. As has been seen, military theorists such as Papillon claimed that lining the walls with earth would not be effective in a siege.

The initial barrage of artillery as used by the Parliamentarians was a very old tactic. The use of 'missiles' – including archers – is discussed by Aelian, who drew on Hellenistic work whilst writing in the second century AD, suggesting that they were used in an attempt to provoke or disrupt the enemy and damage their defences.[1] This appears to have been the primary role of the artillery assault during a siege.

As the evidence indicates that both sides at Worcester were equally matched in terms of artillery firepower during the first siege, it was the successful cavalry charge of the Royalists and the notification of a relief army approaching that caused the Parliamentarians to abandon their assault. The general tactics employed – the use of siege weapons and attempting to assault

1 Christopher Matthew, *The Tactics of Aelian or On the Military Arrangements of the Greeks* (Barnsley: Pen & Sword Books Ltd, 2012), p. 49.

the city – were tried-and-tested methods, although not always successful; the repeated attempts of the English to storm Calais in 1347 is one such example of failure from an earlier era.[2]

Moving to Bristol and the Royalists' successful siege of the city, there was an expanded approach regarding defence from the Parliamentarians. More artillery and more defensive positions were in place there, compared to what was at Worcester. The impact of the geology on what could be constructed in particular positions – and how – was more critical. Like at Worcester, the decision was made to storm rather than approach using mines and saps. Whilst there was some skirmishing, unlike at Worcester the besieged did not attempt full counter-attacks on the Royalists' positions. The effective use of cavalry and dragoons made the successful breach in the defences. Crucially, unlike at Worcester, the Royalists did not have to contend with an artillery barrage when launching their attack, as the topography and the range of artillery meant that this was difficult from the defensive positions taken.

The capture of the Essex Work was a further example of the effective use of horsemen, something that would have been akin to medieval tactics. However, some innovative tactics by the Parliamentarians have been discussed, particularly amending light artillery pieces to effectively turn them into the precursor of heavy machine guns. The Royalists' use of firepikes is also illustrative of innovative tactics designed to harass and terrorise the defenders inside the fortification.

Like at Worcester, the use of earth around fortifications was present; however, the legend of Mrs Dorothy Hazzard and nearly 200 women and girls working to fortify the defences near Frome Gate adds an additional dimension and truly shows that the war and siege warfare affected everybody in society, regardless of age or gender. The capture of Bristol was not due to an inspired tactical decision on the part of the Royalists. In fact, because the attacking southern forces launched early, it nearly failed. Rather, it was down to poor Parliamentary leadership, the ineffective use of the artillery available and the lack of morale of the besieged forces.

The storming of Bristol and the losses endured by the Royalists meant a new tactical approach to siege warfare in the Severn Valley took place at Gloucester – that of a formal siege. This meant a war of attrition, with the time and effort required to construct artillery positions. The lack of lines of circumvallation and contravallation meant that this warfare style was a modification of the approach by Gustavus Adolphus.[3]

Perhaps one of the most significant events of the siege of Gloucester was the preparation of the city to withstand an assault, in this case, the burning of the suburbs. One-third of the city – 241 homes – was destroyed. The creation of this 'field of fire' is an important tactic for the besieged. This is because, if the deployment is successful, the besiegers cannot hide in the abandoned buildings, using them as cover on their approach.

2 Peter Hoskins, *Siege Warfare During the Hundred Years War: 'Once More unto the Breach...'* (Barnsley: Pen & Sword Books Ltd, 2018), p. 58.

3 Jon Day, *Gloucester & Newbury 1643: The Turning Point of the Civil War* (Barnsley: Pen & Sword Books Ltd, 2007), pp. 65–66.

Like at Bristol, the importance that the area's geology has on the construction of both defensive and offensive fortifications was seen at Gloucester. The high water table meant that the attempts of mines, and countermines, in response were stopped.

Despite mining being an issue, there is clear evidence, through the historical and archaeological record, of the use of saps. Henry Hexham wrote that saps must be dry and have no water; considering the high water table, the task would have been difficult, but not impossible. The excavation of the sap, to such precision, illustrates the skill of the sappers and the detail required in warfare during this period. On the other hand, it also shows how much time was wasted in the approach of the Royalists towards conducting a siege quickly and efficiently.

An important tactical act for the Royalists was to cut the water supply of the residents of Gloucester from Robinhood's Hill. By employing a similar methodology, albeit regarding a different source of water, to the events of the siege of Breda (1624–25), the effect here of putting pressure on the community inside would have had the same outcome. The cutting of the water supply affected the local landscape, and the ability of the population to continue their daily lives without making some sacrifice.

In contrast to at Bristol, the defending Parliamentarians under Massey had been launching attacks on the Royalists, attempting to slow down and halt construction of their artillery positions. This strategy appears to have been the only one available. The tactical decision to launch a raid at midnight, under darkness, and the example of the success of the raid by Harcus and Stevens, validates that decision. The only other option available would have been to wait for an all-out assault.

The draining of the ditch at Gooseditch, as has been discussed, presented an interesting strategic and tactical approach. Comparing this to Worcester and Bristol, neither in the historical nor archaeological record from these towns is there evidence that ditches needed to be wet. Dutch fortifications would have had a wet ditch.[4] Interestingly, in Machiavelli's *The Art of War*, in Book Seven, Fabrizio states: "I would have them without water; for they are more secure, and, as it has been observed that in winter time the ditches ice over, the capture of a city is made easy."[5] This evidence implies that ditches should not be filled with water; indeed, the time of year (autumn) and the onslaught of winter was perhaps in the minds of the besieged at Gloucester. In addition, the ditch was constructed immediately in front of the Roman/medieval wall, therefore suggesting that the feature was kept dry so that it remained intact and did not degrade. The archaeological evidence of a V-shaped ditch, like that seen at South Gate, is apparent from the Roman period; the steepness makes it difficult for attackers to navigate over the feature.[6]

4 Christopher Duffy, *Siege Warfare: The Fortress in the Early Modern World 1494–1600* (London: Routledge & Kegan Paul Ltd, 1979), p. 90.

5 Niccolò Machiavelli, *The Art of War*, trans. by Henry Neville (New York: Dover Publications Inc. 2006 modernised reprint, 1674), p. 148.

6 Jeremy Black, *Fortifications and Siegecraft: Defense and Attack through the Ages* (London: The Rowman & Littlefield Publishing Group, Inc., 2018), p. 16.

The use of the half-moon has been seen throughout the examination of the defences of Gloucester. Samuel Fawcett's 1643 list of artillery for Bristol lists a hornwork fortification. What these similarities indicate is that where it was not possible, perhaps due to time and resources, to construct ramparts and bastions according to the descriptions given by Richard Norwood and Robert Ward, the engineers and designers decided to improvise and construct what they could in the available window of opportunity. This adaptation of theory and design is something that can be seen throughout history, with people modifying the normal parameters to suit their needs, such as the conversion of light artillery to something akin to heavy machine guns at Bristol in 1645.

One of the most interesting episodes of the Gloucester siege was Doctor Chillingworth's attempt to use Roman siege techniques. The historian Philip Rance states that Plutarch, the philosopher, was probably describing a *testudo* being used in 36 BC against Parthian cavalry, but it should also be remembered that the term is frequently noted to describe many units that are simply well shielded and compact.[7] However, John Corbet, who was critical of the siege engine, described them as "those unperfect and troublesome engines to assault the lower parts of the City. Those engines ran upon wheels, with planks musket proof placed on the Axel-tree, with holes for musketshot, and a bridge before it, the end of (the wheels failing into the ditch) was the rest upon our breast works."[8]

Interestingly, the historian Jon Day relates the use of this weapon to "sows".[9] According to the historian Christopher Duffy, in 1595 the governor of Connaught had been captured by using a rood screen from Sligo Abbey, placing it on wheels, covering it with hides and moving it against the forces inside Sligo Castle, akin to a tank. The word 'sow' is derived from "the forest of soldiers' legs which dangled from the innards of the beast like piglets' trotters".[10]

The most critical factor in the failures to take Worcester and Gloucester, and hold onto Bristol, is the ineffective use of artillery. Although it appears that the artillery, numerically at least, were evenly matched at Worcester, the placement of a large section of that available at Bristol on or around Bristol Castle appears to have been a tactical mistake.

At Gloucester, the Royalists only fired 17 rounds each day.[11] Indeed, Christopher Duffy noted the "tempo of the whole operation was far too slow".[12] By making this statement, however, it must be kept in mind that it was common for an artillery piece to have at most 50 rounds, and that the

7 Philip Rance, 'The Fulcum, the late Roman and Byzantine testudo: the Germanization of late Roman Tactics?', *Greek, Roman and Byzantine studies*, Vol. 44 (3) (2004), p. 300.

8 John Corbet, *An Historicall relation of the military government of Gloucester: from the beginning of the Civill Warre betweene King and Parliament to the removal of Colonell Massie from that Government to the command of the Westerne Forces* (London: Robert Bostock, 1645), p. 51.

9 Day, *Gloucester & Newbury 1643: The Turning Point of the Civil War*, p. 79.

10 Duffy, *Siege Warfare: The Fortress in the Early Modern World 1494–1600*, p. 145.

11 John Lynch, *Bristol and the Civil War: For King and Parliament* (Stroud: The History Press, 2009), p. 71.

12 Duffy, *Siege Warfare: The Fortress in the Early Modern World 1494–1600*, p. 153.

artillery of this age was not the "battle-winning weapon that it came to be".[13] Nevertheless, it is important to note the failure to deploy artillery effectively in several sieges.

The Sieges of 1645

Moving to examine the 1645 sieges, the one at Shrewsbury was an extremely brief one. The stratagem was akin to taking a fortress by surprise. These tactics were effectively used by Roman and ancient Greek commanders, most notably by Alcibiades at the Battle of Cyzicus in the Peloponnesian War.[14]

Examining the preparation of the defences, it is seen that the Royalists did, in large part, make sufficient preparations to secure Shrewsbury. A variety of technological developments and materials were used in preparing the defences. At a basic level were implements such as turnpikes, whilst in sharp contrast at Frankwell, the construction of a four-sided sconce was in line with modern 17th century military thinking. Wood was also used in the construction of the palisades. Yet whilst palisades are an important element for a variety of Civil War fortifications, they should not be the main line of defence; indeed, perhaps Shrewsbury was a lesson in this regard.

The construction of a redoubt and wall at Roushill, in addition to a sconce at Frankwell, would have limited the approach of the Parliamentarians. But due to reconnaissance, and what the *Mercurius Aulicus* records as a "vulnerable point", it was clear for the Parliamentarians to approach the palisades near the castle by the river. Approaching at night gives the besiegers an advantage, as it is more likely than not that the besieged are asleep, or at the very least have a minimum number on guard. However, it is important not to give away the position during a night assault by approaching with lit matchlocks, as the Parliamentarians did, even though they were not detected. The assault at night is an important parallel with Gloucester, as, on both occasions, the Parliamentarians used the time of day and the cover of darkness as a useful tool in an attempt to cause maximum damage. As Vegetius noted in the fifth century, "For the security of an expedition depends on the concealment of all motions from the enemy."[15]

The use of carpenters importantly illustrates that people with a variety of different skills accompanied soldiers when the decision was made to storm or approach a fortification or town. Interestingly, like all the previous sieges in the study area – except for Gloucester – the storm approach was taken rather than the formal siege.

Like the 1643 siege of Gloucester, and the batteries at the siege of Breda (1624–25), Shrewsbury highlights the importance of turf in the construction

---

13 Stephen Bull, *The Furie of the Ordnance: Artillery in the English Civil Wars* (Woodbridge: The Boydell Press, 2008), p. 164.

14 Konstantin Nossov, *Ancient and Medieval Siege Weapons* (Guilford: First Lyons Press, 2012), pp. 253–54.

15 Flavius Vegetius Renatus, *De Re Militari (Concerning military affairs): the classic treatise on warfare at the pinnacle of the Roman Empire's power* (Leonaur, 2012), p. 73.

and maintenance of the defences. This demonstrates that whether or not someone was reading or referring to Richard Norwood's 1639 *Fortification or Architecture Military* manual in the field, for example, modern 17th century theories regarding fortification were reaching people on the front line, and engineers were trying to construct the best fortifications they could, given the available time and resources.

The additional construction of a stone wall at Roushill demonstrates how the besieged were able to tactically understand and appreciate the landscape surrounding them. The importance of the watchtower is seen here, particularly one made of timber. The ancient Greeks utilised watchtowers, and towers in Roman Britain were timber-framed in the first century AD. Four large posts were the mainframe, which would have been defended by either a ditch or a rampart.[16] Importantly, what is seen here is the continuation of siege warfare strategy for 1,600 years. The necessity of, in this case, creating artificially high ground provides commanders and troops with places to observe and monitor enemy approaches, something that has remained a constant in warfare for thousands of years.

The importance of the medieval castle can still be seen in the siege at Shrewsbury. There is a general perception that the English Civil War is the 'last hurrah' of such castles; the historian Konstantin Nossov commented that "castles had become outdated, their walls unable to withstand such fire"[17] in relation to artillery. However, the castles in the case studies above played an important role in the overall defence of the towns. For the majority of the castles, though, the "Civil War was the last time that most of these fortifications served a purely military use".[18] Despite the incoming new fortifications of the *Trace Italienne* style, none of the old-style castles in the Severn Valley area were taken by direct assault. As the historian Peter Gaunt notes, "[M]any had stood up remarkably well to bombardment and attack from 17th century artillery and armies."[19] The discussion regarding whether or not all castles primarily served a military function is for another time.

Shrewsbury fell because of the tactical weakness in the defences near the castle and river. If further defensive additions had been made, for example earthen fortifications such as redoubts, hornworks or half-moons (although as has been seen, the latter two were not recommended by the 17th century military theorists as standalone features), then it is possible that the events of Shrewsbury could have turned out differently. Indeed, the "vulnerable point" referenced in the *Mercurius Aulicus* (p. 72) may have been nothing more than excellent reconnaissance or the effective use of spies to understand the enemy, something which every commander should aspire to. As Sun Tzu states:

16 David John Breeze, *Roman Forts in Britain* (Oxford: Shire Publications Ltd, 2002), p. 45.

17 Nossov, *Ancient and Medieval Siege Weapons*, p. 71.

18 Peter Harrington, *Archaeology of the English Civil War* (Princes Risborough: Shire Publications Ltd, 1992), p. 15.

19 Peter Gaunt, *The English Civil Wars 1642–51*, p. 87.

> "This knowledge is not to be got at by calling on gods and demons; nor does it come of past experience nor calculation. It is through men that knowledge of the enemy is gained."[20]

Moving on to Bristol, it is seen that the Royalists in their attempts to hold the city attempted unsuccessfully to create a large field of fire by destroying the villages to the north of the city. This is despite Bernard de Gomme noting that the hedges along the defensive line remained, which were therefore a tactical weakness to be exploited by the Parliamentarians.

Like at Worcester in 1643, the attack on Bristol began with an artillery barrage. The effective deployment of troops at Lawford's Gate appears to have overwhelmed the besieged and captured some artillery pieces. A tactical advantage was gained by utilising gaps in the line where it was decayed, whilst the regiments of Birch and Skippon turned Royalist artillery against their former owners. All of these actions limited any attempts by the Royalists to hold back the storming New Model Army. As the approaches were successful, this reduced the ability of the Royalists to counter-attack. By retreating to the Royal Fort and Colston's Fort, the Royalists were able to regroup tactically and reassess the situation, whilst the Parliamentarians were able to target their attacks in a more controlled approach.

The attack on Prior's Hill Fort demonstrates a key aspect of siege warfare that did not change for centuries: that of scaling fortifications. Scaling ladders have been depicted in ancient Egyptian tombs dating to the Old Kingdom (2660–2195 BC). When the Turks besieged Constantinople in 1453 AD, they had 2,000 ladders.[21]

After capturing Prior's Hill Fort, Sprigg noted the importance of launching the assault in the dark. This tactic was also effectively launched at Shrewsbury, indicating that attacking under the cover of darkness meant fewer of the opponents' troops on patrol, and in both cases it limited the effectiveness of the enemy's artillery.

Tactically, one of the most interesting aspects of the sieges at Bristol was that neither side was able to breach the southern sector of the defences. The explanation for this lies in the fact that both strategically and tactically, this was not the most important sector of the defences to breach; it was merely enough to keep some of the besieged troops occupied in that area so that they could not be repositioned to other more important areas of the city. Indeed, if this section of the defences had been breached, the besiegers would still have to cross the River Avon to effectively target Bristol Castle. As has been seen in both the 1643 and 1645 sieges, the castle was not pivotal in holding Bristol. The key was to hold the outer fortifications on the northern sector and the defensive line. Lack of manpower and lack of work on the defences were the main reasons for the failure to repel the besiegers in both cases.

The most crucial similarity between the Royalist and Parliamentarian forces assaulting Bristol was their decisions to storm the city rather than effect

20 Sun Tzu, *The Art of War: including the translated The Sayings of Wu Tzu*, trans. by Everard Ferguson Calthrop (Chichester: Capstone Publishing Ltd, 2010), p. 97.

21 Nossov, *Ancient and Medieval Siege Weapons*, pp. 75–76.

a prolonged siege. In 1645, Sir Thomas Fairfax appears to have preferred the assault method, but there were other factors, including worries that the army could succumb to sickness over the winter, the possibility of a Royalist relief army approaching and the political ambition of Westminster to conclude the war as quickly as possible.[22] What has been seen, then, is that on both occasions Bristol was stormed for a variety of reasons. Regardless of the decision-making process, the actual decision to storm was effective because both sets of besiegers captured the city.

The Sieges of 1646

The siege at Bridgnorth highlights the importance of the medieval landscape, with the re-cutting of the ditch, in addition to new earthworks. There were similar reuses of the landscape at Shrewsbury and Worcester in 1645 and 1643 respectively. Indeed, in all the case studies examined, the importance of the pre-existing landscape was essential, including whether or not to keep that landscape intact or destroy it for tactical reasons.

The reduction in height of the tower of St Leonard's Church at Bridgnorth illustrates the importance of stone in the construction of the defences. The removal of stone can only indicate that it was being used to repair gaps in the medieval stone wall. Revetting new earthworks in this conflict was rare. The tactical advantage of using the tower as a lookout point was apparently deemed less important. This is contrast to what happened at Shrewsbury, where a watchtower was built to observe enemy troop movements. Like all other study sites, albeit significantly so at Bristol, the destruction of property and industries to create a field of a fire was a key ingredient of preparing for war in this period.

The historical documentation suggests that Panpudding Hill was an artillery position. Combining this with the evidence of the excavations conducted in 1983 of the mound, immediately south of the medieval castle earthworks, clearly indicates an important, albeit not revolutionary, understanding of the landscape – the need to command and control higher ground. Control of high ground (even if fortifications were not constructed of sufficient standards) was also seen at Frankwell at Shrewsbury, and the northern circuit of defences at Bristol. At Bridgnorth, the position chosen indicates that reconnaissance of the landscape had taken place, with a conscious decision to use the nearby remains of the motte and bailey castle as cover for movement of artillery pieces and troops.

The construction of approaches and entrenchments near the castle at Bridgnorth signalled the intent of the Parliamentarians for a formal siege. This was in part aided by the fire that destroyed large sections of the town. The use of these techniques follows the methodology seen in earlier sieges on the Continent, namely the siege of Breda (1624–25), as discussed by Robert Ward in *Animadversions of Warre* (p. xix).

22 Lynch, *Bristol and the Civil War: For King and Parliament*, p. 151.

Besieging a castle, such as that at Bridgnorth, has parallels with the siege warfare of the Greek, Roman and medieval worlds. Whilst mining was attempted at Gloucester – but stopped due to the local geology – at Bridgnorth, the effect of mining was more psychological. This is despite the fact that if the mine had reached St Mary's Church, exploding it would have caused similar results to the medieval siege of Rochester by King John in 1215, when a large section of the castle's tower was brought crashing down.

Looking at Worcester, the population of the city made sacrifices and adapted to the dangers of siege warfare, particularly after the events of 1643. This included, as noted by Henry Townshend, the removal of houses, trees and hedges (p. 34) to create a clear field of fire, so that the enemy could not use those features to their advantage. The clearance of land is a common factor, as has been seen at Bristol, Gloucester and Shrewsbury, although the question of how much needed to be destroyed before a siege to save what remained was surely asked by numerous people, with Sir Balthazar Gerbier being one of those individuals.[23]

In Worcester, the historical evidence illustrates the difficulties of being under siege, with the threat made to Smith the Baker that he would be thrown over the wall if he did not continue to help feed the defenders. The psychological impact of being trapped inside the city walls would have been familiar to those in Bridgnorth Castle after nearly three weeks of being besieged, which would have been extremely difficult. As Vegetius noted, "It is much better to overcome the enemy by famine, surprise, or terror than by general actions."[24]

Continuing the analysis of the siege of Worcester compared to those at Bridgnorth and Gloucester, some parallels can be seen. There was construction by the besiegers of artillery emplacements on the surrounding high ground, apart from Fort Royal Hill, which was under the control of the Royalists. High ground, if available, is a dominant feature throughout warfare: high ground obviously provides a position from which to effectively fire artillery onto lower ground. It also means that, theoretically, opposing troop movements can be monitored (something which was not done when the Royalists attempted to capture Gloucester, as they failed to adequately prepare for the relief army). The high ground also acts as natural protection, allows visibility between forts and serves as a psychological deterrent to the enemy.[25] Indeed, looking back in history to the ancient Chinese strategist Sun Tzu, he noted the following:

> "Place the army on high ground, and avoid an enemy in high places.[26]
>
> "... As a rule, the soldiers prefer high ground to low.[27]

23 Stephen Porter, *The Blast of War*, p. 23.

24 Renatus, *De Re Militari (Concerning military affairs): the classic treatise on warfare at the pinnacle of the Roman Empire's power*, p. 103.

25 Stuart Prior, *A few well-positioned castles: The Norman Art of War* (Stroud: Tempus Publishing Ltd, 2006), p. 53.

26 Sun Tzu, *The Art of War*, p. 58.

27 *Ibid.*, p. 59.

> "... If there be rising ground, encamp on its sunny side and in front of it; for thereby the soldiers are benefited, and the ground used to our advantage."[28]

The high ground in the cases studies examined here to a certain extent fulfils the criteria of Sun Tzu's sayings. However, when it is considered that Panpudding Hill was lower than Bridgnorth Castle, and that in both sieges of Bristol, the besiegers had to go uphill to attack, it was often difficult to avoid the enemy in high places.

Archaeologically, an important ditch was discovered in Worcester at The Butts, measuring 16m in width and 3.5m in depth. The construction of a U-shaped ditch some 7.62m wide and 2.43m deep at King's School Grounds adds further to the evidence of significant enhancements throughout the city. In addition, there was the evidence of stakes along with a ditch measuring 9m in width and 3m in depth, where St Martin's Sconce would have been constructed. What this evidence illustrates is the amount of organisation and effort put into the defences by the people of Worcester to hold the remaining suburbs of the city. Similar evidence has been discovered archaeologically at Gloucester, with the creation of a defensive ditch some 10m in width and 4m in depth and the removal of Green Dragon Lane.

Parallels can be drawn between the use of the River Severn, in particular the bridge of boats at Worcester and the similar use of the river at Shrewsbury and the River Avon at Bristol. At Shrewsbury, the initial attack began by attempting to transport men further along the river by boat, whilst plans were made in Bristol to storm the Water Fort amphibiously. However, it was only at Worcester that a bridge of boats, probably like that illustrated in Figure 13 (p. 124), was successful.

One of the most significant aspects of siege warfare is the attempted construction of a circumvallation. This was seen put into effect at the siege of Breda (1624–25) and the siege of Alesia in 52 BC. The construction of seven artillery emplacements at Worcester shows how committed the Parliamentarians were to the siege. The importance of constructing on high ground is seen here, and in the case of Perry Wood Hill, the difficulty of constructing earthworks on and near woodland. Woodland provided an essential resource for fuel for fires and the construction of huts, along with turnpikes and gabions. However, soldiers disliked woodlands because it was easier for the enemy to create traps and ambushes. Formations cannot be kept in woodland, and it is possible for a few men to surround and disrupt a larger body. It is also relatively easy to get lost in woodland. It is important to bear in mind that woodland can cause difficulty for even the most well-trained units, such as was the case with Varus and his Roman legions in the Teutoburger Wald, where they were defeated by Germanic tribes in 9 AD.[29] This evidence of the artillery positions at Worcester indicates the importance that the Parliamentarians placed on holding high ground and constructing emplacements on it.

28 *Ibid.*, p. 60.

29 Jim Storr, *King Arthur's Wars: The Anglo-Saxon Conquest of England* (Warwick: Helion & Company Ltd, 2018), p. 44.

No Lines of Circumvallation or Contravallation

None of the case studies of sieges in the Severn Valley featured the construction of complete lines of circumvallation or contravallation. This is, however, not surprising. Taking Worcester as an example, the construction of the circumvallation was incomplete, as it did not encircle the west section of the city and the River Severn. The construction of a circumvallation would have been an enormous undertaking, let alone a contravallation, which would have been several miles in length.

The only evidence there is for anything that resembles a complete circumvallation during the Civil Wars is at Colchester in Essex, although interestingly, de Gomme refers to the defences of Bristol in 1643 as a "Circumvallation" (p. 36). There is no evidence at all for a contravallation being constructed during the English Civil War.[30]

Looking more closely at the siege of Colchester in 1648, during the Second Civil War, the Royalist defenders, like at Gloucester, utilised the Roman and medieval walls whilst constructing a bastion at the north-east section of the wall. They also positioned artillery stoppers and snipers on church towers to observe the besiegers. At Shrewsbury, this study has seen the construction of a wooden tower for this effect. It is also probable that St Leonard's Church at Bridgnorth was used for a similar function, despite its reduction in height.[31]

The importance of the River Colne can be seen at Colchester, as four forts were constructed on its bank by the besieging Parliamentarians. A further six forts were constructed to the south of the river. All of these fortifications were connected by banks and ditches, meaning that the town was isolated from the outside world.[32] The construction of these fortifications, along with the connecting banks and ditches, illustrates that given the time and resources, a line of circumvallation could be planned and built successfully. However, even here there is nothing like the massive line of circumvallation – with the intricate use of 'lily' pits, 'gravestone' ditches and spurs – that Julius Caesar constructed at Alesia in 52 BC.

The impressive line of circumvallation seen at Colchester in 1648 was probably constructed due to a change in the political landscape in the country. Following the success of Parliament in the First Civil War, any attempted resurgence of the Royalist cause was met with fierce resistance. This led to Parliament twice marching on London, in 1647 and 1648, and ultimately the beheading of Charles I on 30 January 1649.

The Severn Valley

Interestingly, and perhaps not surprisingly, the outcomes of the sieges during this period dictated the outcome of the war. The importance of Shrewsbury to

30 Mike Osborne, *Sieges and Fortifications of the Civil Wars in Britain* (Leigh-on-Sea, Partizan Press, 2004), p. 15.

31 *Ibid.*, pp. 50–51.

32 *Ibid.*

the Royalist cause was established on 20 September 1642, when they installed military and administrative headquarters in the town. The significance of Worcester – and the shire as a whole – before the 1643 siege culminated in the Battle of Powick Bridge on 23 September 1642, the first engagement of the conflict and a Royalist victory. Worcester's strategic importance in being on the main road to monitor Royalist advances from the south-west, and its proximity to the London Road, explains why Colonel Essex decided to set up his headquarters in the town. After Royalist troops left Bridgnorth, Essex left Worcester, and both groups saw service at the Battle of Edgehill on 23 October 1642. After the battle, the Royalists were able to seize Evesham and Bewdley, forcing Essex to withdraw to Gloucester, and the Royalists under Sir William Russell then occupied Worcester.[33]

At the first siege studied, Parliament was attempting to expand its control over the region by attacking Worcester. The unsuccessful assault was compounded by the loss of Bristol in July. Only Gloucester now stood in the way of the Royalists having complete control of the Severn Valley.

The overall Royalist strategy for the region, and the war as a whole, until the siege of Gloucester was clearly replicated in the towns that remained in their hands and fell to them because of the sieges: the successful hold of Worcester in 1643 and the taking of Bristol later in the year.

The 26-day length of the siege of Gloucester is relatively short compared to the Royalists' unsuccessful siege of Hull between 2 September and 11 October 1643 (39 days) and Parliament's unsuccessful siege of York between 21 April and 1 July 1644 (71 days); however, it critically affected the Royalists' strategy.[34] This is where the Royalists failed. The tactical failure to conduct a formal siege rather than storm the city, and the failure to defeat the army of the Earl of Essex at the First Battle of Newbury on 20 September 1643, ultimately meant that victory did not go to the king.[35]

Losing the Battle of Marston Moor on 2 July 1644 – as well as defeats at King's Lynn, Winceby, Chichester and Arundel – caused problems for the Royalists. The Second Battle of Newbury on 27 October 1644 ended in an impasse.

By 1645, the Parliamentarians had remodelled their army – creating the New Model Army, which was some 20,000-strong – and were on the offensive. This is reflected in the study area, with the capture of Shrewsbury on 22 February 1645 and the taking of Bristol on 11 September that year. The Severn Valley was merely reflecting the changes in the war as a whole. Key towns, including Gloucester, Shrewsbury and Bristol, were now under the control of Parliament. This meant that the Royalists lost control of the ports and manufacturing centres of Bristol and Shrewsbury, and that by failing to capture Gloucester, it was difficult for them to obtain any support from Wales.

33 Atkin, *The Civil War in Worcestershire*, pp. 41–42; John Ellis, *'To walk in the dark': Military Intelligence during the English Civil War 1642–1646* (Stroud: The History Press, 2011), p. 72; Peter Gaunt, *The English Civil War: A Military History*, p. 69.

34 John Barratt, *Sieges of the English Civil War*, p. 175.

35 Gaunt, *The English Civil War: A Military History*, p. 152.

The siege of Bridgnorth in 1646 occurred when the Royalists were unable to engage in field battles, but remained in the few loyal garrisoned towns and castles in the central Marches and mid-Wales area.[36] This also explains why Worcester was the last key Royal stronghold to continue the fight for the king.

In summary, the key siege in the study area – and the Civil War overall – was Gloucester. Regardless of whether or not a formal siege was the correct strategic and tactical decision to make, the Royalists made two critical tactical mistakes when conducting their siege. The first was conducting the mining operation. Their mining demonstrated that they failed to understand the low-lying nature of the landscape that Gloucester inhabits. The second major error was the Royalists' inability to use their artillery effectively, or lack of judgment in this field. By failing to conduct an efficient bombardment of the Roman and medieval walls, they were not able to capitalise on their advantage.

The failure to take Gloucester ultimately affected the Royalists' strategy, and was why they were unable to finish the war in 1643. It should be remembered that the reason the Royalists decided on the formal siege rather than to storm the town was because of the events at Bristol earlier in the year. By holding onto Gloucester, the Parliamentarians gave themselves a lifeline to hold onto, an ability to stay in the war.

Impact of Siege Warfare on the Individual

On 23 August 1645, Joshua Sprigg recorded that the artillery from the Royal Fort and Prior's Hill Fort targeted a number of dragoons, shooting off the leg of one. If a soldier's limb was too infected or damaged, it needed to be removed to stop sepsis. Before the operation, the patient would have been required to have a high-calorie diet, including eating yolks. Cleanliness was important for the operation. Two bone saws were required, in case one broke, as well as a variety of bandages and cloth buttons to seal blood vessels. A secure tourniquet would be applied and the flesh would be cut through with a potentially red-hot dismembering knife. Following this, the bone would be cut. An eschar would be encouraged to help the healing process. The blood vessels would either be clogged, cauterised or sutured. The use of a hot dismembering knife, along with antibacterial compounds such as vinegar, illustrates an understanding of infection. Despite this, without anaesthetics, the procedure was extremely dangerous.[37]

The close-combat nature of all of the sieges examined in the Severn Valley usually involved swords. Swords of low quality cut deeply into unprotected areas of the body, whilst high-quality blades could cut to the bone or sever limbs, a particular problem when facing cavalry as the blade would connect

36 Gaunt, *The English Civil War: A Military History*, pp. 222–23.

37 Stephen M. Rutherford, 'Ground-breaking pioneers or dangerous amateurs? Did early modern surgery have any basis in medical science?', in Ismini Pells (ed.), *New approaches to the military history of the English Civil War* (Solihull: Helion & Company Ltd, 2016), pp. 18–182.

with the soldier at significant speed. Surprisingly, the wound was usually left open to bleed. Allowing the wound to bleed does, in part, remove infectious elements from it. The wound would be kept open to air, with a small bandage to stop the sides meeting; the decision to close it would be made later. Closing the wound early, without modern antibiotics, could have led to sepsis; keeping it open would have allowed pus to help cleanse the wound. By not closing the wound early, medical practitioners understood the importance of infection, albeit bacteria would not be identified for another two centuries.[38]

Examining the impact of artillery shot and sword trauma is a reminder of the brutal impact that warfare has on individuals. Warfare necessitates improvements in medical science and battlefield trauma treatment. Statistics regarding the number of men, women and children killed or maimed as a result of the three Civil Wars vividly illustrate the impact of the conflict. The historian Charles Carlton has suggested that 84,738 people died as a direct result of combat. There were a further 100,000 indirect deaths, as a result of disease, for example. Moreover, there were 300 deaths caused by accidents, and some 500 people were killed during the Bishops' Wars that preceded the Civil War. This gives a total of 185,538. If this figure is rounded down to 180,000 and the country's population was reckoned to be approximately five million, this means that 3.6 percent of the nation were killed as a result of the English Civil War. To contextualise this, 2.6 percent were killed as a result of the First World War, and this figure falls to 0.6 percent for the Second World War.[39]

Theoretical Analysis

Throughout this book, reference has been made to the construction of defensive and offensive fortifications, along with the impact of a scorched-earth policy to prepare a field of fire and the psychological effects of siege warfare. The purpose of these references is to expand the discussion and fully encompass the effects of warfare on the individual and groups.

To start with, some facts might be examined:

> 241 homes in Gloucester were destroyed.
> Sconces, ditches and fortifications were constructed throughout the land.
> Human beings were maimed and killed.

On their own, these facts do not provide a great deal of information about the past. It is known that these events occurred, and there is enough historical information to account for them, but the historian needs to know more about them. Why were 241 homes destroyed in Gloucester? Why were all these fortifications constructed? Why were people attacking one another? There is a gulf, a gap, between the evidence that is available today – through

38 Rutherford, 'Ground-breaking pioneers or dangerous amateurs?', pp.168, 171–73.

39 Charles Carlton, 'The Impact of the Fighting', in John Morrill (ed.), *The Impact of the English Civil War* (London: Collins and Brown Limited, 1991), p. 20.

analysis of the evidence that has been examined in each chapter, each case study – and the past. An interest in the past is what shapes people to question and interrogate what is known, to find out more about what they think they know. When looking at the landscape and the surviving structures from the past, they are seeing them through modern eyes, not those of the people who constructed them and lived their lives in their shadow. The modern view of a castle, for instance, is very different to that of the medieval person who may have constructed it, lived inside it and died in it.[40]

In essence, before the 1960s, archaeology was concerned with culture history – the classification of artefacts, facts, data and their sequence. There was also the introduction of Marxist theories. From the 1960s onwards, there was the introduction of 'New Archaeology' or 'Processual Archaeology'. Essentially, this stressed the importance of a scientific approach: testing hypotheses about the past. This was followed by the feminist approach to archaeology, along with post-processualism. At a simplistic level, post-processualism rejects the purely scientific approach of processualism. Broadly, it focuses on meaning, how different people view the same thing differently, their thoughts and values, the individual, material culture and context.[41]

Deriving an approach from this, this examination will focus on material culture or materiality – the study of objects, and how those objects in turn make us and shape human experience.[42] Phenomenology – which involves looking at human behaviour, and how someone interacts with artefacts and buildings – will also be employed. By understanding their environment, it is hoped to gain a better comprehension of what motivated people in the past.[43]

The historical and archaeological record have revealed the effects of the scorched-earth policy at Worcester and Shrewsbury. One such example was the destruction of 241 homes in Gloucester, dated to 10 August 1643, to prevent the Royalists from using those buildings as cover on their approach to the town. The archaeological record illustrated evidence of burning and fallen masonry (p. 49). In these cases, the alteration and destruction of the urban landscape illustrates that the citizens involved were creating their own identity. Specifically, they were creating their own social identity. By altering the landscape, they were expressing their own political identity as a sign of resistance against the Royalists approaching their home.[44] The message of destroying one-third of the city to create a clear field of fire was a clear indication that the citizens were preparing for a long siege and the warfare to come.

---

40 Matthew Johnson, *Archaeological Theory: An Introduction* (Oxford: Blackwell Publishing, 1999), pp. 7, 14.

41 Clive Gamble, *Archaeology: The Basics* (London: Routledge, 2004), pp. 22, 30, 32; Johnson, *Archaeological Theory*, pp. 40, 102–07.

42 Daniel Miller, 'Materiality: An Introduction', in Daniel Miller (ed.), *Materiality* (Durham: Duke University Press), pp. 1–50; Lynn Meskell, *Object Worlds in Ancient Egypt: Material Biographies Past and Present* (Oxford: Berg, 2004), pp. 2, 4.

43 Bruce G. Trigger, *A History of Archaeological Thought* (New York: Cambridge University Press, 2006), pp. 472–73.

44 Wendy Ashmore and A. Bernard Knapp, 'Archaeological Landscapes: Constructed, Conceptualized, Ideational', in Wendy Ashmore and A. Bernard Knapp (eds), *Archaeologies of landscape: contemporary perspectives* (Oxford: Blackwell Publishers Ltd, 1999), pp. 14–15.

When examining the historical and archaeological evidence regarding the construction of ramparts, bastions, sconces, half-moons, ditches and numerous other types of fortifications, it can be seen that the building of these fortifications on the landscape took an immense amount of effort – mainly using pickaxes and shovels. When constructing the landscape, it is important to remember that people would have experienced numerous senses – visual, as well as sounds, smells and taste – that change and adapt to what people experience at particular moments.[45] An understanding of the senses can also be critically applied to the engagements of warfare. Some of the senses would have probably been overwhelmed: by the smell of smoke and sound from muskets and cannons, trying to hear orders from commanding officers, confusion and fear, the screams of individuals hit by shot, close combat with swords and moving through or over bastions and ramparts, including mounting scaling ladders. Similarly, the effect on the senses of a sapper or tunneller would have been profound, working underground in dark, hot and difficult conditions, particularly if they could hear the enemy working on a countermine.

By examining the consequences of warfare, namely the surgery required after being involved in combat during the 17th century, the intention of this study is to focus on the individual. Human beings today are a product of the post-medieval world and the technologies that now exist.[46] The surgery performed on an individual due to being hit by a musket ball or cannon shot was the direct result of another individual or individuals. It is necessary to recall that siege warfare and the methodologies employed had lasting impacts on the individuals who died, and those that survived, with or without any physical and/or mental issues that arose because of the conflict.

This is where the landscape, the setting of siege warfare, becomes one of transformation. The landscape itself was transformed.[47] The effects of these sieges changed the political and social maps of the country. The physical transformation was short-lived, as the majority of the fortifications were destroyed soon after the war. A record in the Gloucestershire Archives dating to 1653 illustrates the cost of removing some of the fortifications from the landscape:

> Charges for levelling the Sconce at Eastgate Total 4–13–2. [£–shillings–pence]
> Charges for levelling the Sconce at Southgate Total 8–1–6.
> Charges for levelling the Sconce at Northgate Total 13–13–0.
> Charges for levelling the Sconce at the Fryers Orchard Total 5–16–6.
> Charges for levelling the Sconce at St. Oswalds and making good the way Total 2–6–8.[48]

45 Timothy Darvill, 'The historic environment, historic landscapes, and space-time-action models in landscape archaeology', in Peter J. Ucko and Robert Layton (eds), *The Archaeology and Anthropology of landscape: shaping your landscape* (London: Routledge, 1999), p. 107.

46 Ian Hodder and Scott Hutson, *Reading the Past: Current Approaches to Interpretation in Archaeology* (Cambridge: Cambridge University Press, 2003), p. 99.

47 Ashmore and Bernard Knapp, 'Archaeological Landscapes', p. 18.

48 Gloucestershire Archives, Accounts (1635–1653), Reference: GBR GA F4/5 f.483–5.

The desire of the citizens of Gloucester in this case may have been to return the landscape to its previous state, attempting to remove the physical reminders of the war from their consciousness. The landscape is remade and the symbolic reminders of the past are removed.[49]

There were also attempts to rebuild and revise the landscape, such as the reconstruction of St Leonard's Church at Bridgnorth (Plate 29), as well as a statute of Charles II in St Mary's Square (Plate 30) in Gloucester, marking the return of the monarchy. The statue was originally positioned on Southgate Street on a corner of the Wheat Market.[50]

It is important to remember that the current dilapidated tower of Bridgnorth Castle is a product and a reaction to the events of the Civil War, not how the castle was left as a result of the 1646 siege. Looking at the remains of Bridgnorth Castle today, it is reminder of Britain's national identity.[51] The sounds of tunnelling, gun and cannon fire, the burning of the High Town and the men trapped inside the castle for three weeks are a distant memory, and whilst the reasons for slighting a castle can be complex, the role(s) of the castle that became home for the men under siege bombardment must continue to be reassessed.[52]

Looking again at the facts presented at the beginning of the section, it can be seen that these have taken on new meaning. By adding theory, the facts have become more evocative.[53] This improves the modern understanding of the events described, and why people did what they did at the time.

Summary

Looking at all the sieges of the study area together, it can be seen that all of the towns were dramatically affected by the conflict. Crucially, there is evidence of the construction of new defences and enhancement of the old. Looking at Worcester, redoubts, half-moons and sconces were constructed. Significant sums of money were provided for the building of the defences. A key element was the reuse of the medieval walls, being lined with earth, along with the re-cutting of the ditch. For Bristol, the construction of defences, particularly the surrounding hills to the north, and the defensive line were essential. If the defences had not been constructed on the nearby hills, these positions would have doubtless been used by enemy forces. At Gloucester, the construction of new defences can be seen, along with the incorporation of existing medieval and Roman features. At Shrewsbury, there were modifications to the medieval castle, along with a new wall at Roushill, a timber watchtower and a sconce at Frankwell. Finally, Bridgnorth witnessed the re-cutting of the medieval ditch, along with the construction of defences at the North Gate.

49 Ashmore and Bernard Knapp, 'Archaeological Landscapes', p. 19.

50 Atkin and Laughlin, *Gloucester and the Civil War: a city under siege*, p. 159.

51 Matthew Johnson, *Ideas of Landscape* (Oxford: Blackwell Publishing Ltd, 2007), p. 23.

52 Lila Rakoczy, *Archaeology of Destruction: A Reinterpretation of Castle Slightings in the English Civil War* (Unpublished PhD: University of York, 2007), p. 265; Johnson, *Archaeological Theory: An Introduction*, p. 160.

53 Johnson, *Archaeological Theory: An Introduction*, p. 7.

Plate 29 The rebuilt St Leonard's Church, Bridgnorth (facing north-east). (Author's photo)

Plate 30 A statue of Charles II, illustrating the restored Monarchy at Gloucester (facing west-north-west). (Author's photo)

A key aspect of this study is the evidence regarding the removal of suburbs, beginning with outside of the medieval city walls. Although there is evidence of some destruction at Bristol – for example the windmill at Windmill Hill – the towns of Gloucester and Worcester were more dramatically affected. The destruction of houses and industries would have displaced numerous people. There was also the destruction of property at Frankwell and Abbey Foregate in Shrewsbury. Although not by design, the loss of the majority of the High Town in Bridgnorth due to a fire was caused directly by the Civil War and would have had a devastating impact on the population. The impact was seen for years to come, as a rent record dating to 1670 at Worcester notes that "all the houses without st martyns Gate were Bruned Down or Destroyed in the tyme of the Late unhappy warre".[54]

As the long-term effects of siege warfare on the Severn Valley case studies are seen, it is important to reflect and compare them to other actions around the country. The events at Colchester in 1648 illustrated that it was possible to construct something representing a line of circumvallation. This, however, was only possible once the main war of 1642–46 was over, and Parliament was consequently able to deploy more resources, men and equipment to this task.

By focusing on the individual, the long-term effects of siege warfare are clear to see. The sights, tastes, sounds and smells from warfare are apparent, and add elements to improve the understanding of what it must have been like experiencing warfare. The decisions made to remove the fortifications and features from the landscape so soon after the war had ended are a reminder of the effect of war on people and places.

The short two-day siege of Worcester in 1643 was unsuccessful for two reasons. The first was the ineffective artillery barrage: an artillery train of only eight cannons appears to have been insufficient. The second reason for its failure was the tactics employed by the Royalists, in particular the cavalry charge from St Martin's Gate. The combination of poor artillery fire and the cavalry charge was enough for the Parliamentarian siege to end in defeat.

The Royalists followed a similar approach to the Parliamentarians in their successful attempt to capture the city of Bristol. Their tactics were to storm the city, rather than have a prolonged formal siege. Whilst they only brought a small artillery train, it included two demi-cannons – siege-specific pieces. Although the Parliamentarians had 96 artillery pieces, these consisted mainly of sakers, minions and robinets – light field weapons. Another double-edged sword was the landscape the Parliamentarians were required to defend. The creation of a 3-mile (4.82km) defensive circuit lined with forts, and occupying the surrounding high ground, was necessary, but also problematic. A combination of not enough troops and lack of the necessary weapons and morale caused the city to surrender to the Royalists.

The bloodshed at Bristol resulted in a change of tactics at Gloucester. However, the Royalists' formal siege approach, which included saps and mining, was here too slow regarding the artillery barrage. In addition, a stout

54 The Hive, Worcestershire, The Present Rents 1670 Reference: BA36174.

defence from the outnumbered Parliamentarians, and the failure to complete a line of circumvallation or monitor the approach of a relief army, meant that the siege was unsuccessful.

The successful siege of Shrewsbury by the Parliamentarians was resulted from a tactic that was new in the Severn Valley region; they took the Royalists, and the city, by surprise. They combined this with good reconnaissance and the identification of a weak spot in the defences, although the medieval castle and the newly constructed sconce at Frankwell held out for as long as possible.

Turning to the second siege of Bristol, the Parliamentarians employed the same tactics as the Royalists had in 1643 – the storm approach. Like the Royalists, they were successful in their approach. Despite two years of work on the fortifications, the Royalists were unable to hold onto Bristol, and the city was returned to the hands of the Parliamentarians. Neither side defending the city could have held onto it without a significant increase in resources, men and equipment.

When examining the siege of Bridgnorth, the Royalists made additions to the town with the construction of new fortifications, and clearance of some buildings to create an effective field of fire. Despite this, the town was overrun and the surviving Royalists retreated to the castle. Rather than storm the castle, the Parliamentarians began to conduct a formal siege. Crucially, most of the High Town was destroyed in a fire. The bombardment of the castle by artillery, and the psychological impact of the excavation of a deep mine, forced the Royalists to surrender the castle after holding out for three weeks.

The final siege at Worcester followed the successes of Parliamentarian troops at Shrewsbury, Bristol and Bridgnorth. Formal siege tactics were again used. This included the construction of seven artillery positions. There was also the partial construction of a line of circumvallation, from north to south via the east. The long-term effects of bombardment, combined with failing food supplies and lack of morale, eventually led to the Royalists inside the city surrendering. The Parliamentarian besiegers had the ability to wait and see the food supplies dwindle in the city, which caused unrest and infighting among the defenders. The overall approach of cutting off supplies was similar to that of the Syracusan tyrant Dionysius I when he attempted (unsuccessfully on that occasion) to capture Rhegium in southern Italy in 391 BC.[55]

55 Nossov, *Ancient and Medieval Siege Weapons*, p. 255.

Chapter 5

Conclusion

The English Civil War was an overarching battle for nationhood and the right to determine who governs whom. Following Charles I's theatrical raising of the standard at Nottingham on 22 August 1642, the race was on to secure towns and cities throughout the country to provide each side with the necessary resources, equipment and men. Following the indecisive first major battle of the war at Edgehill on 23 October 1642, and despite Worcester and Bristol changing hands, the Royalists controlled Shrewsbury, Worcester and Bridgnorth heading into 1643, whilst Parliament held Bristol and Gloucester.

Strategy

Parliament began on the offensive in 1643; however, it failed to capture Worcester. The Royalists then focused on the south of the Severn Valley, including Bristol. Their successful siege of Bristol meant that only Gloucester then stood in the way of the Royalists' domination of the Severn Valley.

The failure of the Royalists to take Gloucester was a critical point in the war, as well as for the region. In time, this allowed the Parliamentarians to implement their own strategy. Turning to 1645, the Parliamentarians focused on the north and south of the study area. Firstly, they captured Shrewsbury, soon followed by Bristol. This left the Royalists still holding only two major towns in the area, Bridgnorth and Worcester.

By having the ability to focus on the pockets of Royalist resistance, first overcoming Bridgnorth and then Worcester, Parliament was able to present its terms to the king. Holding sway in the Severn Valley region meant having control over the supply of gunnery tools and swords from Shrewsbury, bullets from Bridgnorth, gunpowder from Worcester and the manufacturing hubs of Gloucester and Bristol, in addition to the strategically important road and river networks. All this ensured that Parliament was also in control of the war.

All the towns of this case study were strategically important because of the positions they occupied along the River Severn, with the exception of Bristol, which had the River Avon. The rivers, along with the road network, were essential for the transportation of supplies, communication and troops.

Tactics – Defensive

For each siege, the besieged employed a variety of tactics. The key tactics and their effects are summarised below.

Reuse of Medieval Castles, Walls and Ditches

For all of the case studies, it was logical to reuse existing features that could have provided some form of defence against the artillery of the age. The medieval castles at Bristol, Shrewsbury and Bridgnorth were refurbished and occupied. As the evidence has demonstrated, the castles at Bridgnorth and Shrewsbury were able to withstand, respectively, assaults from an artillery bombardment and a surprise storm. The tactical decision of the Parliamentarians to position a good portion of their artillery in the castle during the 1643 siege of Bristol appears to have been a mistake; however, that decision should be considered as part of the overall ineffective use of artillery at that siege.

The medieval walls – particularly of Worcester, Gloucester (including the Roman wall) and the Portwall of Bristol – did actually offer significant resistance to the sieges. There was success for the defenders at Worcester in 1643 and at the section between East Gate and South Gate at Gloucester in the same year, while neither side was able to breach the southern defences of Bristol in 1643 or 1645. The lining of the walls with earth, and the success of those features, was despite the engineer David Papillon's statement that this would offer no protection from cannon fire,[1] as well as Robert Ward highlighting "the imperfections of our walled Townes here in England" and "that we may not bee deceived in putting our confidence in the strength of them".[2] The tactical theories presented in the military manuals of the period in relation to the reuse of medieval walls for defending a town can thus be seriously questioned. Whilst the archaeological evidence of 38–44 Eastgate Street at Gloucester shows that 17th century artillery was able to penetrate a medieval tower, the walls of medieval castles such as that at Bridgnorth do not appear to have succumbed to a large and sustained artillery bombardment, illustrating their effectiveness against the weapon.

The evidence has shown that the time and effort put into recutting medieval ditches would have provided some defence against troops storming the towns. This tactic was employed at Bridgnorth and Gloucester. At Gloucester, the Gooseditch was re-cut and drained of water. Tactically, this presents an interesting premise. Corbet states that the main ditches contained water, and that the Dutch favoured wet ditches, and evidence from the state of the ditch of Worcester in 1643 suggests that sections of it would have been boggy. However, Fabrizio in Machiavelli's *The Art of War* says that a ditch should be dry. As the ditch was in front of a Roman wall at Gloucester, the

1 Papillon, *A practicall abstract of the arts of fortification*, pp.11–12.
2 Ward, *Animadversions of Warre*, p. 55.

decision to keep it dry could have been made to ensure that the wall did not sink or collapse. It therefore appears that whether or not the ditch was wet remained a matter for individual engineers' judgment.

Scorched-Earth Policy

It has been seen that the scorched-earth policy to create a field of fire was used throughout the case studies, but most prominently at Gloucester, Worcester and Shrewsbury. The *Chamber Order Book of Worcester* records the names of individuals and the property they lost through this stratagem. The recording of names makes the impact of this policy more tangible. Historical evidence is backed up by archaeological finds through a thin layer of burning at Southgate Street in Gloucester, giving a date of 10 August 1643, indicating the removal of the suburbs in tandem with the creation of the field of fire. Another example was the destruction of property at Frankwell in Shrewsbury to make way for a new sconce-style fortification.

New Fortifications

The construction of earthen fortifications was obviously not a new invention; indeed, as has been seen, large-scale earthworks were used by the Persians around 497 BC during their siege of Paphos in Cyprus. What was new was the large-scale use of the *Trace Italienne* style of fortification, or at least attempts to mirror it. This was referenced in the military manuals of Henry Hexham, who in 1637 wrote *The Principles of the Art Militarie; practised in the warres of the Vnited Netherlands*, and Robert Ward's 1639 work titled *Animadversions of Warre; or, A militarie magazine of the truest rules, and ablest instructions, for the managing of warre*, to give but two examples.

The earliest fortifications constructed in the Severn Valley study area were in Worcester by the Parliamentarians in 1643. Documentary evidence records the construction of half-moons and a sconce and redoubt. Unfortunately, there is no surviving description of the dimensions of the fortifications, although according to the military manuals, such as that of Robert Ward, half-moons in particular should have been constructed *in addition* to main segments of the fortification, such as bastions.

The first evidence that details specific dimensions comes from the engineer Bernard de Gomme, after the Royalists' successful siege of Bristol in 1643. Whilst mindful regarding the amount of weight that should be given to this source, the fortifications around the northern circuit do not conform to the measurements given in the military manuals. However, it must be remembered that the reality of war, and what can be accomplished, is different to what can be theorised on paper. It has been seen how the topography instigated the need to construct fortifications encompassing hills to the north of the city, and that the geology had an effect on the size of the ditches that were constructed. The importance of combining and examining all available documentary documents has been stressed, as Samuel Fawcett's list of artillery made on 28 July 1643 is the only contemporary source that survives referring to fortifications "Over the Bridge".

The lining of walls with earth is seen through the documentary sources of Corbet, Dorney and Backhouse, and analysis of the cartographic source Plan D 12862. Whilst military engineers and theorists such as Papillon and Ward would have argued against this tactic, the evidence of a successful defence illustrates that it did disrupt and slow the Royalists' advance at Gloucester. There was also the construction of bastions by Captain Singleton, and underneath the site of the former castle. Archaeological evidence revealed the construction of a defensive ditch some 10m in width on Southgate Street. The documentary evidence of maids running to obtain turf to support the earthworks illustrates an understanding and appreciation of 17th century military theory.

The evidence from Shrewsbury in 1645 has demonstrated a variety of new features, including palisades, a watchtower, a sconce at Frankwell and a new wall at Roushill. A combination of historical, cartographic and archaeological evidence has highlighted the wall at Roushill, which completed the circuit of riverside defences. The construction of a sconce on the high ground illustrates the use of modern theories. However, the erection of palisades, without the addition of earthworks near the castle, was a fatal flaw in the defence of Shrewsbury, as demonstrated by how quickly the town fell to the Parliamentarians.

Returning to Bristol, and after two years of work by the Royalists under the supervision of the engineer Bernard de Gomme, it is seen from his own account that the fortifications of the city were not of a sufficiently high standard. This is despite the archaeological evidence from the Royal Fort demonstrating that the ditch was cut 2.5m into natural geology, and at one section was 11–12m in width, with a bastion 12m in length. However, this bastion is significantly shorter than the 93¼ yards (85.3m) suggested by Richard Norwood in his 1639 manual *Fortification or Military Architecture*.

The addition of new fortifications at Bridgnorth was small in scale, but the evidence indicates that the new earthworks outside the North Gate were able to hold back the approach of the Parliamentarians for a limited time.

The evolution of the fortifications at Worcester appears from the cartographic and archaeological information to be impressive. Whilst questions marks exist over the placement of two bastions – namely 'The Butts Bastion' and the 'bastion at The Butts/Farrier Street' – due to their close proximity, a significant amount of time and resources were channelled into their construction. This included the reworking of the fortifications at Fort Royal Hill into the sconce, along with the excavation of an important ditch at The Butts, some 16m wide, surpassing the literary recommendations of Robert Ward. Archaeology has also illuminated the defences constructed on Severn Street, including a glacis, palisades, stakes and a significant ditch.

The immense of amount of work that was invested in the construction of new fortifications throughout the Severn Valley area has been seen. Whilst some fortifications were constructed that matched, and even surpassed, the idealised versions set out in the military manuals of the period, the evidence has illustrated that, by and large, people constructed what fortifications they could with the resources available. The realities of war always reveal clear differences from the written and illustrative works available.

Countermines

The Persians were recorded as having effectively used mining, and it was a common theme of medieval warfare. The evidence for countermines in this study comes from Gloucester. The use of countermining, whilst causing tactical problems for the Royalists, was halted due to problems with the high water table and the local geology.

Tactics – Offensive

Moving from the defensive tactics employed, it is now time to summarise the evidence there is for offensive works and operations during the sieges in the Severn Valley.

New Fortifications

The first substantial Civil War siegeworks in the Severn Valley were constructed at Gloucester by the Royalists in their unsuccessful siege of 1643. The historical record reveals the construction of entrenchments near Gawdy Green and Issold's House, to the south and east of the city respectively, between the defensive gates of South Gate and East Gate. However, there is no precise information regarding the dimensions of these fortifications for comparison to the military manuals of the period.

At Bridgnorth there was the reuse of a ringwork and bailey of an earlier 12th century fortification, along with the construction of a new position on a mound immediately south of this feature. The sites were chosen because they occupy high ground. The archaeological evidence from the mound indicates the construction of raised banks to protect the artillery inside. Further investigations of both sites could provide valuable information in relation to the 1646 siege.

The evidence from Worcester illustrates that there were seven siegeworks constructed during the 1646 siege. There is also evidence of siege lines between Perry Wood Hill and Red Hill Cross. The siegework at Tamar Close requires further investigation to understand its construction. Most interestingly, there are no complete lines of circumvallation or contravallation. There is certainly no evidence of siegeworks in any of the case studies to match the scale of those at the siege of Alesia conducted by Julius Caesar in 52 BC.

Saps

The archaeological evidence of approaches in the form of saps comes from Gloucester, where a steep-sided 1m × 1m feature was excavated at Southgate Street. The evidence discovered provides a real, tangible link to the past. It also illustrates that the sap followed, or at least appeared to follow, the guidelines seen in Henry Hexham's manual that such a work should be cut to a depth of 3ft (0.91m).

Mines

The use of mines was seen at Gloucester and Bridgnorth. Turning to Gloucester first, although mining was employed, it was stopped – like the countermining – due to the geology. The use of mining appears to have been a tactical mistake here, as the operation was too slow; because of the geology, this tactic was never going to be an effective approach.

Conversely, the use of a mine at Bridgnorth effectively brought the siege to a quick conclusion. Despite the fact that it was 34ft (10.36m) below the surface, the psychological effect on the Royalists holed up in the castle meant that it brought their resistance to an early conclusion. It is important to remember, however, that the conditions for those excavating the mine would have been extremely difficult.

Scaling Ladders

The use of scaling ladders is one of the oldest tactics in warfare. They were employed effectively at Shrewsbury in 1645. However, that same year at Bristol, the Parliamentarians storming the city did not appreciate the size of the fortification at Prior's Hill Fort, and brought ladders that were too short. This led to harder fighting at this position and was a tactical mistake by the Parliamentarians.

Approach

Maurice of Nassau

The evidence has demonstrated that the Parliamentarians employed the siege techniques of Maurice of Nassau during their 1646 siege of Worcester. This was executed within their overall strategy by controlling the surrounding landscapes to organise a formal siege, rather than conduct a battle.

Gustavus Adolphus

Prince Rupert employed the techniques of Gustavus Adolphus at Bristol, particularly with the early assault, and also attempted to employ the Swede's siege methods at Gloucester. Gustavus Adolphus relied heavily on bombardment during sieges. This was a tactical mistake by the Royalists

– they were unable to effectively bombard the artillery positions and walls manned by the Parliamentarians. This mistake ultimately cost the Royalists the chance to finish the war in their favour in 1643.

Impact of Artillery

Substitute missiles or arrows for cannon shot, and the basics of siege warfare had not changed for centuries. The introduction of artillery was not a military revolution, but the response to this new weapon was only gradual in the style of fortification. As has been seen, the stone-built medieval castles of Shrewsbury and Bridgnorth were able to withstand artillery bombardment – particularly at the latter.

The five tables and information set out in the Introduction to this study are a reminder of the importance of artillery during the Civil War. Those who disregard the importance of this weapon clearly do not understand the period. However, what is so striking from the sieges in the Severn Valley region – both from the perspective of the besieged at Worcester and Bristol in 1643, and of the besiegers at Gloucester a few months later and at Bridgnorth in 1646 – is how ineffective both sides were at using artillery.

If the Parliamentarians had organised a better bombardment of the southern defences of Worcester in 1643, they may have been able to retake the city. However, their ineffective bombardment meant that a Royalist cavalry charge was able to repel their assault.

The realities of war have been discussed in relation to the construction of new fortifications, and have been borne in mind when examining the use of artillery. Nonetheless, at Bristol, the Parliamentarians had 96 cannons of a variety of sizes located throughout the city, but they did not use them effectively.

The worst tactical mistake during the sieges in the Severn Valley, and indeed of the war as a whole, was that the Royalists only fired 17 shots per day when besieging Gloucester, when theoretically they could have fired 100. This was the opposite of the heavy bombardment advocated by Gustavus Adolphus. Consequently, by ineffectively using their artillery, the Royalists lost the war.

Approach of Landscape Archaeology Methodology

As referenced throughout this chapter, and the book as a whole, the use of landscape archaeology has been vital to uncovering more about the sieges in the Severn Valley. The importance of understanding and appreciating geology has been abundantly clear when taking a look at the fortifications constructed at Bristol in relation to the defences, and the decision to storm the city rather than conduct a formal siege. Its critical influence on warfare has also been seen at Gloucester and with the mining at Bridgnorth.

An understanding of the topography has explained why the decision was made to fortify the hills surrounding Bristol to the north. It also accounts for the siegeworks at Bridgnorth, and the need to construct fortifications at Fort Royal Hill and the various siegeworks at Worcester. The importance of an area's topography can never be underestimated.

The cartographic sources have been invaluable in this study. Whether looking at the evidence for the fortifications at Gloucester or for the construction of the wall at Roushill in Shrewsbury, these sources provide another method to better understand the landscape.

Historical written accounts have shown their obvious importance, but have also served as a reminder to interrogate and reassess the narrative they present. Finally, the archaeological evidence has provided tangible links to the past, whether the evidence of the burning of the suburbs of Gloucester on 10 August 1643 or the reinterpretation of the extant feature at Brandon Hill in Bristol; further excavations should continue to reveal valuable information.

However, it is only through the combination of all of these methodologies that a full appreciation can be gained of the impact of siege warfare, in relation to the Civil War and other conflicts. The influence of the sieges in the Severn Valley clearly affected the outcome of the English Civil War. That outcome changed the direction of the whole country, going far beyond the walls of Shrewsbury, Bridgnorth, Worcester, Gloucester and Bristol.

Bibliography

Articles and Books

Anonymous, *A copie of the articles agreed upon at the surrender of the city of Bristol* (London: 1643).

Anonymous, *A true and full relation of the manner and taking of the towne and castle of Shrewsbury* (London: 1644).

Anonymous, *The Garrisons of Shropshire, During the Civil War, 1642–48* (Shrewsbury: Leake and Evans, 1867).

Ashmore, Wendy and Bernard Knapp, A., 'Archaeological Landscapes: Constructed, Conceptualized, Ideational', in Wendy Ashmore and A. Bernard Knapp (eds), *Archaeologies of landscape: contemporary perspectives* (Oxford: Blackwell Publishers Ltd, 1999), pp. 1–32.

Atkin, Malcolm, 'Excavations in Gloucester, 1988', *Glevensis*, Vol. 23 (1988), pp. 2–11.

Atkin, Malcolm, *Trial Excavations on the Bank of England site, Southgate Street, Gloucester, 1988: An Interim Report* (Unpublished Report: Gloucester Excavations Unit, 1988).

Atkin, Malcolm, 'Excavations in Gloucester 1989 – An Interim Report', *Glevensis*, Vol. 24 (1990), pp. 2–7.

Atkin, Malcolm, 'David Papillon and the Civil War Defences of Gloucester', *Transactions of the Bristol and Gloucestershire Archaeological Society*, Vol. 111 (1993), pp. 147–64.

Atkin, Malcolm, *The Civil War in Worcestershire* (Stroud: Alan Sutton Publishing Ltd, 1995).

Atkin, Malcolm, *Worcestershire under Arms: an English County During the Civil Wars* (Barnsley: Pen & Sword Ltd, 2004).

Atkin, Malcolm, *Worcester 1651* (Barnsley: Pen & Sword Books Ltd, 2008).

Atkin, Malcolm and Howes, Russell, 'The use of archaeology and documentary sources in identifying the Civil War defences of Gloucester', *Post-Medieval Archaeology*, Vol. 27 (1993), pp. 15–41.

Atkin, Malcolm and Laughlin, Wayne, *Gloucester and the Civil War: a city under siege* (Stroud: Alan Sutton Publishing Ltd, 1992).

Backhouse, Captain, 'A true relation of a wicked plot intended and still on for against the city of Glocester to betray the same into the hands of the Cavaliers' (1644), in J. Washborn (ed.), *Bibliotheca Gloucestrensis* (Gloucester: J. Washborn, 1825), pp. 283–324.

Baker, Nigel, *Shrewsbury: an archaeological assessment of an English border town* (Oxford: Oxbow Books, 2010).

Baker, Nigel, Brett, Jonathan and Jones, Robert (eds), *Bristol: A Worshipful Town and Famous City: An Archaeological Assessment* (Oxford: Oxbow Books, 2018).

Baker, Nigel and Holt, Richard, *Urban Growth and the Medieval Church: Gloucester and Worcester* (Aldershot: Ashgate Publishing Ltd, 2004).

Barker, Philip, 'The Origins of Worcester', *Transactions of the Worcestershire Archaeological Society*, Vol. 2 (1968/1969).

Barker, Philip A., 'Excavations on the Town Wall, Roushill, Shrewsbury', *Medieval Archaeology*, Vol. 5 (1961), pp. 181–210.

Barratt, John, *Sieges of the English Civil War* (Barnsley: Pen & Sword Books Ltd, 2009).

Barratt, William, *The history and antiquities of the city of Bristol* (Bristol: William Pine, 1789).

Beardsmore, Clive, 'Documentary Evidence for the History of Worcester City Defences', in M.O.H. Carver (ed.), 'Medieval Worcester: an archaeological framework: reports, surveys texts and essays', *Transactions of the Worcestershire Archaeological Society* (3rd Series) Vol. 7 (1980), pp. 53–64.

Bellett, George, *The Antiquities of Bridgnorth* (Bridgnorth: W.J. Rowley, 1856).

Bishop, Jeff, *Bristol through Maps: Ways of Seeing a City* (Bristol: Redcliffe Press Ltd, 2016).

Black, Jeremy, *Fortifications and Siegecraft: Defense and Attack through the Ages* (London: The Rowman & Littlefield Publishing Group, Inc., 2018).

Blackmore, David J., *Arms and Armour of the English Civil Wars* (London: The Trustees of the Royal Armouries, 1990).

Bond, Shelagh (ed.), *The Chamber Order Book of Worcester 1602–1650* (Leeds: The Worcestershire Historical Society, 1974).

Bourne, William, *The arte of shooting in great Ordnaunce* (London: Thomas Woodcocke, 1587).

Bracher, Terry and Emmett, Roger, *Shropshire in the Civil War* (Shrewsbury: Shropshire Books, 2000).

Bradbury, Jim, *The Medieval Siege* (Woodbridge: The Boydell Press, 1992).

Breeze, David John, *Roman Forts in Britain* (Oxford: Shire Publications Ltd, 2002).

Breeze, David John, *The Roman Army* (London: Bloomsbury, 2016).

Brett, Mark, *Gloscat Gloucester Archaeological Evaluation* (Unpublished Report No. 06022: Cotswold Archaeology, 2006).

Brown, T.M. and Watson, Michael D., 'The Civil War Roushill Wall, Shrewsbury', *Transactions of the Shropshire Archaeological and Historical Society*, Vol. 66 (1989), pp. 85–89.

Bryant, John, *Archaeological Evaluation of Park Row and Woodland Road, Clifton, Bristol* (Unpublished Report: Bristol and Region Archaeological Services, 1994).

Bull, Stephen, *The Furie of the Ordnance: Artillery in the English Civil Wars* (Woodbridge: The Boydell Press, 2008).

Buteux, Victoria, with contributions by Derek Hurst, Richard Morriss, Elizabeth Pearson and Paul Stamper, *Archaeological assessment of Bridgnorth, Shropshire* (Extensive Urban Survey – The Central Marches Historic Towns Survey 1992–6, 1996).

Caesar, Julius, *The Gallic War*, edited and translated by Carolyn Hammond (Oxford: Oxford University Press, 2008).

Carlton, Charles, 'The Impact of the Fighting', in John Morrill (ed.), *The Impact of the English Civil War* (London: Collins and Brown Limited, 1991), pp. 17–31.

Carlton, Charles, *Going to the Wars: The Experience of the British Civil Wars 1638–1651* (London: Routledge, 1992).

Champion, W.A. and Coulton, Barbara, with contributions by James Lawson, 'Shrewsbury 1640–1780', in W.A. Champion and A.T. Thacker (eds), *The Victoria History of the Counties of England. A History of Shropshire Volume VI, Part I* (Woodbridge: The Boydell Press, 2014), pp. 180–230.

Corbet, John, *An Historicall relation of the military government of Gloucester: from the beginning of the Civill Warre betweene King and Parliament to the removal of Colonell Massie from that Government to the command of the Westerne Forces* (London: Robert Bostock, 1645).

Corbet, John, 'An Historicall relation of the military government of Gloucester: from the beginning of the Civill Warre betweene King and Parliament to the removal of Colonell Massie from that Government to the command of the Westerne Forces' (1645), in J. Washborn (ed.), *Bibliotheca Gloucestrensis* (Gloucester: J. Washborn, 1825), pp. 1–152.

Cornes, Richard, 'A short topographical account of Bridgnorth in the county of Salop', *Transactions of the Shropshire Archaeological and Natural History Society*, Vol. 9 (1886) pp. 193–210.

Dalwood, Hal, *Desk-Based Assessment of Sainsbury's Supermarket Site, The Smithfield, Bridgnorth, Shropshire* (Unpublished Report: Worcestershire County Council, 2007).

Daly, Tegan, *St Leonard's Church Bridgnorth, Shropshire Archaeological Watching Brief* (Unpublished Report: Headland Archaeology Ltd, 2012).

Darvill, Timothy, 'The historic environment, historic landscapes, and space-time-action models in landscape archaeology', in Peter J. Ucko and Robert Layton (eds), *The Archaeology and Anthropology of landscape: shaping your landscape* (London: Routledge, 1999), pp. 104–18.

Day, Jon, *Gloucester & Newbury 1643: The Turning Point of the Civil War* (Barnsley: Pen & Sword Books Ltd, 2007).

De Gomme, Bernard, 'The State and condition of the Line of fortifications about the City of Bristoll, as likewise of the great Fort (as appeares by the subscriptions of the Engineers, who had taken an exact survey of them were as followes)', in *A Declaration Of His Highnesse Prince RUPERT* (1645), pp. 9–10.

De Gomme, Bernard (Charles Firth and J.H. Leslie (eds)), 'The Siege and Capture of Bristol by the Royalist Forces in 1643', *Journal of Army Historical Research*, Vol. 4 (1925), pp. 180–203.
Dinn, James, 'News from City', *Worcestershire Recorder* (Newsletter from the Worcestershire Archaeological Society, Edition 86, Autumn 2012), p. 5.
Dorney, John, 'A briefe and exact relation of the most materiall and remarkeable passages that hapned in the late well-formed (and as valiently defended) siege laid before the city of Glocester' (1643), in J. Washborn (ed.), *Bibliotheca Gloucestrensis* (Gloucester: J. Washborn, 1825), pp. 205–32.
Duffy, Christopher, *Siege Warfare: The Fortress in the Early Modern World 1494–1600* (London: Routledge & Kegan Paul Ltd, 1979).
Eldred, William, *The Gunners Glasse* (London: Robert Boydel, 1646).
Ellis, Henry, 'Letters from a subaltern officer of the Earl of Essex's army, written in the summer and autumn of 1642; detailing the early movements of that portion of the Parliament forces which was formed by the volunteers of the metropolis; and their further movements when amalgamated with the rest of the Earl of Essex's troops', *Archaeologia*, Vol. 35 (1853), pp. 310–34.
Ellis, John, *'To walk in the dark': Military Intelligence during the English Civil War 1642–1646* (Stroud: The History Press, 2011).
Flintham, David, 'They have sent to Holland for Engineers', in Serena Jones (ed.), *'Britain Turned Germany: The Thirty Years' War and its impact on the British Isles, 1638–1660*, Proceedings of the Helion and Company 'Century of the Soldier' Conference (Warwick: Helion & Company Ltd, 2019), pp. 89–121.
Gamble, Clive, *Archaeology: The Basics* (London: Routledge, 2004).
Garrod, Anthony P., *Inner Relief Road Bruton Way to London Road Junction Gloucester Site 23/1982* (Gloucester City Historic Environment Record Entry, 1982).
Garrod, Anthony P., '31 Parliament Street, Gloucester', *Glevensis*, Vol. 19 (1985), p. 47.
Gaunt, Peter, *The English Civil Wars 1642–51* (Oxford: Osprey Publishing Ltd, 2003).
Gaunt, Peter, *The English Civil War: A Military History* (London: I.B. Tauris & Co Ltd, 2014).
GSB Prospection, *Bridgnorth, Shropshire: geophysical survey* (Unpublished Report: 2000/109 Bridgnorth Shropshire, 2000).
Hale, John Rigby, 'The early development of the bastion: an Italian Chronology *c.* 1450–*c.*1534', in John Rigby Hale, John Roger Loxdale Highfield and Beryl Smalley (eds), *Europe in the late Middle Ages* (London: Faber and Faber, 1965), pp. 466–94.
Hannaford, H.R., *Shrewsbury Town Walls: A Conservation Management Plan* (Unpublished Report: Shropshire Council, 2015).
Hardwicke, William, 'Collections for a History of Bridgnorth, Salop', a MS by William Hardwicke, annotated by Wilfred Watkins-Pitchford, *Transactions of the Shropshire Archaeological Society*, Vol. 49 (2) (1938), pp. 189–216.
Harrington, Peter, *Archaeology of the English Civil War* (Princes Risborough: Shire Publications Ltd, 1992).
Harrington, Peter, *English Civil War Fortifications 1642–51* (Oxford: Osprey Publishing Ltd, 2003).
Haslam, Jeremy, 'The articulation of burgages and streets in early medieval towns, part 1: the case of Bridgnorth, Shropshire', *Landscape History*, Vol. 37 (1) (2016), pp. 51–68.
Hayes, Laurence, *Premier Inn Shrewsbury Archaeological Excavation Report* (Unpublished Report: SLR, 2012).
Heighway, Carolyn, *The East and North Gates of Gloucester and Associated Sites Excavations 1974–81* (Bristol: Western Archaeological Trust, 1983).
Henry, Chris, *English Civil War Artillery 1642–51* (Oxford: Osprey Publishing Ltd, 2005).
Hexham, Henry, *The Principles of the Art Militarie; practised in the warres of the Vnited Netherlands* (London: M.P. for Matthew Symmons, 1637).
Hexham, Henry, 'The Second Part of The Principles of the Art Militarie, Practised In the Warres of the United Provinces: Consisting of the severall formes of battell, represented by the illustrious Maurice Prince of Orange, of famous memorie, and his highnesse Frederick Henrie Prince of Orange that now is, Lord Generall of the Armie of the high & mightie lords the States Generall, of the United Netherlands, &c. Together with the order, and forme of quartering, encamping, and approching in a warre offensive, and defensive', in *The Principles of the Art Militarie; practised in the warres of the Vnited Netherlands* (London: Printed by Robert Young, at the signe of the Starre upon Bread-street-hill, 1639), pp. 1–40.
Hexham, Henry, 'The Third Part of The Principles of the Art Militarie practised in the warres of the United Provinces, vnder the lords the States Generall, and his Highnesse the Prince

of Orange, treating of severall peeces of ordnance, carriages, engines, quadrants, morters, petards, as also instructions for master gunners, and canoniers, with diverse instruments, and materials belonging to a warre with their severall vses, and practises most briefly, and lively demonstrated by letter and figure. Together with a list of all necessarie preparations, appertayning to an armie, with a quarter for the generall of the ordnance, and of all officers belonging to his traine', in *The Principles of the Art Militarie; practised in the warres of the Vnited Netherlands* (Hagh: Printed by Francis vander Spruyt, 1640), pp. 1–82.

Hexham, Henry, *The Third Part of the Principles of the Art Military practised in the warres of the United Provinces vnder the Lords the States Generall and His Highnesse the Prince of Orange* (Rotterdam: Printed by James Moxon, 1643).

Hislop, Malcolm, *Castle Builders: Approaches to Castle Design and Construction in the Middle Ages* (Barnsley: Pen & Sword Books Ltd, 2016).

Hodder, Ian, and Hutson, Scott, *Reading the Past: Current Approaches to Interpretation in Archaeology* (Cambridge: Cambridge University Press, 2003).

Hoskins, Peter, *Siege Warfare During the Hundred Years War 'Once More unto the Breach…'* (Barnsley: Pen & Sword Books Ltd, 2018).

Hosler, John D., *The Siege of Acre 1189–1191: Saladin, Richard the Lionheart and the Battle that Decided the Third Crusade* (London: Yale University Press, 2018).

Howes, R., *Weekly Intelligence from Severall parts of this Kingdome, and other places, from the 10 of Octob. to the 18.* (London: 1642).

Hughes, Quentin, *Military Architecture* (London: Hugh Evelyn Ltd, 1974).

Insoll, Allan N., with additions by Robert Jones, 'Chapter 2: The setting of Bristol: its geology and topography; deposit model', in Nigel Baker, Jonathan Brett and Robert Jones (eds), *Bristol: A Worshipful Town and Famous City: An Archaeological Assessment* (Oxford: Oxbow Books, 2018), pp. 23–38.

Iremaine, S., *An Exact relation of Prince Rupert His marching out of Bristoll* (London: 1645).

Jackson, Robin, *Evaluation at The Butts, Worcester* (Unpublished Report: Hereford and Worcester County Council, 1992).

Johnson, Matthew, *Archaeological Theory: An Introduction* (Oxford: Blackwell Publishing, 1999).

Johnson, Matthew, *Ideas of Landscape* (Oxford: Blackwell Publishing Ltd, 2007).

Kemp, Barry J., *Ancient Egypt: Anatomy of a Civilization* (Abingdon: Routledge, 2006).

King, Andy, *Archaeological Excavations at 30 Gloucester Lane, Old Market, Bristol* (Unpublished Report No. 1084/2003: Bristol and Region Archaeological Services, 2003).

King, Andy, *Archaeological Evaluation at Brandon Hill, Bristol for Bristol City Council* (Unpublished Report No. 2515/2011: Bristol and Region Archaeological Services, 2011).

King, Andy, *Archaeological Excavation at the site of the Royal Fort, St Michael's Hill for University of Bristol* (Unpublished Report No. 2142/2012: Bristol and Region Archaeological Services, 2012).

King, Andy, '"Not fullye so loftye": excavations at the Royal Fort, St Michael's Hill, Bristol', *Post-Medieval Archaeology*, Vol. 48 (1) (2014), pp. 1–44.

Kishlansky, Mark, *A Monarchy Transformed: Britain 1603–1714* (London: Penguin Books Ltd, 1996).

Lee, Adam, *Archaeological Watching Brief of Sainsbury's Supermarket, The Smithfield, Bridgnorth, Shropshire* (Unpublished Report: Worcestershire County Council, 2009).

Louth, Warwick, 'Organised Chaos: Applying seventeenth-century military manuals to conflict archaeology', in Ismini Pells (ed.), *New approaches to the military history of the English Civil War* (Solihull: Helion & Company Ltd, 2016), pp. 115–50.

Louth, Warwick, *The Arte Militaire: The Application of 17th Century Military Manuals to Conflict Archaeology* (Solihull: Helion & Company Ltd, 2016).

Lowry, Bernard, *Discovering Fortifications from the Tudors to the Cold War* (Princes Risborough: Shire Publications Ltd, 2006).

Lynch, John, *Bristol and the Civil War: For King and Parliament* (Stroud: The History Press, 2009).

Machiavelli, Niccolò, *The Art of War*, translated by Henry Neville (New York: Dover Publications Inc. 2006 modernised reprint, 1674).

Malim, Tim, *The Habit, Bridgnorth Archaeological Evaluation* (Unpublished Report: SLR, 2014).

Mason, Cai, *Water Fort, Brandon Hill, Bristol: Historic Environment Desk-Based Assessment and Topographical Survey* (Unpublished Report Ref: 109410.01: Wessex Archaeology, 2015).

Mason, John Frederick Arthur, *The Borough of Bridgnorth, 1157–1957* (Bridgnorth: Bridgnorth Borough Council, 1957).

Matthew, Christopher, *The Tactics of Aelian or On the Military Arrangements of the Greeks* (Barnsley: Pen & Sword Books Ltd, 2012).

McGrath, Patrick, *Bristol and the Civil War* (Bristol: Bristol Branch of the Historical Association, 1981).

Meskell, Lynn, *Object Worlds in Ancient Egypt: Material Biographies Past and Present* (Oxford: Berg, 2004).

Miller, Daniel, 'Materiality: An Introduction', in Daniel Miller (ed.), *Materiality* (Durham: Duke University Press), pp. 1–50.

Morris, Robert, *The Siege of Gloucester 1643* (Bristol: Stuart Press, 1993).

Mundy, Charles, *Trial excavations in Worcester 1985* (Unpublished Report: Hereford and Worcester County Council, 1985).

Mundy, Charles, *Worcester Archaeological Project 1985/86* (Unpublished Report: Hereford and Worcester County Council, 1986).

Neale, Frances, *William Worcestre: The Topography of Medieval Bristol* (Bristol: Bristol Record Society, 2000).

Norwood, Richard, *Fortification or Military Architecture* (London: Andrew Crooke, 1639).

Nossov, Konstantin, *Ancient and Medieval Siege Weapons* (Guilford: First Lyons Press, 2012).

Nye, Nathaniel, *The Art of Gunnery* (London: William Leak, 1647).

Nye, Nathaniel, *The Art of Gunnery* (London: William Leak, 1670).

Nye, Nathaniel, *The Art of Gunnery (1647) together with A Treatise of Artificall Fire-Works*, introduction and transcription by Cliff Mitchell (Farnham: The Pike and Shot Society, 2004).

O'Connell, Robert L., *Of Arms and Men: A History of War, Weapons, and Aggression* (Oxford: Oxford University Press, 1989).

Osborne, Mike, *Sieges and Fortifications of the Civil Wars in Britain* (Leigh-on-Sea: Partizan Press, 2004).

Papillon, David, *A practicall abstract of the arts of fortification and assailing containing foure different methods of fortifications with approved rules, to be set out in the feild all manner of superficies, intrenchments, and approaches by the demy circle, or with lines and stakes* (London: R. Austin, 1645).

Parker, Geoffrey, *The Military Revolution: military innovation and the rise of the West 1500–1800* (Cambridge: Cambridge University Press, 1996).

Parker, Geoffrey (ed.), *The Thirty Years' War* (London: Routledge, 1997).

Porter, Stephen, *The Blast of War: Destruction in the English Civil Wars* (Stroud: The History Press, 2011).

Potter, Kevin, *Archaeological Watching Brief during geotechnical trenching at the proposed Maths & Biosciences Building, Tyndall Avenue, Bristol* (Unpublished Report No. 1871/2007: Bristol and Region Archaeological Services, 2007).

Prior, Stuart, *A few well-positioned castles: The Norman Art of War* (Stroud: Tempus Publishing Ltd, 2006).

Rakoczy, Lila, *Archaeology of Destruction: A Reinterpretation of Castle Slightings in the English Civil War* (Unpublished PhD: University of York, 2007).

Rance, Philip, 'The Fulcum, the late Roman and Byzantine testudo: the Germanization of late Roman Tactics?', *Greek, Roman and Byzantine studies*, Vol. 44 (3) (2004), pp. 265–326.

Reinking, William, *A more exact and particular relation of the taking of Shrewsbury, then hath hitherto been published. With the manner and performance thereof by Lieutenant Collonel William Reinking commander in chief in that designe* (London: Published by Authority, 1645).

Renatus, Flavius Vegetius, *De Re Militari (Concerning military affairs): the classic treatise on warfare at the pinnacle of the Roman Empire's power* (London: Leonaur, 2012).

Rhodes, John, 'The Civil War Defences of Gloucester', *Transactions of the Bristol and Gloucestershire Archaeological Society*, Vol. 132 (2014), pp. 159–87.

Roe, Annette, 'Bridgnorth (Panpudding Hill)', *West Midlands Archaeology*, Vol. 26 (1983), pp. 86–87.

Roy, Ian (ed.), *The Royalist Ordnance Papers 1642–1646 Part 2* (Oxfordshire Record Society, Vol. 49, 1975).

Roy, Ian, 'England Turned Germany? The Aftermath of the Civil War in Its European Context', *Transactions of the Royal Historical Society*, Vol. 28 (1978), pp. 127–44.

Russell, James, *The Civil War Defences of Bristol: Their Archaeology & Topography* (Bristol: Author, 2003).

Rutherford, Stephen M., 'Ground-breaking pioneers or dangerous amateurs? Did early modern surgery have any basis in medical science?', in Ismini Pells (ed.), *New approaches to the military history of the English Civil War* (Solihull: Helion & Company Ltd, 2016), pp. 153–85.

Seyer, Samuel, *Memoirs Historical and Topographical of Bristol and its neighbourhood from the earliest period down to the present time* Vol. 2 (Bristol: John Mathew Gutch, 1823).
Smith, Thomas, *The Art of Gunnery* (London: William Ponsonby, 1600).
Staynred, Philip, *A compendium of fortification, both geometrically and instrumentally, by a scale: the making whereof is shewed by the tables, and their use, both of the tables and the scale, for speedy protracting of any fort consisting of 8 bulwarks, whose bastion-angles shall not exceed 90 degrees, and so the like for bastion-angles of 12 bulwarks* (London: Printed by E. Cotes, 1669).
Spencer, Michael, *Early Firearms 1300–1800* (Oxford: Shire Publications Ltd, 2008).
Sprigg, Joshua, *Anglia Rediviva; Englands Recovery: being the history of the motions, actions, and successes of the army under the immediate conduct of his excellency Sir Thomas Fairfax, KT* (Oxford: Oxford University Press, Forgotten Books 2012 Reprint, 1647).
Spring, Laurence, *The First British Army 1624–1628: The Army of the Duke of Buckingham* (Solihull: Helion & Company Limited, 2016).
Stone, Nicholas, *Enchiridion of Fortification or, A handfull of knowledge in martiall affaires* (London: Richard Royston, 1645).
Storr, Jim, *King Arthur's Wars: The Anglo-Saxon Conquest of England* (Warwick: Helion & Company Ltd, 2018).
Thucydides, *History of the Peloponnesian War*, translated by Rex Warner (London: Penguin Group, 1954).
Trigger, Bruce G., *A History of Archaeological Thought* (New York: Cambridge University Press, 2006).
Tzu, Sun, *The Art of War: including the translated The Sayings of Wu Tzu*, translated by Everard Ferguson Calthrop (Chichester: Capstone Publishing Ltd, 2010).
Wanklyn, Malcolm, 'Urban Revival in Early Modern England: Bridgnorth and the River Trade, 1660–1800', *Midland History*, Vol. 18 (1993), pp. 37–64.
Wanklyn, Malcolm and Jones, Frank, *A military history of the English Civil War 1642–1646: Strategy and Tactics* (Harlow: Pearson Education Limited, 2005).
Ward, Robert, *Animadversions of Warre; or, A militarie magazine of the truest rules, and ablest instructions, for the managing of warre* (London: John Dawson, 1639).
Watkins-Pitchford, Wilfred, 'Bridgnorth Castle and Ethelfleda's Tower', *Transactions of the Shropshire Archaeological and Natural History Society*, Vol. 46 (1) (1931), pp. 3–12.
Watkins-Pitchford, Wilfred, 'A visit to Bridgnorth', *Transactions of the Shropshire Archaeological Society*, Vol. 52, 1947–1948 (1948), pp. 153–78.
Willis Bund, John William (ed.), *Diary of Henry Townshend of Elmley Lovett 1640–1663* (London: The Worcestershire Historical Society, 1915).
Willis Bund, John William (ed.), *Diary of Henry Townshend of Elmley Lovett 1640–1663*, Vol. 2 (London: The Worcestershire Historical Society, 1916).
Woodiwiss, Simon, *Assessment and Updated Project Design for a programme of archaeological mitigation at St Martin's Quarter, Worcester* (Unpublished Report: Worcestershire Archaeology, 2014).
Worton, Jonathan, '"The Strongest Works in England"?: The defences of Shrewsbury during the Civil Wars, 1642–1651', *Transactions of the Shropshire Archaeological Society*, Vol. 87 (2012), pp. 95–112.
Worton, Jonathan, 'The Royalist and Parliamentarian War Effort in Shropshire during the First and Second Civil Wars, 1642–1648' (PhD Thesis, University of Chester, 2015).
Worton, Jonathan, *To Settle The Crown: Waging Civil War in Shropshire, 1642–1648* (Solihull: Helion & Company Limited, 2016).
Yuill, Veronica, *Excavations at 106, Southgate Street, Gloucester* (Unpublished Report: Gloucester Excavation Unit, 1983).

Archival Sources

Gloucestershire Archives, Accounts (1635–1653), Reference: GBR GA F4/5 f.483–5.
Shropshire Archives, A copy of an Old Map of the Borough of Bridgenorth in possession of the Corporation, *c.* 1660, Reference: SRO P40.V.2.5.
Shropshire Archives and the Museum Curator, Prospect of the Town of Shrewsbury as it appeared in the Great Frost, 1739, Reference: PH.5.13.5.22.219.

The Hive, Worcestershire, An Exact Ground Plot of the City of Worcester, As It Stood Fortified 3. Sep: 1651, Reference: 899:41 BA510.
The Hive, Worcestershire, The Present Rents 1670, Reference: BA36174.

Computer Programmes

Memory Map Inc. © Crown Copyright Ordnance Survey 2008 Licence No: PU100034184 (Central England).